FAREWELL TO FOGGY BOTTOM

ALSO BY ELLIS BRIGGS

Shots Heard Around the World

FAREWELL
to
FOGGY BOTTOM

The Recollections of
A Career Diplomat

ELLIS BRIGGS

DAVID McKAY COMPANY, INC.

NEW YORK

FAREWELL TO FOGGY BOTTOM

LIBRARY OF CONGRESS CATALOG CARD NUMBER: 64–24994

MANUFACTURED IN THE UNITED STATES OF AMERICA

Portions of this book have appeared in *Esquire, Foreign Service Journal, New York Times Magazine, Show, The Reader's Digest, The Saturday Evening Post*. A portion of Chapter XVIII was first published in article form by *The Associated Press*.

For

Lucita and Sally and Ted

for reasons that may occur to them

TABLE OF CONTENTS

TABLE OF CONTENTS

FOREWORD

ELLIS BRIGGS has been a friend of mine for many years and I have always been a great admirer of his unusual competency as a career Foreign Service officer. I only regret that I never had a chance to shoot or fish with him in any of those many areas where he has so vastly enjoyed himself, and the joy of which he has recorded elsewhere in a wonderful luring way.

His present book is a compilation of two somewhat different and yet related matters of substance. The first has to do with his own conclusions as to the importance of our career Foreign Service and how it could be made more effective. The second is a series of anecdotal reminiscences of particular episodes in his own career which sometimes seem extraneous, sometimes just amusing, and sometimes illustrative of the serious conclusions which he has reached after an amazingly varied and useful experience.

With many of the things which he says in this book regarding some of our foreign policies or individuals responsible for our foreign policies, I must disassociate myself. I cannot agree with some of his disparaging remarks regarding our policies in South America or his completely negative attitude towards the Peace Corps experiment. At times I feel that his prejudices have arisen from disagreement with bureaucrats in Washington and have warped his better judgment. I also find myself subscribing somewhat less than wholeheartedly to his criticisms of my own actions while I was Secretary of State, or of my recommendations as appearing in the later "Herter Committee" report. In spite of these reservations, however, I found his book extremely useful, as well as readable.

There is no doubt in my mind that the American Ambassador of today is seriously over-cluttered with too many people from too many agencies of the Government. Even though he has full responsibility, in accord with successive Executive

Orders, for the direction of this somewhat heterogeneous group, nonetheless, it is impossible for him to follow their actions in detail or, in fact, to demand their full loyalties when their careers are governed by agencies completely separated from the State Department. Ellis Briggs makes this point most convincingly. He is equally effective when he stresses the downgrading of our Ambassadors by Washington's habit of sending special spokesmen to the country to which the Ambassador is accredited. Only too often the message which they are presumed to have special qualifications to convey could much better have been conveyed by the Ambassador himself. He also makes an extremely eloquent case for the professionally trained diplomat as against the politically appointed diplomat. In all of these areas his conclusions are, in my opinion, soundly grounded, and if this book achieves no other purpose than to help restore in some measure the dignity and importance of the career-trained diplomat, it will have served a very useful purpose.

However, for those who are not necessarily interested in the future of our Foreign Service, there is much in this book of entertaining reading in the humorous and easy style in which the personal anecdotes are recounted. Even where the anecdotes appear entirely irrelevant, they do illustrate the infinite variety of problems and responsibilities of varying degrees of importance which face any diplomat. Because Ellis Briggs has an amazing record of seven Ambassadorships, with an eighth accepted which ill health precluded him from fulfilling, he has had as wide an experience in posts of responsibility as any of our career diplomats. That he preferred a small staff and wide leeway in the handling of his duties is only a natural accompaniment of his own independence and brilliant performance in his chosen field.

CHRISTIAN A. HERTER

Washington, D. C.
August 26, 1964

FAREWELL TO FOGGY BOTTOM

I.

Terms of Reference

A MAN does not work in diplomacy for nearly forty years without reaching certain conclusions about how foreign affairs should be run. That they could be run better, few would deny. That they could also be run a great deal worse is less generally recognized than it should be, for in the nature of things the Foreign Service cannot develop a grass-roots constituency. When things come apart it is easier to blame faulty performance by Foreign Service personnel than to question the validity of the objective. Conversely, there is a tendency to emphasize the romantic aspects of a career over the routine that is often the staple fare of the professional diplomat.

Having been an ambassador for over half of my official service, I have had opportunities to watch the machine operate, and on occasion to tinker with the ignition. My impressions, after treading both the uncertain terrain of policy and the narrower and more frequented alleys where the flow of bilateral questions takes precedence over the traffic in generalities, are in these pages. If greater understanding of the factors that produce our dilemmas should emerge, so much the better.

My observations do not claim to be objective, except in the sense that I have no magic elixir to peddle, no politics to promote, and few panaceas to offer. I am skeptical of elixirs, whether the label be Alliance for Progress or Volunteers of the Peace Corps. The crusading spirit does not inhabit my locker. And too many of the panaceas are either narcotic — like Manifest Destiny or Massive Retaliation — or else they are

1

"founded neither on realities of power nor on a true community of interest among its members," like the United Nations. (Which is not to imply that there is at the moment a better bunker than U.N. to hide in.)

I do not believe that one political party or the other has a monopoly either of statesmanship or of the ability to stumble and turn a spectacular somersault over an international hurdle. I apprehend that several of the most difficult problems are probably insoluble in the existing conjunction of ingredients. A major task of diplomacy in our time is to deal realistically with those shifting components.

One way *not* to deal with foreign affairs is through a barrage of public statements. When something out of the ordinary occurs, American officials experience an almost irresistible impulse to rush to a loudspeaker. No amount of inglorious experience restrains them. Shouting "Once more unto the breach, dear friends," Uncle Sam time and again mistakes his kiddycar for an armored charger:

The citizens of Country B having at last overthrown a reprehensible demagogue, unfriendly to the United States, the sagacious Washington attitude is clearly one of private elation accompanied by official silence. Now is the time to remember that any statement of public pleasure plays into the hands of those who habitually accuse the United States of having fomented an event it praises. Here is the opportunity to use that magic formula: No Comment. Here is the occasion to recognize that of all the woes afflicting statesmen, the most painful are those that come from not having the wit to keep their mouths shut.

Instead, almost before the deposed demagogue takes refuge in a foreign embassy in Tegucifagasta, the President of the United States is pawing the valley like Job's horse, clothing his neck with triumphant thunder. And the Secretary of State, not to be outdone, goes as pink and giggly as a high-school girl dating the football captain.

2

Whereupon the glorious revolution turns sour, and Uncle Sam is left with egg on his whiskers. And if it does not turn sour, the foreign government will probably resent the gratuitous pat on the back, the patronizing thanks-for-nothing. The fact that the revolution was overdue has nothing to do with the question, which is the undesirability of rushing into sound and print over another country's business.

My observations are thus dedicated to professionals — to the men and women of the American Foreign Service. They should be better known, that fine body of public servants who on behalf of our government perform in far places an infinite variety of tasks both large and small. They deserve well of our country. My observations are also offered in the hope they may stimulate debate, and that out of argument may come further improvements in the technique of foreign operations.

That does not mean that I favor another reorganization of the Foreign Service. Having survived three reorganizations during my own career, I am allergic to planners; let us at least wait until the last infusion of calories is digested.

The heresies herein are strictly my own. They possibly flow from the belief that albeit diplomacy is a most serious business, to be entered into with dignity and respect and even with trepidation, the diplomatist is under no obligation to take himself seriously. In this he has an advantage over the bureaucrat, who is often a solemn fellow with a tendency to pontificate, like an owl trying to nest in the Parthenon; and over the politician, who is a marathon runner compelled, poor wretch, to stop every few yards to ask the spectators, "How am I doing?"

Let us begin by considering some of the kinds of preoccupations that are likely to face an ambassador as he surveys his responsibilities from his desk in an American embassy. If his office was built since the war, it will be an eye-catching architectural triumph, likely as not adapted from the Tomb of an Unknown Soldier, or from a pavilion at a fair, with an immense United States shield on the avenue side, and a great

3

expanse of unprotected plate glass all around it. The incumbent ambassador, after his first stricken look at the premises, will have appealed to Washington for a fence, like the one enclosing the White House. He will have been informed by the Foreign Buildings Office of the State Department, by now busy erecting a comparable coliseum in Ouagadougou: No Funds. Which is where the matter will remain until after the first brickbats hurled by students angered by the curtailment of the foreign aid program.

Behind his desk, the ambassador is considering alternatives and weighing courses of action:

Whether to warn the Foreign Minister about the effect of a threatened expropriation on pending American investment, or to await receipt of the promised views-with-concern from Washington;

Whether to tip off the Palace that the Traveling Senator whom Their Majesties incautiously invited to luncheon is an inveterate knee-pincher;

How far to accept the overtures of that rising but disreputable opposition leader, who may resent having the American embassy represented at his birthday rout by a bilingual First Secretary. Ambassadorial presence, on the other hand, may be distasteful to the government to which the ambassador is accredited.

Whether to slap down the general who has just made a silly speech, or to mollify the Prime Minister by reminding him that the old boy has only a few months to go before exchanging his assimilated diplomatic pretensions for a pecan grove in Alabama, where the parade-ground voice will galvanize only the squirrels.

Routine embassy business. But unlike crossword puzzles and questionnaires in the Sunday magazine section, a diplomat cannot find the answers by turning to page seventy-nine or waiting for next week's issue. An ambassador must handle the problems as they arise. He accordingly decides:

4

To see the Foreign Minister, without waiting for Washington; to let the Palace find out for itself about the Senator; to send the First Secretary to the politician's birthday party; to mollify the Prime Minister *and* put a cork in the general.

As these daily decisions multiply, an ambassador slowly strengthens the foundations of his house of experience, the dwelling place a-building ever since his vice consular days and now filled with things accumulated at seventeen posts on five continents — some battered and some bent and some in need of fresh upholstery, but each piece lived in or lived with, and cherished at the moment of acquisition.

There comes a time, nevertheless, when one cleans out the attic and surveys the things possessed. One discards a good deal of rubbish, parting with reluctance from each shopworn but comforting prejudice. And one does his best to evaluate the remainder. Thus the retired Foreign Service Officer, looking back to the 1920's and ahead to the unrecorded decades before us.

Consider the widely-believed statement that "an ambassador is merely a Washington messenger boy." That was clearly invented by someone who never served in an embassy. The person who is content to carry messages is in fact a messenger boy, but he has no business being an ambassador. *How* an envoy delivers a message can be as important as the communication itself. What the ambassador says when he delivers the views of his government can cause the representations to prosper or to fail, regardless of the eloquence of the prose confected in Washington.

During World War I, President Wilson became aroused by British seizure of American property on the high seas, and he directed Ambassador Page to take action. Page sympathized with the British. He went to the Foreign Office with the Wilsonian script, which he brandished like a dead mouse removed from a mousetrap. Then he and Sir Edward Grey concerted together to bury it.

5

In contrast to Ambassador Page, who killed the Wilsonian message by inertia, there are many awkward or infelicitous Washington messages that are rescued from failure by experienced ambassadorial handling. It is the responsibility of the ambassador, as his government's senior agent abroad, to protect his principal from the effects of his folly as well as his wisdom — and always to have Washington think it has cornered the market on clairvoyance.

Another myth, brewed in the same pot with the ambassadorial messenger, is that "ambassadors do not make policy." If a representative is worth the white wafer seal at the bottom of his presidential commission, policy is precisely what an ambassador does make. He may not make it every hour on the hour, like a baker baking bread, and the proportion of his policy decisions to his operational choices may be small. There are more Peace Corps Volunteers to discipline than there are treaties to sign or international conferences to attend. But policy is implicit in many of the ambassador's operational decisions. The raw material of policy is found in his interpretation of events, his judgments about foreign intentions, his assessment of the foreign potential. And all those intangibles are gathered together and sent to Washington by the ambassador, for use in arriving at policy.

The fact that policy can also fit like an old pillow under the bottom of a lethargic Potomac bureaucrat or become the legend that frustrates an overdue decision, is beside the point. Policy can likewise be the harbinger of a change in the climate or the beacon inspiring the pilot navigating international waters. But whatever the form that policy takes, ambassadorial influence should be felt in the shaping of it. Otherwise a man has no business being an ambassador.

Recognition of these things gives encouragement to candidates for the Foreign Service examinations and to junior diplomats as they slowly climb the rungs of the foreign service ladder. The view from each level is more stimulating than it was from the one below, the responsibilities more challenging, the rewards more gratifying. That is why diplomacy continues to attract superior talent, notwithstanding the parsimony of the Congress, the stultifying weight of bureaucracy, and the not infrequent indifference of the public.

The conduct of foreign affairs has changed little over the decades. When people talk about The New Diplomacy, they are often trying to find an excuse for flunking the entrance requirements.

As the research member of the family, my wife maintains that had it not been for an irrational and uninhibited enthusiasm for bird shooting — mine, not hers — she might never have been an ambassadress. When eyebrows lift, she points to a course in international law that I took while in college. It was an elective course, and the initial attraction was not the prospectus but the schedule, for in that autumn of my junior year I was carefully preserving, free of sordid academic preoccupations, three afternoons a week. Those afternoons were dedicated to the pursuit of partridge and woodcock around the birch knolls and alder thickets of Grafton County, New Hampshire, along the east bank of the upper Connecticut River.

There being no conflict between Professor Washburn's morning exercise with Grotius and my afternoon shotgun program, I signed up, and was instantly delighted. The more I heard of a diplomatic career — Washburn in his youth had served in Hohenzollern Germany and was impressively articulate about it — the more enthusiastic I became. It was an enthusiasm which led, a quarter of a century after I met Albert Washburn, to my first ambassadorial toga.

That, at any rate, is the way my wife tells it.

Other candidates may find easier trails to Parnassus. There are a variety of impulses that can set a young man's face toward the Foreign Service. Testifying recently before a Senate committee, a senior diplomat cited three: a sense of adventure,

7

ambition to become an ambassador, and desire for public service. Not necessarily in that order of importance.

Ambition, certainly. Baton in the knapsack; ballpoint pen in the cutaway coat. And for those who do not become chief of mission, there are fascinating jobs and specialties along the way: if financial adviser to Liberia inflates no dormant urge, then set your sights on the Consulate General in Montreal or São Paulo. The expectation, or at any rate the possibility of getting to the top, is a proper part of a candidate's interest in a competitive service.

A sense of adventure, by all means! There is no more important ingredient, nor one which when present is more likely to be satisfied anywhere else than in the Foreign Service. And let each young man pray that a comparable spirit may stir in the heart of his bride, who will be summoned to make a new home every time an officer is transferred — in the tropics one year, maybe in Finland the next one.

As for a desire for public service, I would substitute "a belief in the importance of transacting the government's business abroad." That may be another way of saying the same thing, but without the whiff of sacrificial endeavor. In diplomacy the prerogatives of official position — the prestige of the office, the immunities while abroad, the diplomatic passport while traveling — are legitimate attractions. They, too, play a part in a young man's decision.

Since "Why do you want to be a Foreign Service Officer?" is often asked during the oral examination, these comments can be useful in formulating the diffident reply a candidate is expected to make to that question.

I have forgotten the order of my own predilections, but I do remember that getting started in diplomacy turned out to be a lengthy undertaking. In the year of the Versailles Treaty the maximum salary was four thousand dollars; it was paid to the Counselor of the American embassy in London, whose expenses were several times greater. An apprentice consul received eighteen hundred, and there were no allowances. When an officer was moved, he paid his own way to the next post of assignment. Furthermore, the notion that twenty or twenty-five years of experience qualified an officer to be chief of mission was just beginning to penetrate the presidential custom of appointing ambassadors from the ranks of party stalwarts and campaign contributors.

By 1921, when I graduated from Daniel Webster's institution for dedicated grouse hunters, diplomatic prospects were at last improving in Washington. Legislation was in prospect that was to create a professional non-partisan career. Salaries were to be increased, and there were provisions, gradually implemented by Congress during the next four decades, for allowances and benefits that have gone some distance toward making the Foreign Service self-supporting. Most ambassadorships can now be held by men without large private resources.

The Rogers Act, as this initial legislation was called, was enacted in 1924, five years after my course with Professor Washburn. By combining five hundred consular officers with approximately one hundred diplomats, the Rogers Act created the American Foreign Service. With Washburn's words refurbished, and with an assist from a fabulous Washington teacher named Angus Macdonald Crawford, I took the examinations the following year. My first commission as "Foreign Service Officer of the United States of America" was signed by President Coolidge on September 11, 1925.

The Foreign Service has since grown from six hundred to almost four thousand officers, more than a six-fold increase. The State Department has expanded in the same period from seven hundred working for Charles Evans Hughes, to ten time as many working for Dean Rusk. The Hughes aggregation had elbow room and occasionally time to think. The present personnel, exiled in 1947 from their traditional headquarters beside the White House, are already bursting the partitions of that ugly new complex on Virginia Avenue known as Foggy Bottom. They make so much work for each other that they have little time to think, and they are so crowded they have no elbow room whatever.

Secretary Rusk, obediently switching off the lights to save electric current, complains that his myrmidons are "layering." Other observers make less ambiguous comments.

It is one of the beliefs ventilated in these pages that, notwithstanding the multiplicity of countries spawned in the last twenty years (many of whose inhabitants would be better off had they remained colonies for another generation) and the increase of American international responsibilities since the end of World War II (which increase is always taken for granted but rarely defined), four thousand Foreign Service Officers, plus a supporting cast almost double that size in the home office, is an overabundance of manpower.

This personnel inundation is especially drenching in the State Department areas of administration, housekeeping, "career development," management, and other fields of occasionally useful but hardly substantive accomplishment.

Consider, for example, the organization of the Latin American section of the Department of State. When last I served there, the duties of the Assistant Secretary for Latin America were described in nine words: "In charge of relations with the other American Republics."

The 1964 equivalent of those nine words is a pamphlet of twenty-five printed pages. It contains a table of contents, an introduction, a statement of principles, eight charts, and fifteen pages of text, the purpose of which (hopefully, as the bureaucrats say) is to describe who does what to whom among the swarming drones of the Bureau of Inter-American Affairs of the State Department, the Bureau for Latin America of the Agency for International Development, and the Alliance for Progress.

10

Twenty-five pages of diagrams and prose, against nine words which sufficed in 1947.

Or consider the managerial dream of coping with too many top secret papers floating about in the archives. This is from an ultimatum recently addressed to employees by the Assistant Secretary of State for Administration:

Subject: Automatic Downgrading, Declassification and Decontrol

Laxity on the part of drafting officers to comply with the criteria for the automatic time-phased downgrading, declassification and decontrol of classified and administratively controlled documents has been of genuine concern to the Department. It is mandatory that each classified and administratively controlled document bear a special notation which identifies its status in the automatic time-phased downgrading, declassification and decontrol system.

No wonder the Secretary of State employs nearly eight thousand assistants. If half of them played leapfrog from Acapulco to Arequipa while the other half sang "Polly Wolly Doodle All Day," practically nobody would know the difference.

There are nevertheless more bureaucrats clamoring to get in, and more innocents seconding the motion. Although in almost every American embassy aquarium the world over there are more tadpoles than there is water, it was recently recommended by a committee of investigation that this burgeoning wonderland be still further congested by recognizing as permanent — and in fact as parallel and companion services to the Foreign Service — the inhabitants of the Handout Empire and the Propaganda Establishment. These are otherwise known as AID for Agency for International Development (successor to ICA for International Cooperation Administration, successor to ECA for Economic Cooperation Administration) and USIA, for United States Information Agency (successor to

11

OWI for Office of War Information, which was in turn the stepchild of a patriot called George Creel, who was Chief Censor in World War I).

A sounder objective might be to disband AID before the taxpayers lose what remains of their shirts (a thought now happily occurring to Congress) and to whittle down the propaganda megaphone toward the time when it can be held without straining the elbows. Against this the affected personnel, along with the supernumeraries already in the State Department, are frantically seeking to invent new alphabetical disguises, to perpetuate themselves, and to multiply. Benjamin Franklin is not their ideal, but *cavia porcellus*, the guinea pig of the philoprogenitive fable.

That, however, is getting ahead of my story. Between that course on international law at Dartmouth College in 1919, and the stricken duodenum that remanded me to the same New England pastures over forty years later, the Foreign Service took me from Washington to Peru, back to the State Department, to Liberia, to Cuba, to Washington once more, to Chile, to Cuba a second time, to the Dominican Republic, to China for the last months of the war, to the State Department for yet another assignment, and then to Uruguay, to Communist-dominated Czechoslovakia and Communist-attacked Korea, to Peru twenty-nine years after my first consular exequatur, and finally to Brazil and to Greece.

In seven countries I served as ambassador. An eighth embassy, Spain, was pending at the time of my retirement. Seventeen posts, even in thirty-seven years of commissioned service, is hardly the best way to run a diplomatic service. There is comment on that in chapters hereafter, along with remarks about the profligate way in which American representatives are uprooted every few months and packed off to another assignment.

Come to think of it, one of the few posts I did *not* reach was the first and only preference I ever put on State Department paper. That was Harbin, in Manchuria, toward which in 1926 I cast a yearning eye as I sat in Bill Dawson's Foreign Service School in the basement of the old State War Navy building. My twelve young colleagues and I, the lucky survivors of the examinations the previous summer, were invited, as the time approached for us to go abroad, to submit a list of posts, in order of preference.

I chose Harbin for the same reason I picked Professor Washburn's course on international law. I had read of the great flyway of the Sungari valley, connecting the Siberian nesting grounds with the deltas of the Yangtze and Yellow Rivers. Harbin, by a fortunate coincidence, was on the banks of the Sungari. There was also an American Consulate General.

But since an embryo Vice Consul does not write of flyways and wild geese for the official record, I cited the Chinese, Mongols, Japanese, Russians, and Koreans, all riding to and fro on the Chinese Eastern Railway, and all contributing to the mounting political pressures in the cockpit of North China. Hence, I respectfully represented, Harbin ought to be a good spot to be in, for a man ambitious to witness international politics and to practice political reporting.

The State Department despatched me instead to Callao, in Peru. There I dealt with recalcitrant American seamen, studied Spanish, and watched President Augusto B. Leguia operate the most efficient dictatorship then existing in South America. I also learned about the guano business, the mining of copper, the Tacna Arica dispute and the overthrow of the Inca Empire by Pizarro. Peru was the most interesting country in South America, and in a short time I forgot about Manchuria.

Not so my wife, who for years was apprehensive lest some eager beaver catch up with my Asiatic preference.

"Poor old Briggs," she could hear a kindly bureaucrat saying. "All this time he's wanted to go to Manchuria. Let's send the so-and-so to Manchuria. . . ."

The Communists got us off the hook by gobbling up China

13

in 1949. I had been right, at that, about the international political pressures, and also about the bird shooting. In Korea, in 1952, those pressures were manifested by Communist artillery and machine guns which did not, however, prevent my paying my respects to the mallard and teal, pausing on the war-torn peninsula on their way from Siberia to the South China coast. And in Pusan, our first Christmas, we ate wild swan, courtesy of the Vice Admiral commanding the Seventh Fleet. It was a noble bird. It reconciled me, a quarter of a century after that first post preference, to having missed Harbin and its flyway.

But seventeen posts for one career were still too many.

Turning to substantive matters, as separate from the mechanics and management of foreign operations, it is evident that all is not well with the American image, overrated though the importance of that image may be. Pick up almost any metropolitan newspaper and likely as not the front page will report the stoning of an American embassy somewhere.

The foreign capitals may be as far apart as Ghana and Indonesia, or Panama and Cyprus, but the pattern of foreign behavior repeats itself: rocks through the chancery window; gleeful demolition of the American propaganda headquarters; "Yankee, Go Home" scribbled in conspicuous places.

The question arises (belatedly) why the response to over one hundred billion dollars in aid programs since the war has become so hostile. In recorded history, no country has worked more unselfishly to accomplish good, and none has ever contributed a fraction of the resources poured out by the American people to assist other nations. None has striven so diligently to produce on the screen of international life so benevolent a likeness.

What has blunted these efforts and tarnished the image? Because relations between no two pairs of countries are alike, there is no easy answer. One man's meat is another man's hardtack. What is pertinent to Cambodia may be irrelevant to Bo-

14

livia — a circumstance the confectioners of aid projects and canned propaganda sometimes overlook. The program that seems wonderful in Korea may give the Burmese people economic if not political indigestion.

The Communists have tried to smear our efforts, of course. Wherever in the world they find an American stream, the Communists seek to pollute it. But the Communists are by no means the whole story.

In the New World, the American Guilt Complex has played a part, as has envy in the breast of the pampered Good Neighbors. If *Alianza para el Progreso* were the stimulant the Potomac medicine men profess to believe, the hemisphere ought to resound with the cheers of happy workmen; instead, it echoes alternately with whimpers of self pity and snarls of abuse and recrimination.

Racial troubles at home have contributed to American overseas unpopularity, especially in those newly established countries of Africa. Nationalism, the virus brand propagated by demagogues on every continent, has added to American troubles. And in the backward lands, where much of the anti-American agitation has occurred, the failure of the "revolution of rising expectations" to produce a perceptible improvement in the human situation has generated disappointment, exploding in attacks on the readiest available target — the Overstuffed American Presence.

That presence may be defined as the existence in foreign capitals of vast and conspicuous agglomerations of United States officials and their dependents, often living on a level that appears to the host citizens — particularly if they themselves are unshod — as unattainable affluence and luxury. (The answer is not to depress the standard of living of American officials abroad, but to reduce their numbers and dismantle their gaudier PX's.)

So the host citizens, frustrated in their aspirations and often incited by leaders whose ineptiude has exacerbated their prob-

15

lems, vent their resentment by painting "Yankee, Go Home" or by burning the ambassador's Cadillac.

The only suggestion Washington has made lately is that maybe the ambassador ought not to have a Cadillac — an observation as irrelevant, but not so bright, as Pat Hurley's remark in 1944 that if you could straighten the bent axles of China, Chiang Kai Shek could forget about the "agrarian reformers."

It has taken the American people approximately a generation (counted from 1933, when President Roosevelt established official relations with Soviet Russia) to challenge the notion that a crusading spirit is a substitute for foreign policy. Historians are beginning to recognize, as skeptical diplomats have long perceived, how many of the woes of the United States derive from failure to distinguish between the two.

A crusading spirit is a motivating force. It has produced such manifestations as the aid programs, Truman's Point Four project, the gravy train piloted through Latin America during World War II by Nelson Rockefeller as Coordinator of Inter-American Affairs, and its current successor, *Alianza para el Progreso*. The crusading spirit likewise incubated, hatched out, and now feeds rich angleworms and plump sunflower seeds to the Peace Corps.

A foreign policy, on the other hand, is not a motivating force but a course of action with respect to another country or area — the Monroe Doctrine or the Good Neighbor Policy, for example. A crusading spirit is mixed up with moral fervor; in fact, mixed up is just the phrase for it. Moral fervor should have little part in the calculations producing a foreign policy, which should be undertaken coldly, objectively, without losing sight of the human equation but also without allowing that equation to dominate the exercise or dictate the answers. A sound policy may in time become a motivating force, but that is a different question.

The United States has been afflicted for several decades with

16

the irrational belief that wishing well equals doing good, and that doing good equals international progress, and that therefore wishing well is the equivalent of international progress.

President Roosevelt's Grand Design is a case in point. His plan for the post-war world was based on the premise that Russia, having been treated generously as an ally, would collaborate with the non-Communist world in building a new order. The golden glow of victory would continue to illuminate the faces of men of good will in every victorious nation.

That ghastly miscalculation led to the enslavement of Eastern Europe, left Berlin stranded one hundred and ten miles within Communist territory, nearly deprived the free world of Greece, and led via the 38th parallel to the Korean War. That war in turn led to the adhesive dilemmas still confronting the United States in Southeast Asia. A Grand Design indeed.

The examples of statesmanship in the late 1940's — the Marshall Plan, support for Tito when he became a Kremlin heretic, the rescue of Greece, the establishment of NATO — in historical perspective were only incidentally policy decisions. They were primarily reactions to Communist broken promises, offensive behavior, or miscalculations. But the very success of European rehabilitation once more lured the United States off the firm ground of pragmatism, and into the crevice of the Crusading Spirit. Before we could climb out, the do-gooders had sunk us to the ears in the underlying muskeg. The welfare workers established the doctrine that since an aid program worked gloriously in Europe, comparable programs should be undertaken elsewhere in the world, wherever a hand-out was demanded.

Soon there were so many hands in Uncle Sam's pocket that a Hindu goddess looked by comparison like the one-armed paperhanger. Successive Chief Executives, in command of the jukeboxes of federal persuasion, deafened the opposition with sonnets about how the world would collapse unless it kept a pipeline into the American Treasury. Successive Congresses

17

were solemnly assured that after one more, just one more injection of dollars, the economy of Bolivia (or Iran, or Brazil, or India) would be saved, its future viability guaranteed, and the inhabitants suffused with permanent satisfaction.

These promises generally turned out to be euphemisms for "one more diaper and the baby will be housebroken." A hopeless improvident or a delinquent spendthrift was salvaged to enjoy The Abundant Life, while an army of spenders was recruited, and the Crusading Spirit flourished.

At long last there are signs that the American people are losing their zeal for emptying dollars into the Alice-in-Wonderland rabbit holes of underdeveloped countries. Little seeps out except owls' tears, on sight of which the foreign politician denounces the American engineers for the inadequacy of the sanitation.

Behind the anti-American demonstrations there are consequently a variety of forces. The frustrated revolutionaries-of-rising-expectations, recalling that the American government inspired the expectations, blame the United States for not producing Utopia-on-the-half-shell. Those who found it unsportsmanlike to shoot Santa Claus as long as Congress kept replenishing his bag of toys, are now drawing a bead on the ailing Kris Kringle. Still others, like Lawrence's Arabs who could not resist firing at Allied war planes because they made such provocative targets, are stimulated by the Overstuffed American Presence, including the acres of plate glass in those garish embassy chanceries.

When any of these groups show signs of running out of breath or brickbats, the Communists, whose implacable hatred of the free world is undiminished by slogans like Peaceful Coexistence, are quick to rally around with fresh warcries and new ammunition.

To the extent that anti-American activity in foreign lands accelerates the eradication of the American Crusading Spirit, it is probably worth it, even if the United States has to rebuild an embassy now and then or ship abroad a replacement ambassadorial Cadillac.

That does not necessarily mean that all foreign aid should be abandoned. A limited program can probably be justified on grounds of self-interest, which is the only legitimate basis for having one. Much depends on the kind of aid that is being considered: military aid or economic aid; soft loans, hard loans or give-away programs. Likewise the kind of country that is being assisted.

The most successful aid enterprises were the aforesaid Marshall Plan, followed by the rehabilitation of Greece. And the NATO alliance, notwithstanding the tall woodpecker pecking away at the girders, still serves to remind the Communists of the validity of the Atlantic Community.

Contrariwise, the most difficult area to assist is a backward land whose inhabitants are inexperienced, incompetent, or inert. Yet precisely those countries have been the target, year after year, of plans that have no chance of succeeding:

First, until a cork is put in the population bottle, aid in whatever amount to a retarded country is vitiated by the multiplication of mouths to feed. Aid without population control is futile.

Second, the regimes operating in underdeveloped countries are usually incapable of manipulating the tools of government, and frequently corrupt as well. They are unable to assimilate foreign aid or to make profitable use of it.

Third, whenever the purveyor of aid, seeking to prevent an incompetent beneficiary from wasting it, insists on controlling implementation, his efforts are shortly denounced as "intervention." Xenophobia takes control, and the air is dark with stones flung at the Ugly Purveyor. (A comforting thought, by the way, about those Russian advisers in Cuba.)

Again, there ought to be a minimum standard of deportment established for beneficiaries. The United States gains little in the world's respect, and it diminishes its own, when

19

it underwrites a regime which behaves arbitrarily or without responsibility in matters affecting the interests of American citizens. Inviting an expropriator to Washington jeopardizes property rights the world over; giving that country an aid program compounds the imbecility.

Americans are generous. They want to help less fortunate peoples. But to what extent is the United States accountable for so disproportionate a share of the world's burdens? What makes the American people believe they have the resources to continue to carry them? Is the free world really fortified against Communist penetration by American handouts? Is the welfare state a feasible state, or merely the state of mind of the government spender?

Until he has answers to some of those questions, a taxpayer is handicapped in discussing the sensations he experiences while perched on the horns of the foreign aid dilemma.

Another enterprise overdue for scrutiny is the Food for Peace program, which at first glance makes more sense than some of the projects causing leaks in the Treasury plumbing. A lush brochure by the administering agency calls Food for Peace "the creative use of American abundance in international development." Loud cheers. But the brochure neglects to remind the public that the agricultural price support policy of the federal government created the surpluses in the first place, and continues to reproduce them. It likewise fails to report that the Creative Use whereof the brochure brags so prettily, now approaching its tenth year and x-millionth taxpayers' dollar, has not yet appreciably reduced those mastodon carryovers the elimination of which the scheme was ostensibly designed to accomplish.

In 1955, when the enabling legislation was still damp on the books, the White House undertook to reassure foreign governments. Meticulous care would be exercised, went this declaration, to ensure that Traditional Markets would not be disrupted by the disposal of American wheat, peanuts, soy

20

beans, cotton, or what-have-we. There would be, the world was told, No Dumping. It had a noble ring, this official defense of Public Law 480, but on the numerous occasions when I was instructed by Washington to sell that defense to foreign officials, they always looked at me as if they thought I thought they were half-wits.

The operation of Public Law 480, I quickly discovered, was capable of converting an American ambassador into a Public Hero one week and a Public Enemy one week later.

In Peru the grain crop failed. In the *altiplano,* from Cuzco to Lake Titicaca, the *serranos* were hungry. To the rescue galloped *Tío* Sam, his saddlebags heavy with foodstuffs.

Eat this year. Pay in 1970. The Creative Use of American Abundance.

It was one of the shortest triumphs on record. While the American envoy basked in the sunshine of his unearned increment, salesmen of the Department of Agriculture were busy beside the Potomac, peddling not only surplus wheat but also surplus cotton. Presently they peddled some surplus cotton to Chile. Now Peru also grows cotton. Peru is proud of her Tanguis and Pima, and one of her regular cotton customers, year after year, is her next-door neighbor the Republic of Chile.

When Lima learned that the United States was selling surplus cotton to Chile, six thousand miles from Galveston and New Orleans, on terms that no Peruvian producer five hundred miles away could come within years of approaching, that fine wheat patriot the American ambassador was discovered to be a cotton scoundrel and an enemy of the Peruvian people. He and Washington were pilloried for dirty work at the economic crossroads. Nor were the Peruvians soothed when they found out that at the same time the United States was selling wheat to them, repayable in dollars, another South American country was buying the same wheat, repayable in its local currency.

21

Eat this year. Pay in something or other in 1970. The Creative Use of American Abundance.

Although Food for Peace owes some of its support to that shopworn friend the Crusading Spirit, the reasons why the program continues to engage the affable attention of Congress are more practical. Notwithstanding its failure to reduce — far less abolish — the surplus, Food for Peace helps postpone the adoption of a sensible but politically painful American agricultural policy, and it generates what are known as Counterpart Funds — those lovely local currencies that are advanced to traveling Congressmen as they move from country to country, studying foreign conditions. Counterpart funds have proved the greatest boon to congressional travel since the invention of the credit card and the airplane, and Food for Peace produces the counterpart.

Less clear is what the United States is going to do with all the rupees in India, which will soon be pledged against the billions of bushels of wheat sold on credit to neutralist Nehru. Statisticians predict that by the end of the decade practically the entire supply of rupees will be in hock to the United States.

Perhaps we should offer to buy the Taj Mahal. After the World's Fair, we could move it upriver to Yonkers. Or Congress might transfer itself to the Vale of Kashmir and hold sessions there, all expenses paid, until the year 2000. The Creative Use of American Abundance!

As to other ways in which the operation of our foreign affairs establishment might be improved, ensuing chapters offer various suggestions. In this, it is comforting to know that I am not alone in my researches. Not only have colleges and universities been busy putting stethoscopes to the cornerstone of the State Department, but public groups and volunteer committees have swarmed all over the Ship of State, offering everything from a shave and a haircut to a permanent wave for the blades of the propeller.

22

A committee under former Secretary of State Herter produced a whole volume of ideas, some of them splendid. Unfortunately they became bemused at the prospect of founding a graduate school to train robot diplomats to draft treaties, achieve disarmament, and juggle protocol; and they became attracted by the New Diplomacy slogan "Anything you can do, two can do better; ten can do anything better than two." In the main, however, the Herter recommendations merit greater implementation than they appear to be getting.

The erudite Council on Foreign Relations held meetings in New York for over six months on "The Role of the Ambassador," without exhausting the subject, the participants, or Bill Burden's generous hospitality These communicants concluded, *inter alia*, that an American ambassador abroad has all the authority he needs, if he has the gumption and hardihood to use it, but that an American ambassador in Washington lacks even the right to a table-d'hôte in the Executive Dining Room, far less a parking permit in the State Department cellar. Other conclusions are eagerly awaited.

And there is a Senate subcommittee which under the civilized chairmanship of Senator Henry Jackson (D., Washington) has been holding bipartisan hearings since 1963, collecting a vast array of testimony. Summoning philosophers, administrators, professors, politicians, plus a honking gaggle of large and small ambassadors, the committee has already published a study on the Secretary of State (in the alas-poor-Yorick tradition), and a treatise on "The Ambassador and the Problem of Coordination."

The latter, which contains a compilation of Executive Orders, regulations, and other applicable documents, is the most convincing explanation so far of why so many diplomatic envoys, having gone abroad on the wings of the morning, soon look like the central figure of the Laocoön group. In fact, Laocoön, a realist who warned the Trojans against the wooden

23

horse and then perished strangled by the serpents of Apollo might well be taken — like the caduceus of Mercury for the medical fraternity — as the emblem of twentieth-century diplomacy. Change the serpents to red tape, and the two sons of Laocoön to Policy Planning and Career Development, and the rest would be up to Praxiteles, by and with the advice and consent of the Senate.*

On planning, the committee republishes that wonderful precept under which a State Department promotion panel was once instructed to reshuffle the diplomats in order to select candidates for career minister, the rank which represents the penultimate twig at the top of the Foreign Service tree. The qualifications are too long to quote — nine paragraphs of lilting State Department prose that squeeze out like a ribbon and lie flat on the soothsayer's toothbrush — but the characteristics established would probably have scared hell out of Elihu Root or Henry L. Stimson and given twinges of gout to Benjamin Franklin, Charles Evans Hughes, and considerably more recent company. Having myself been a career minister for over ten years, it would perhaps be ungracious to take exception to the super-superior talents alleged to reside in the holders of that exalted position, but the precept became fair game when it concluded with a sentence to the effect that the successful candidate "will have demonstrated complete awareness of the new dimensions of diplomacy in the 1960's, in both the substantive and management-administrative fields."

We are further indebted to Senator Jackson for placing a Foggy Bottom proponent of this thesis on the stand, whence he illuminates the New Diplomacy with the following testimony:

---

* Since the foregoing was written, the subcommittee has published its findings on "The American Ambassador" — an invaluable treatise on the hopes and harrassments of those who preside over our embassies abroad. Administrators may not like it, but ambassadors will.

"Running parallel," he declares breathlessly, "to this flexible approach in dealing with crisis situations, are highly important changes that will strengthen over the long run the organizational structure for dealing with foreign affairs on a day-to-day basis."

But enough of Bureaucrats, or my Ark will be overloaded with them.

Once I had a secretary who produced a unique contribution to the enlightenment of mankind. This maiden served briefly while my regular assistant was in the United States on leave; she took dictation, misspelled a good many words, and was gracious with callers; when not tapping away on her electric typewriter, she stoked her comely and tidy person with whatever brand of perfume was most powerfully displayed at our local Post Exchange. Guerlain, Houbigant, Chanel, Coty — I never knew what brand my Muskmouse favored, but pretty soon you could sniff the ambassadorial suite clear across the chancery.

Among those alerted were the United States Marines, present as embassy security personnel. Marines on duty, one of whom was supposed to stay in the entrance lobby downstairs while another prowled through the building looking for unattended safes and bits of classified paper, invented all sorts of reasons, many of them demonstrating a high degree of ingenuity, to make visits to the Muskmouse's cubicle adjoining my office. Marines off duty were with difficulty restrained from congregating outside my waiting room, respectfully, but with a basset hound expression. The behavior of the Muskmouse continued exemplary.

Then she got herself engaged to a little man in the Budget and Fiscal Office, and since he was of suitable background and deportment, approval was forthcoming and a date for the wedding was set. It was pleasant to see them, walking hand in hand in the park below the chancery or dancing demurely together on a Saturday night. They looked as sleek and self-satisfied as a couple of chipmunks.

Moreover, the first thing the accountant did was insist on less perfume, so that everybody around the ambassadorial suite breathed more freely. But as the wedding day approached, the secretarial talents of the bride progressively disintegrated. Her rendering of ambassadorial dictation became more and more erratic, until presently I dictated the phrase: "Man shall not live by bread alone," in the middle of a report to Washington. It was about an accusation of the opposition party that the government was doing little to enrich the spirit of the people, and I was rather proud of my ability to introduce a biblical allusion into political reporting. Busy with this and that, I hurriedly signed my mail and hastened to the airport for an hour between planes with a traveling Senator; it was not until the following morning that I read the carbon copy of my report, which by that time was half way across the Atlantic.

The bride had typed more eloquently than she had heard. The focus was on wedding cake and trousseau, not St. Matthew or the local opposition. "Man shall not live by bread alone," sifted through keys electric with impending nuptials, reached official embassy stationery in a context wider than politics. Typed the Muskmouse briskly (and I hoped prophetically): "Man shall not love in bed alone."

By the same token, a book should not consist of exposition alone, and I have accordingly included various episodes which may serve to illustrate — or perhaps only to confuse — some of the prejudices ventilated in the rest of the chapters. The last word on diplomacy is certainly yet to be said. In serving around the world, a Foreign Service Officer encounters a great variety of people, many of them seen under stress and others in unusual circumstances. Some of them inhabit these pages. Others, waiting along the sidelines of memory and experience, may, I hope, be welcomed in further installments.

It has been a rich and wonderful life, and the people who shared it with me made it so. For their friendship and forebearance, they deserve more than footnotes in a biography. History may belong to those who make it, but history is enjoyed by those who see it.

II.

The Fledgling Ambassador.

The State Department has embarked on a program seeking to popularize the Foreign Service as a career. Although this activity sometimes smacks more of Madison Avenue or Ian Fleming than it does of international relations, the infinite variety of Foreign Service work, which is one of its strongest attractions, renders diplomacy extraordinarily difficult to describe to those who have never flipped the pages of a codebook, or visited a foreign hospital at two A.M. searching for a vanished compatriot, or heard the menacing growl of a crowd that is getting out of hand in front of an American embassy.

As part of the same effort, Washington has a college-relations program, designed to encourage superior young men and women to take the examinations. One hazard of this undertaking is that the colleges may take seriously the emanations of some of the spokesmen of the State Department itself. One such official, having derided before a congressional committee the "supposedly dignified past" and the "gentlemanly pace" of old-fashioned diplomacy, declared that the first task of the overseas representative is to promote "internal development" — that is, the "various activities undertaken by the United States to encourage other nations to modernize their institutions."

Fumigated of obscurities, this seems to endorse the idea of wreaking good on thy neighbor, especially thy underdeveloped neighbor, regardless of his squawks of protest. That is one of the reasons why the Cambodians throw rocks through Amer-

28

ican embassy windows, and why "Yankee, Go Home" gets daubed beside chancery doorways.

A more damaging doctrine than that which holds it to be a duty of the diplomat to accelerate someone else's social revolution would be impossible to imagine.

Another foolishness fed by the State Department to the colleges is the proposition that Management Equals Diplomacy, an equation derived from the truly astonishing proliferation, first within the Department of State and then in its offices abroad, of administrative types who inflate themselves with all sorts of rich and resonant titles like Career Evaluators, and General Services Specialists, and even Ministers of Embassy for Administrative Affairs. These glorified janitors, supply clerks, and pants-pressers yearn to get their fingers in the foreign affairs pie, and when they do, the diplomatic furniture often gets marked with gummy thumbprints.

The Secretary of State recently complained about the multiplicity of officials separating him from the gist of whatever problem he was trying to unravel. What Mr. Rusk failed to note, or if noting, failed to decry, was the population explosion in his own bailiwick, and the way in which his own ravening bureaucratic termites have chewed their way into the woodwork of the Comprehensive Country Programming System, as the latest revelation of the professorial planners is labeled.

The universities might do well to encourage the development of a new type of statesman who would at the same time be a bureaucrat-exterminator. Otherwise there is the risk that the State Department become, as Vice Consul Peachpit once brashly warned Secretary Herter, so "overstaffed, overstuffed, and overstymied" that there may be little time left for foreign relations.

This year several thousand young men and women will compete for entry into the American Foreign Service. Possibly five per cent may survive the examinations. Perhaps

29

two hundred may finally be commissioned by the President. After six months of State Department indoctrination, these fledgling ambassadors will be issued gold and black diplomatic passports and assigned as probationers to embassies and consulates, all the way from Abidjan to Zagreb.

Theirs is a difficult and exacting profession. It speaks well for the fascination of the work and the enthusiasm of the participants that notwithstanding the award of one third of the ambassadorships to outsiders, so many excellent candidates continue to apply for the Foreign Service. Perhaps by 1985, when members of the entering class of 1964 should be reaching ambassadorial rank, a President may forego the luxury of appointing amateur engineers to design cloverleafs for his international highway.

How well our government is accomplishing the recruitment and training of Foreign Service officers is already an important factor in the effectiveness of our representation abroad. That accounts for the interest in a proposal to establish a Foreign Service Academy, which would monopolize the preparation of candidates. The proponents declare that an official school, run by the government, would simplify the selection of officers, now a somewhat cumbersome operation.

In theory, that might be so. The State Department would indicate its numerical and specialized requirements, and then wait for the Academy Superintendent to fill up the hopper. From that receptacle the master of diplomatic genetics would obediently extract so many homogenized political scientists, economists and vice consuls; so many administrators to harass the scientists, economists and vice consuls; and so many officers capable of translating into Swahili or Amharic the enduring aphorisms of Soapy Williams and Senator Ellender.

That would be fine if it worked, but few who have operated a foreign affairs establishment are in favor of a "West Point for diplomats," no matter how beguiling the prospectus. As the strength of our country has been fortified by the diverse ethnic groups who have merged to create the American citizen, so has the Foreign Service benefited from drawing its officer corps not from a single trade school, but from approximately four hundred institutions of learning, literally from Maine to California. That strength would be diluted if a Foreign Service Academy furnished all of the officers.

Diplomacy — that is, the substantive tasks of foreign relations in contrast to administering give-away programs or engaging in bureaucratic management — should be operated from the broadest possible educational and geographic base. The best candidates for diplomacy are those who, whatever their origins, possess a mixture of imagination, energy, durability, and flair for the work. The best undergraduate training for diplomacy is in the liberal arts, plus emphasis on history and social sciences as directional tools in charting a course through the rapidly changing world.

It is probably easier to pass the Foreign Service examinations after studying at an Atlantic seaboard or Pacific Coast college, because institutions in those areas have long encouraged training for diplomacy, with courses oriented in that direction. According to a State Department survey of the six years between 1957 and 1962, during which approximately nine hundred Foreign Service Officers were commissioned, 295 of them or 32 per cent were graduates of eight institutions in New England, the New York and Washington areas, and California. Harvard led with 60, followed by the University of California, 56; Princeton, 44; Yale, 41; Georgetown, 28; Leland Stanford, 23; Dartmouth, 22; and Columbia, 21. It speaks well, however, for the talents and ambitions of youths from other sections of the country that representation now covers every state in the Union; the Foreign Service is truly a national service.

One of the most important qualifications for a Foreign Service officer is the ability to write clear English. No irreparable damage is done by a sloppy or ambiguous statement ut-

31

tered by a public official *inside* the United States. (Otherwise, our country might be in a bad way.) But uness the American representative *abroad* can express himself so precisely that his interpretation formulated perhaps ten thousand miles from Washington can convey an exact impression when it reaches the Potomac, that envoy had better stick to career development, whose practitioners move their lips when they read, or else peddle the snake oil of *Alianza para el Progreso* to the Alacalufas of Tierra del Fuego, who scarcely read at all.

Slovenly writing is the most insistent criticism of the preparation of candidates for the Foreign Service.

Competence in at least one foreign language is a tremendous asset. Notwithstanding this, in recognition of the difficulty of learning foreign tongues in many parts of the United States, the language requirements for entering the Foreign Service are not high; if they were, the advantage would lie heavily on the side of the cosmopolitan polyglot, who might or might not be talented in other particulars. The *ability* to learn languages is rightly prized, and an excellent language training program is operated for those already in the Service.

Another criticism is that the State Department is over-administered and that the elapsed time between taking the examinations and certifying the results is too long. That is a valid complaint. There is an all-day written examination, followed some months later for those who pass by a searching oral examination. This oral test before a panel of examiners is the heart of the evaluation process. After further delay the candidate faces physical, security, and "suitability" examinations, the last in the square-pegs-in-round-holes tradition.

To the extent that this procedure can be shortened toward a maximum of one month, the loss of valuable candidates through attrition ought to be diminished. Telescoping the process involves, however, the danger of "computerizing" it, with too much reliance on formulas and mechanical gadgets to measure the intangibles of leadership potential and intellectual depth. The robot mind has no place in diplomacy.

Until recently, junior appointments (to Class 8, the lowest grade in the Service) have accounted for four-fifths of the total number of entering officers. In practice, a bachelor's degree has hitherto sufficed, after which "in-service training following competitive intake," to employ the jargon of the witch doctors of bureaucracy, has been regarded as the best preparation for increasing responsibilities. This means that experience on the diplomatic job at a succession of foreign posts, with an occasional stint at the State Department in Washington, is still the most effective training that a future ambassador can have.

It seems likely that a larger proportion of future candidates will have education beyond a bachelor's degree, a development consonant with trends in other fields that attract superior talent. Entry at Class 7 or Class 6 has been suggested to accommodate those with advanced education who pass the examinations.

Once launched on a career in the Foreign Service, there are rewarding opportunities for graduate work to supplement the "in-service training," or to achieve experience in such esoteric specialties as the anthropology of Southeast Asia or quadruple-entry bookkeeping to assist underdeveloped Ministers of Finance. The National War College and the separate service colleges now admit senior Foreign Service Officers, and the relationship thus established has been profitable in both directions: the military no longer automatically regard the diplomatic service as out of touch with reality, and the diplomats no longer automatically patronize the Pentagon.

As to the argument about "specialists" versus "generalists" in foreign affairs, that debate is largely academic: the great need in overseas work is for more people of the highest quality — people capable, as Senator Fulbright recently observed, of separating the myths from the realities of international life. The State Department, with hundreds of factotums assigned

33

to handling personnel, spends too much time designing charts and promoting projects like "mid-career training" and "senior officers' courses." Unlike the initial orientation — the famous A-100 seminar to which all successful candidates are exposed before they go afield — mid-career and senior training is frequently a waste of the officer's time and the taxpayers' money. Moreover, unlike attendance at the war colleges, it seldom attracts outstanding officers.

In that connection, there exists no compelling reason for the establishment of the "National Foreign Affairs College on the Graduate Level" — a mastodon post-graduate supermarket with ivory towers manned by hot-and cold-running professors — which was one of the less inspired proposals of a committee reporting last year to the Secretary of State.* Commenting without enthusiasm on this subject, Dean Acheson suggested that the government first make use of existing official facilities, together with those available through private colleges, universities and foundations, before launching so top-heavy a leviathan.

Before leaving the subject, let us not forget the Peace Corps. The foregoing is, after all, advice for the pedestrian Foreign Service candidate, who has not yet hitched his chariot to a star. For him who puts spurs to Pegasus and feels weightless only when contemplating his orbit, there is now a new road to diplomacy.

The Director General of the Foreign Service is "eager," so he has publicly declared, to have Peace Corps Volunteers apply. In fact, he hopes the Peace Corps will become "one of the major sources of recruitment." Many of the assignments which the Volunteers have undertaken should, he avers, "add significantly to their qualifications for the Foreign Service."

* The Herter Committee, chaired by the former Secretary of State, was constituted in 1961 at the request of Secretary of State Rusk. Its recommendations, entitled "Personnel for the New Diplomacy," were published in December, 1962.

This sputnik of confetti was launched in time to greet Peace Corps Volunters who are now returning from their caves and jungles, their enlistments completed and their appetites allegedly whetted for further adventures. Which of their experiences will "add significantly" to solving the problems of diplomacy, the Director General left to conjecture. It seems clear, however, that a special moth-resistant red carpet is being laid along Virginia Avenue by a politically-conscious State Department, for returning Peace Corps Volunteers to walk on.

Possibly that is all to the good. Having acquired an immunity to Parkinson's disease in Borneo, perhaps the Peace Corps should be invited to take on Parkinson's Law in Foggy Bottom.

III.

"This Is a Professional Game"

Ambitious young men, entering the Foreign Service through a competitive examination so rigorous that it eliminates ninety-five per cent of the candidates, have a right to aspire to be ambassadors. To reach eligibility they will have had thereafter a minimum of two and nearer three decades of professional service in foreign countries and in the Department of State. Yet upwards to thirty-five per cent of ambassadorial posts still go to non-professionals, most of whom have no prior diplomatic experience.

Of the 111 posts recently listed by the State Department, only sixty-seven were held by professional ambassadors. And of the so-called normal posts — in contrast to the sixty-three "hardship posts" — forty-one per cent were occupied by non-professionals. The outsiders, that is, hold a higher proportion of the attractive world capitals than they do of those in malarial tropics, or bleak plateau regions, or other under-developed areas. In fact, the reluctance of some outsiders to take on tough assignments was illustrated years ago in a cartoon by Peter Arno. A hard-looking character is offering a pen to a fluttery campaign contributor with a checkbook; the latter is complaining: "But I don't want to be American minister to Bolivia."

Campaign contributors, across the years, have continued to prefer Switzerland, Ireland, and Denmark to Korea, Iraq, and Bolivia.

No single factor is more discouraging to those in the career service than the practice of awarding ambassadorial posts to non-professionals. It is especially disheartening when the beneficiary is either an outright purchaser or one whose claim to consideration rests on dubious or publicly weakened foundations.

The time has already overtaken us when it ought to be just as archaic for a President to dispose of a diplomatic mission as it would be, reverting to the usages of nearly two centuries ago, for him to sell a regiment or auction off a colonelcy. Moreover, it can be imagined what the effect on armed service morale would be if command of an Army corps, or of a fleet, were entrusted to an un-uniformed outsider — to a Foreign Service Officer, for example. The infamy of it would be proclaimed from Bangor to San Diego, and the roof of the Pentagon would glow like the tail of a comet. Yet the reverse of this practice, equally abrasive to the morale of professional diplomats, is hardly an unusual occurrence.

Apologists for the non-professionals sometimes endeavor to divide them into categories. They would disqualify the candidate who comes, pocketbook in hand, to exchange a campaign contribution for a diplomatic mission. They would likewise reject the postulant who, having mismanaged the affairs of the Department of Agriculture or of the Thermal Dynamic Commission, is awarded an important embassy in order to guarantee his absence from the disenchanted Potomac environment for the balance of the administration. (Any Washington correspondent can identify specimens grown in that test tube.)

Those two categories of non-professionals are *bad,* say the apologists, and no more of them ought to be appointed. But there is a third group, they declare; they are the *good* non-professionals. During recent testimony before a Senate subcommittee, a former public servant expressed this thought as follows:

"In my own mind," he said, "I divide ambassadors into three

37

categories. The professional, the Foreign Service Ambassador, who has risen to the top. I think the vast majority of ambassadorial posts should be filled by career officers.

"The second category would be the appointment of someone for services rendered, either financial or to a political party, and whose qualifications otherwise are not outstanding. I don't believe there should be any of those appointed. . . .

"Then there is a third category of ambassadors for whom I think there is a place. I think an outstanding man who has made a great success in other areas, whether it is the academic field or some other field, who has the talents and the abilities and perhaps special qualifications for a special post, I think there should be a place for them."

The witness then mentioned several eminent Americans who had in fact served their country well, in Bonn, Buenos Aires, London, New Delhi, and Paris. They are patriotic and civilized individuals, and no one familiar with their abilities could fail to be impressed by them. That, however, is beside the point. The point is that practically no outsider, however talented, can be so effective at representing the United States abroad as can the outstanding professional trained for the job — the officer who has risen to the peak of a competitive professional career and who has already proved in important missions successfully completed, his fitness for the topmost positions in the diplomatic service.

The Congress in 1955 established the rank of career ambassador to accommodate such officers and also to serve as an added incentive toward retaining highly superior talent in government service. The enabling legislation specified that no Foreign Service Officer would be eligible to be a Career Ambassador unless he had served at least fifteen years in a position of responsibility in a government agency or agencies, including at least three years as Career Minister (the next highest grade in the Foreign Service), and finally, unless he had "rendered exceptionally distinguished service to the Government."

The sights were set high by Congress in aiming at the top of the Foreign Service. Commenting on the establishment of the new grade, the *Foreign Service Journal,* unofficial publication of the diplomatic service, hailed the first selection of "our five-star professional ambassadors." Here is that first list, appointed by President Eisenhower in 1956:

James Clement Dunn entered the then separate Diplomatic Service in 1919.* Assistant Secretary of State, 1944. Ambassador to Italy, 1946; to France, 1952; to Spain, 1953; and to Brazil, 1955.

Loy W. Henderson entered the Consular Service in 1922. Director of the Office of Near Eastern and African Affairs, 1945. Ambassador to India, 1948; and to Iran, 1951. Deputy Under Secretary of State, 1955–1961.

H. Freeman Matthews began in the Diplomatic Service in 1923. Director of the Office of European Affairs, 1944. Ambassador to Sweden, 1947. Deputy Under Secretary of State, 1950. Ambassador to The Netherlands, 1953; and to Austria, 1957.

Robert D. Murphy entered the Consular Service in 1920. Personal Representative of the President in North Africa in 1942; U. S. Political Adviser on German Affairs with rank of Ambassador, Supreme Headquarters American Expeditionary Forces, 1944. Ambassador to Belgium, 1949; and to Japan, 1952. Deputy Under Secretary of State, 1953.

The experience of those four officers at the time of their appointment as career ambassadors totaled one hundred and forty years, or an average of thirty-five years for each. Each had been a career minister for a full ten years before his appointment.

* The Diplomatic and Consular Service were separate until 1924, when the present American Foreign Service was established by the Rogers Act.

In addition, mention should be made of the veteran diplomatist Jefferson Caffery, who, entering the diplomatic service in 1911, was chief of mission in six successive countries from 1926 until his retirement twenty-nine years later, just before the rank of career ambassador was established.

Since the original four appointments in 1956, however, no President has made more than minimal use of the career ambassador legislation. In the ensuing years, only twelve career ambassadors have been selected, from a Foreign Service of over three thousand six hundred officers.* Nine career ambassadors, including the first four, have retired. Of the remaining seven still on active duty, only three are occupying embassies of first-line importance.

A more effective utilization of the career ambassador provisions was envisaged by Congress when it enacted the legislation. That this has not yet occurred has been disappointing to the Foreign Service.

Two additional factors have affected the morale of the diplomatic career. In a coveted post, a non-professional usually "bumps" a career chief of mission, not vice versa. And only in rare instances has another post been found for the displaced professional, at the time when the impending shift becomes known.

The career officer often learns of his approaching eviction through a Washington leak. That occurs most frequently in the White House itself, where it happens with such regularity as almost to enjoy the status of policy. The leak may also trace to the eager political appointee, who is so captivated by the idea of becoming Mr. Ambassador that he cannot resist telling his friends about it. In either case, the prospect of a change in ambassadorial representation is immediately reported by cable to the foreign capital concerned. Nine times out of ten, that is the first the incumbent ambassador has heard of it. An

* Seven career ambassadors, including the author, were appointed in 1960.

40

enterprising reporter from *El Universal,* or *Le Matin,* or *Rude Pravo,* or *To Bema,* phones the ambassador, reads him the cable, and asks for comment.

This incident is belatedly followed by an official announcement from Washington which, after describing the new appointee in several hearty paragraphs, concludes with the single sentence: "Ambassador Smith will be reassigned."

That is the worst possible way to conduct a career service, for the future usefulness of Ambassador Smith — an able officer with twenty-seven years of service whose only deficiency was that he occupied a post wanted by an influential outsider — can be compromised by even the rumor that he is about to be replaced. The announcement, devoted to the charms and talents of the new appointee but lacking any indication of a further assignment for Ambassador Smith, can put the finishing touches on his effectiveness. No foreign government will give credence to the views of an outgoing ambassador whose successor has already been named. Yet Ambassador Smith is not infrequently required to remain weeks and sometimes months at his post, his prestige destroyed by heedless Washington handling.

At the very least, the President should plug the White House leak factory, and the Secretary of State should require the ardent successor to possess his spirit in patience until another post is found for Ambassador Smith. The official announcement should be deferred until it can include the statement that Smith is being transferred to Burma, or Colombia, or whatever the country may be. That has rarely happened in recent practice, and the corridors of the State Department are filled with Ambassador Smith and his professional cousins, still waiting to be reassigned.

Nor is this all. The Washington leak can be embarrassing to the receiving government, which may or may not have been queried — as international usage as well as courtesy requires — whether the proposed new assignment is agreeable to it.

41

Although it is true that when at long last the official request for the agrément is received, it is generally granted, the premature publicity has forced the host government's hand. The episode has left a bad taste, and the clumsiness of the operation does not redound to the credit of the United States.

In any case, the non-professional appointment is likely to be unwelcome to the foreign government, already disillusioned by past experience with amateurs. Seeking to make the best of it, a government may hope the new envoy can be restrained by a knowledgeable deputy, or that he will soon return to his campus, fleshpot, or factory. The present situation is exceptional only in the quality of the prose that launched the original nominations — since which time one non-professional ambassador to France bowed out after only seventeen months, one ambassador to India departed after twenty-six, and one ambassador to Yugoslavia after twenty-seven, to mention only three of those who were originally billed as star-studded performers, with the implication that they might remain with the circus as long as the elephants did not take over.

Those three ambassadors, and others who could be listed by the time this book is published, will nevertheless probably be remembered as *good* non-professionals, even though their here-today-gone-tomorrow schedule eroded their usefulness.

There is, alas, an opposite grouping of diplomatic representatives, before whom even the most charitable historian may flinch and throw his recording tablets into the river. Sample fauna in the *bad* ambassadorial menagerie include some very ripe specimens indeed. In deference to their descendants, their characteristics have been scrambled, so that identification will not be automatic.

There was the former chiropractor whose wife, mislaying a piece of jewelry during a reception, summoned the police and sought to have her guests — Cabinet ministers, fellow diplomats, and their ladies — searched before they were allowed to leave the embassy residence. Her mate was later apprehended attempting to smuggle art treasures out of the country, concealed in his diplomatic luggage.

There was Monkey-gland Archibald, the perpetual satyr, whose overworked hormones were still so hot that no embassy stenographer was safe, not even with his office door open. This antediluvian wonderman, senile and incompetent in other particulars, was the protegé of a politician so powerful that Archibald headed not one but two diplomatic missions before his arteries finally melted.

There was the amiable drinker who used to disappear from the capital for days at a time, sending playful telegrams from here and there about the country: "Bet you can't guess what I'm doing tonight. Sammy." When, at the end of the administration, Sammy was eventually told he must go, his staff locked him in an embassy bedroom, took away his clothes, and then peddled them back to him a garment at a time and a highball at a time, against the signing of the innumerable forms that had to be completed before the American ambassador, once more fully clothed and again in his cups, was able to leave the country.

And there was the horse-doctor who fought with everybody, except maybe horses. When General Marshall became Secretary of State he demanded from subordinates a count of chiefs of missions, with a view to disinfecting the list. Told that the veterinary was "the worst ambassador we have — anywhere," General Marshall next discovered that the political backing of the horse-doctor was impregnable, and he could not be got rid of.

Not all these gaudy specimens were on the diplomatic racetrack at one time, nor focused in the binoculars of a single observer. But nearly every newspaper correspondent and American business leader abroad has a private memory stable where a stall is filled with equally spavined ambassadorial chargers, as good raw material for a glue factory as for a diplomatic mission. Even though the proportion of these spectacular emis-

43

saries to the total diplomatic population may be relatively small, their effect on the prestige and good name of the United States has been beyond computation.

Integrity, Prudence and Ability, indeed . . . (as it says in the ambassadorial commissions).

Why have foreign governments put up with these people? These governments are quick to resent disparaging remarks or unfriendly behavior, but one of the hallmarks of a certain kind of non-professional is his naïve and ardent admiration for the country to which he is accredited, which he yearns to praise on every occasion. By assiduously cultivating this proclivity, by repeatedly calling the ambassador "Excellency," and by otherwise buttering up his dipolmatic immunities, the Prime Minister is quickly able to get this amateur statesman into his pocket. To keep the American envoy there may be worth a tolerant attitude toward some of his extra-curricular activities.

Again, a foreign government is always informed about the antecedents of the American representative, including the amount and texture of his political backing. It may appear imprudent to jeopardize this American support by being severe with the ambassador at a time when for instance, a foreign-aid melon is about to be apportioned.

Or the foreign government may simply be discouraged at the possibility that the successor to Monkey-gland Archibald, should he be declared *persona non grata,* might turn out to be a dentist from Itching Springs, Oklakota, with a penchant for mixing laughing gas with the bourbon and serving it instead of champagne at his dinners. That government accordingly assigns a professional diplomat from its own service to Washington and handles its business through him, instead of through the American embassy in its own capital. Monkey-gland Archibald, no longer summoned to the Foreign Office, is happily able to extend his researches beyond the desk-tops of his own chancery. The business of the foreign government with the

44

United States — in contrast to the business of the United States with the foreign government — is adequately protected. The only losers are the American government and people.

In deference to the present situation and perhaps also to the spirit of progress, it may be observed that most non-professional ambassadors are trying to do their best, and that there are possibly fewer bad non-professional representatives than there were, say, a generation or even fifteen years ago. But the breed is by no means extinct. And today the stakes are infinitely higher, so that the prospect of wear and tear, damage or loss to the national purposes — to say nothing of the national heritage and ideals — is greater than ever.

It is thus a shameful thing that the American government, for the greater satisfaction of a handful of politicos of the dominant party, goes on handicapping itself in its dealings with other nations.

There are several reasons why few amateur ambassadors can compete on even terms with professional Foreign Service Officers who have risen to be chief of mission. The most obvious is that the newcomer lacks experience in the practical functioning of diplomacy. The atmosphere is strange to him. The tools are new to his hand and often seem oddly shaped. The terms of reference are different from those to which he is accustomed. Granted that by its nature diplomacy is an imprecise business (although its purpose is the rendering of precise agreements that will endure between countries), there is nevertheless a feel for and a familiarity with it, acquired by skilled operation of the machine of foreign affairs and in no other fashion.

A professor has declared that the three elements of diplomacy are *persuasion, compromise,* and *threat of force.* Very well. Assuming that this oversimplification is true, where is the textbook or teacher who will tell the would-be diplomat how to blend these ingredients for use in a given situation?

How much persuasion is enough? When do you introduce

45

even so little as the faintest whiff of the potent additive of threat? And compromise, when do you start compromising? How far can you safely tiptoe down the compromise path that for so many has suddenly become a roller-coaster, just around that safe-looking corner?

And when do you produce the threat itself, in all its hairy-chested menace? When do you tell those gentlemen across the table from you: "OK, boys. This is it. Take your muddy galoshes off my national doorstep — or else!" (And what do you do when one of them answers, "Horsefeathers . . ."?)

Furthermore, no two situations are alike. The mixture of tactics that produced that fine eupeptic effect on the negotiations last Thursday may act as a narcotic or conversely as too powerful a propellant if used on a problem arising the following Tuesday. In fact, almost the only thing that is predictable about diplomacy is its unpredictability. That is one of the things that a Foreign Service Officer learns day by day and year by year as he progresses through the grades of a competitive service. That is one of the things that cannot be learned overnight, not even by the most gifted amateur envoy.

A less manifest reason for the superiority of the professional over the volunteer is that the latter rarely realizes that personal popularity is not essential to successful ambassadorial performance. Popularity is like the olive in a martini; it's all right if you happen to like olives, but the martini drinker can easily survive without them, and an olive displaces some of the gin.

Respect, not popularity, is the essential ingredient in diplomacy. That is especially difficult for a politician-turned-diplomat to accept, for without enough popularity to swing the votes, even the statesman-politician soon finds himself on the domestic mulchpile. Consequently a political ambassador is often convinced that cultivating his public-relations garden is the most important activity in which he could possibly engage abroad. And if the appointee happens to be a lame-duck diplomat — not an unheard-of phenomenon — he is likely to spend practically his entire time trying to grow popularity wild rice to feed the natives or attempting to enhance his golden-glow image in the local duck pond, instead of attending to his government's business.

In Washington I once had occasion to survey the effectiveness of American representation over a period of years in one of the most important capitals of Latin America. Two ambassadors had performed there more competently than the rest. One was feared more than he was liked, and the other received little acclaim from foreign officialdom or press. Each proved a successful envoy, for each was *respected*. In contrast, the most popular American ambassador ever to serve in that capital, without whose genial presence no party was ever complete, accomplished virtually nothing.

That is not to say that *un*popularity is a gauge of success in diplomacy, or that ambassadors ought to go around like Cyrano de Bergerac, exclaiming: "Here comes, thank God, another enemy!" It is merely to observe that there are factors other than the approbation of foreigners that enter into profitable diplomatic achievement.

An ambassador is an appointed official. Moreover, he is not accredited to the *people* of a foreign country but to their *government,* which is not operating a popularity contest or seeking to determine whether Mr. Universe will turn out to be the Chargé d'Affaires of Upper Volta or the ambassador of the United States. What the foreign government is trying to find out is what the United States will do if the tariff on frozen poultry is raised, and what it wants from the American representative within its gates is dependability and accuracy of judgment in reflecting the Washington point of view — just as the American government values the same attributes in the foreign diplomatic representatives assembled in Washington.

Respect, not popularity, is what counts in diplomacy.

It takes time for these things to be learned. Thus the intelligent non-professional, if he remains a diplomat longer than most members of his class are willing to serve abroad, could conceivably end by being a fairly successful representative, beginning four or five years after his appointment. But why our government should be conducting a training course to convert amateur diplomats into professionals, when it already possesses a corps of professionals whose training has long since been accomplished, is not always easy to comprehend.

It reminds one of an abrasive phrase flung like a handful of gravel by an American ambassador at his colleague in a neighboring country, a good many years ago. As the junior officer present, I encoded the message for my hot-tempered chief and then sat back to listen for the answering echo. I remember the incident not so much for the flurry it caused in then pending negotiations, nor the anguish it produced in Secretary Kellogg who was frantically trying to achieve a solution before he yielded his office to Secretary Stimson, as I do for an interpretation of the difference between professional and non-professional performance.

"This is a professional game," declared my ambassador in anger, "and amateurs only interfere . . ."

He might have added that the havoc created by the amateurs, including some with the best of intentions, is not always confined to interference.

There remains one reason, more potent than the others, why the conduct of foreign affairs should be undertaken by professional diplomatists, trained in diplomacy. Political appointments are generally made for the good of the nominee, or the good of the dispenser of the patronage, or the good of the party in power. Professional appointments are made for the good of the country.

48

IV

Never Give a Comrade a Break

1. PROVOCATION

NEXT come tales of Communist Czechoslovakia. They are accompanied by the observation that although it is now fashionable to bask in the sunshine of relaxed tensions and peaceful coexistence, it seems prudent to this observer to cast back his memory now and then, and to recall how our enemies have acted.

It may be, as George Kennan appears to hope, that enough serfs of enough Communist masters may be permitted to retain enough of the goods they produce to render the serfs dependable members of society. Should they thereafter be permitted to conserve what they have, and even add to it, conceivably their masters might cease promoting the destruction of the rest of us.

I hope that miracle may come to pass. I pray that genuine collaboration may in fact be sought by Communist leaders who today seem less outwardly malevolent than they did in the days of Stalin in Moscow and Gottwald in Czechoslovakia. But until that miracle does come about, I prefer to be warned by the texts that the Communists themselves continue to live by. They view our world with implacable hostility.

This tells how the comrades tried to make our lives miserable in Prague, and how our embassy there was able — sometimes — to make the Communists wish they hadn't. In 1958, when parts of this chapter appeared as magazine articles, the Czechoslovak government protested. I found that both pleasant and ironic: pleasant because I had hoped the incidents might

49

inflame the comrades; and ironic that the government that indulged in an orgy of fabrications, false charges, "confessions" obtained under duress, and extermination of innocent men and women, should mistake for slander the derision poked at some of the unimaginative oafs who tried to annoy us.

It was in 1949 that I first reached Czechoslovakia, one year after the Communists took over. The first autumn snow was sifting through the spruces as I waited on the bridge beside the closed barrier at Rosvadov, with the brown fields of Bavaria behind me. A Communist sergeant took my papers and went away with them. Other soldiers in long coats manned either side of the lowered gate, holding machine guns. The barrier across the highway was a section of railroad track mounted in concrete; the rail replaced a wooden gate demolished by a departing fire engine filled with citizens of Pilsen who had decided they wanted no further part of the Communist Utopia.

I was to cross the frontier at Rosvadov many times in the next three years, and par, while the comrades shuffled my papers, was never less than sixty tedious minutes. On subsequent trips I took along the *Reader's Digest,* improving my word power and generating a powerful dislike for all Unforgettable Characters, but that first afternoon, as the gray shadows lengthened and snow powdered the empty Communist highway ahead of me, I looked at the soldiers, who stared back, fingering their weapons. On the left was the customs house with a flagpole beside it; opposite was the barracks. On either side, the dark spruces. Not a cheery spot, Rosvadov. The Iron Curtain.

In Prague I found a staff of eighty Americans, which the Communists shortly reduced to thirteen (as recounted in Chapter X).

The technique of the comrades merits dissection. Stalin used it when he decided to exterminate his friends in the

50

1930's. It became standard Communist practice. But whereas Uncle Joe was able to put the kiss of death on his Kremlin companions, his pupils abroad had to be content, insofar as foreign diplomats were concerned, with expulsion.

The Czech Communists, having decided what they wanted to do, invented in advance a plot involving American diplomats. The script of a spy trial was drafted. It described imaginary circumstances but named real names. Ingenuity went into this effort; later it made spectacular reading. A preparatory campaign was undertaken in *Rude Pravo* hinting at subversive monkey business emanating from the American embassy in Prague. American diplomats were spies, *Rude Pravo* averred, plotting with reactionary enemies of the state. But the Republic was vigilant. The designs of the American embassy would be frustrated by the defenders of the triumphant proletarian revolution. Watch for tomorrow's edition!

Thus the gestation of events was foreshadowed. The next step was the seizure of three innocent Czech employees of the United States Information Service, a part of the embassy. Two young men and a girl, homeward bound from the chancery, were intercepted by the secret police. Next day the embassy inquired of the Foreign Office, which replied, blandly, that it had no idea what had become of them. The Foreign Office reminded us, not so blandly, that the embassy had no jurisdiction over citizens of Czechoslovakia, even when they worked for the embassy.

Breaking down the three employees was eager work for the police apparatus. A few days later what was left of Karel and Jaroslav and Magda signed a catalog of evil, the spy trial script prepared in advance of the arrests. According to their confessions, the People's Democratic Republic of Czechoslovakia was to be delivered into the hands of the imperialist reactionaries. Local names were mentioned: American diplomats and prominent Czechs, the latter selected for destruction beforehand.

It was all there in the script, signed by Magda and Karel and Jaroslav as their "voluntary confessions."

The Czechs mentioned in the confessions were arrested. They, too, were remanded to cellars and put to the question.

At the trial, the broken defendants pleaded guilty in toneless voices. Magda, whose clear young soprano singing "Good King Wenceslaus" at our first embassy Christmas party we remembered, got fifteen years. Karel and Jaroslav received twenty-three years, reduced from life imprisonment because they "cooperated with the authorities following their confessions."

Other Czechs, officials of the former government, were executed. They included Maria Horakova, heroine of anti-Nazi resistance. A letter to President Gottwald was published, described as coming from Mme. Horakova's twelve-year-old daughter. This letter demanded that in view of "the infamy of mother's crimes against the state," executive clemency should be withheld. Maria Horakova was hanged.

The Czech Foreign Office was now ready to take over. An indignant note, citing the confessions produced at the trial, was delivered to the embassy by the Ministry of Foreign Affairs. It declared that American personnel had been vilely abusing the generous hospitality of the noble Republic of Czechoslovakia, in despicable contravention of the lofty principles of international law to which civilized Czechoslovakia subscribed. Ergo, five-sixths of the American embassy staff were declared obnoxious and given two weeks to get out of the country.

What did the Communist government of Czechoslovakia expect to gain by attacking the American government with accusations so patently preposterous? The explanation lies in the political situation as the Communists found it. In 1938 Chamberlain, seeking to avoid war with Hitler, delivered Czechoslovakia to the Nazis. No Czech could forget the betrayal at Munich. When World War II ended in 1945, the

Red Army occupied four-fifths of the country. President Benes, still shaken by Munich, devised a theory that Czechoslovakia, allied by culture with the West but by Slav inheritance with the East, could serve as a bridge of understanding between them. Benes was among the first to be shackled by "peaceful coexistence."

New elections were due in 1948, and the Communists recognized that in circumstances of free choice they would be defeated. To avoid defeat the Communists engineered a Russian-supported coup d'état against the ailing President Benes, who died a few weeks later.

Now in possession of the Czechoslovak government, the initial task of the commissars was the elimination of opposition leadership. The first objective of the spy trial was to remove known anti-Communist leaders; Maria Horakova, for example. That was why their names were written into the script as plotters against the Republic. The second objective, and the principal aim of several succeeding spy trials, was intimidation. The Communists sought to establish that it was dangerous for a citizen of Czechoslovakia to maintain relations with the West, especially Western diplomats living in Czechoslovakia.

A third spy-trial objective was to humiliate free-world diplomatic mission and thereby to discredit them, to show how strong were the Communists and how weak their adversaries.

The Czechs as a race are gentle people. Individually as brave as the lion of their legend, collectively they are the doormats of Europe. For three hundred years after the Battle of White Mountain, they were serfs to the Hapsburgs. Good Soldier Schweig was their hero, not Kossuth or Pilsudski. Not the baring of the chest but the prudent raising of the coat collar became their response to adversity.

So Tomáš Masaryk's dream of freedom for Czechoslovakia became the nightmare of the sickle and hammer. Hence the spy trials. Hence intimidation. Hence the premeditated attack on free-world diplomatic missions, which had the choice of withdrawing from the country or remaining under difficult conditions. That the American government chose to remain in Prague with its reduced staff, we who were there believed was the correct decision. As long as we stayed, the American flag floated daily over the embassy, in sight of the Communist emblems on Hradcany Castle.

A policy of harassing American diplomats having been adopted, it remains to consider how that policy was implemented, and what we were able to do about it. Harass us it was evident they would, for the fuel that operates the Communist vehicle is fear — a powerful and corrosive propellant — and those entrusted with the task were apprehensive of the consequences to themselves, in the hierachy, if they showed little zeal or bungled the operation.

The instrument of our annoyance, the Communist-inflicted thorn in our side, was an unlovely character called Hajdu, who was then Vice Minister for Foreign Affairs in Czernin Palace, the Czech Foreign Office. A Slovak Hungarian with a permanently volcanic complexion, no sense of humor, and a literal view of orders from the Central Committee, Comrade Hajdu relished his assignment. Following the Kremlin formula of the reiterated lie that by repetition becomes the standard premise — "as is now well known from the confessions of the convicted Czech traitors, all American diplomats are spies" — the embassy premises were subjected to heavy doses of Communist surveillance. Four policemen in civilian clothes were stationed across the street from the chancery. They intercepted people who came out of our offices. In a short time we had few visitors.

Next the Communists stepped up surveillance of our remaining American personnel. They followed us about on foot and in Tatras, frequently stopping us to demand identification. "Got your carnet with you?" became an automatic warning to anyone leaving the chancery.

In addition to surveillance, the Foreign Office presently

54

established a special agency for our annoyance. It was called *Burobin,* organized ostensibly to provide foreign diplomats with services for their comfort and convenience. A smug note described the attributes of the new agency. It dwelt on the solicitous concern of the People's Republic for the welfare of its diplomatic guests, who would henceforth rent their houses, hire their servants, and purchase their supplies through the kind intermediary of *Burobin,* theirs to command.

The housing provision did not bother us. The American government owned more real estate in Prague than our remaining thirteen officials knew what to do with: we had a baroque palace with 159 rooms for a chancery, plus an immense residence over the hill from Hradcany Castle, with two smaller houses and a private park around it.

But on servants and supplies we were vulnerable. Our servants were Czechs. Unlike the Communist diplomatic service, which organizes each diplomatic establishment as a unit complete with everyone from gardeners and chauffeurs to the ambassador, non-Communist missions depend on local citizens for their household requirements. One by one our Czech servants were seized by the secret police. Their "confessions" enlivened the pages of *Rude Pravo.* This did little to encourage volunteers to replace them.

That was where *Burobin* came in. That *Burobin's* candidates were police spies we took for granted, but most of them were lamentable servants as well — unwashed, or bad cooks, or else they got into the embassy liquor. Also they kept putting microphones in our houses.

The *Burobin* supply bottleneck was equally trying. Because of *Burobin* we made many extra trips to Nuremberg, two hundred miles away in Bavaria, where our Army maintained a commissary. With only thirteen people in the embassy, the commissary run, with a two-ton truck borrowed from our military establishment, pressed heavily on our depleted personnel.

Coal was a perpetual crisis; because of its bulk it was impractical to transport it from abroad. The Czech who built the embassy residence owned Bohemian coal mines. He not only erected an impressive house, but he also installed furnaces that looked like the boiler room on an ocean liner. There was a private underground railway like the toonerville trolley that connects the Senate Office Building with the Capitol, to supply our furnaces from a nearby coal dump. Even with the most parsimonious contriving it took over one ton of coal a day to keep our pipes from freezing. (A profligate ambassadorial predecessor burned five tons a day.)

Burobin rationed our coal supply. Our Administrative Officer spent hours on the *Burobin* doorstep, packets of Czech *coronas* in hand, trying to keep us from freezing.

At the opposite end of the *Burobin* supply scale was beer — genuine Pilsen. The famous brewery operated full-time under the Communists, but the product on sale, inside Czechoslovakia, would not have elected Miss Rheingold once in a decade. It resembled what remains in the washing machine after you take the socks out and let the suds settle. The Communists made good beer — *Prasdroj* Pilsen — but they made it for export, for dollars. The only way we could get it was to buy it from *Burobin,* at one dollar a bottle.

Burobin had the last word on our coal and our Pilsen.

2. Response

Our beleaguered Prague embassy did not spend its time turning the other cheek or accepting with resignation the taunts of the comrades. See-sawing over the Sudeten hills between the frontier and Prague on my first afternoon in Czechoslovakia, I composed a message to the American High Commissioner in Germany on the subject of border arrangements. Thereafter Czech diplomats, permitted now and then by their commissars to penetrate the Iron Curtain, spent an equivalent sixty minutes waiting for the gate on the German side to be opened.

The Czech Foreign Office complained. It said that formalities on the German side had suddenly been multiplied, without reason. The Foreign Office characterized the newly established one-hour wait before a Czech diplomat could cross from Rosvadov to Waidhaus as a "deliberate and premeditated provocation." That on the Czech side it took sixty minutes to scrutinize candidates for admission to the People's Democratic Republic was irrelevant. What counted was that the previous procedure for prompt entry into Germany had been modified, unilaterally, to the detriment of Czechoslovakia. The Ministry protested.

This was a valuable lesson for an official serving his first stint among the comrades. It indicated that Communists reason like paranoics, logically, but from a false premise; also that their official communications suffer from adjective trouble. The incident implied likewise that whereas goading a free-world diplomat into making a protest is regarded by the Communists as a triumph, a Communist loses no caste — among Communists — by denouncing Imperialist Obstructionism. Absorbing this early lesson, the embassy never delivered a protest.

We let the word get around Prague that the embassy would be glad to lend to each traveling Czech diplomat a dog-eared number of the *Reader's Digest,* which he was at liberty to translate into Unforgettable Slovak. That terminated the episode.

When, following the spy trial, the Communists ordered the expulsion of five-sixths of the embassy staff, we retaliated by reducing the Czech embassy in Washington to the same size as ours in Prague — twelve persons plus the ambassador.

Second, we closed the Czech consulates in the United States, and to forestall the next Communist move announced that we were closing our own single consulate in Bratislava, across the Danube from the Russian zone of Austria. That was a blow to the comrades, for whereas our Bratislava office was of marginal interest to us, the Czech consulates in New York, Cleveland, and Chicago extracted each year huge remittances from Czech-Americans who were worried about their relatives in Czechoslovakia.

There are more Czechs in Chicago than in any city in Czechoslovakia except Prague, the capital. The Czech consuls spent their time gathering lists of American families with relatives in Czechoslovakia. The bite was then put on Aunt Sofia in Kladno, or Uncle Frantichek in Rokicany, to the end that American nephews shortly received pitiful letters. Responsive to these appeals, Czech-Americans warm-heartedly came across with dollar remittances which to reach the recipients had to be handled through the Czech consulates. Payment for American dollars was made in paper *coronas,* at the *official* rate fixed by the Communists, who then pocketed the dollars. The profit averaged ninety per cent, in hard currency, which was added to the Communist war chest. This racket evaporated when we closed the Czech consulates in the United States.

Finally, we answered the Foreign Office note evicting our staff with a vigorous communication in return. The text was broadcast that night in Czech by the Voice of America, to which everyone in Czechoslovakia listened.

When Hajdu organized surveillance of the chancery, we paid off the secret police by giving them lessons in deportment, via the Voice of America. Ascertaining that the Czech equivalent of Eeny-Meeny-Miney-Moe is Eneky, Beneky, Kleeky, and Bey, we christened the four policemen Eneky, Beneky, Kleeky, and Bey. The Voice then proceeded to criticize their appearance, which was slovenly, and their sidewalk picnic manners, which were untidy.

At a time when *Rude Pravo* was exhorting all patriotic workers to put forth special efforts so that the Five Year Plan could be completed in three years, here, the Voice of America pointed out, were four able-bodied idlers cluttering up Mala Strana day after day, loafing in the street, molesting pedestrians, and tossing orange peels and bits of *knedlicky* out of the windows of their green or gray Skoda (or black Tatra). Embassy personnel took photographs of the police, ostentatiously, from the safe haven of our chancery windows.

Czechs passing in Mala Strana were encouraged to make remarks; they pointed at the orange peels and the *knedlicky*. Eneky, Beneky, Kleeky, and Bey became self-conscious and uneasy. The Voice of America gleefully reported their discomfiture, which in turn rendered the four policemen aggressively eager to lay hands on a likely victim.

They shortly found one in Dr. Prochaska, an owlish professor who was appointed Czechoslovak ambassador to Washington. It was after the arrest in Prague of Bill Oatis, an Associated Press correspondent, on trumped-up espionage charges. Official relations were tense, and Dr. Prochaska stayed away from the American embassy, where protocol demanded that he make an official call before leaving for the Potomac. Protocol likewise demanded that our embassy give Prochaska a farewell dinner, but he waited to make his call until the day he left Prague for the United States, so he wouldn't be able to accept the invitation.

Dr. Prochaska spent a desultory half hour with me, preserving amenities. He showed me his steamship ticket; so sorry about the dinner invitation, but he was sailing on the *Queen Mary*. I predicted he would have a rough time in Washington unless his government released Bill Oatis. Prochaska made pectoral noises. Oatis, he declared, was a spy; his confession proved it. Oatis, I retorted, was an honest newspaperman; his confession, obtained under torture, proved nothing.

I accompanied Dr. Prochaska to the chancery gate. I watched him walk down Mala Strana, his Bohemian fedora on the back of his head. When the Ambassador came abreast of

59

the police car, out popped Eneky, Beneky, Kleeky, and Bey in their brown-belted overcoats: they had spruced themselves up under Voice of America coaching.

The four policemen surrounded Ambassador Prochaska. What had he been doing in the American embassy? Where was his authorization to go there? Did he carry identification papers? Quickly, Comrade, produce your credentials! A candidate for the cellar. The policeman loved it. They thought they were acting like G-men.

Ambassador Prochaska fished into his pockets, one after another. He had forgotten to carry his passport, and he had neglected to bring his carnet. Out presently came his steamship ticket. Beneky pounced upon it, while his three companions pounced upon Dr. Prochaska. In a country where no citizen is permitted to move from one district to another without papers stamped by various ministries, there are few documents more incriminating than a ticket for travel outside a People's Democratic Republic.

The last glimpse I had of my opposite number, Ambassador Prochaska was being bundled into the Skoda by Beneky and Kleeky, leaving Eneky and Bey to continue chancery surveillance. We heard later that Prochaska almost missed the *Queen Mary* at Cherbourg.

The Voice of America enjoyed that episode, and so did the Czech people who listened to it. An account of it preceded Prochaska to Washington. For several days thereafter, when members of the embassy staff were stopped in the street by the secret police, my colleagues replied: "Careful, Comrade, for all you know I might be the Chechoslovak ambassador to Washington."

Further attempts to enforce surveillance of embassy personnel outside the chancery led to spirited cross-country chases in which the police Tatras, light in the bow and with rear-end motors, lost out to our high-compression American engines. The police recommended to the Czech Foreign Office that a circle be drawn around Prague, beyond which the embassy would be forbidden to travel. I was summoned to Czerin Palace for another interview with the Vice Minister, who gleefully outlined the projected restrictions. Since all American diplomats are spies, went his thesis, the capital of the country would henceforth contain us.

Fine, I told him. And on the day your government puts Pisak out of bounds to the American embassy, the first Czech diplomat from Washington who turns up in Baltimore gets thrown in the hoosegow.

That fixed it. Since it was much more important to the comrades to have Czech diplomats enjoy *all* of the United Sates to roam around in than it was for them to anchor American diplomats within Prague suburbs, the notion of drawing a circle around the capital and enclosing us in it was abandoned. We had small flags mounted on the embassy automobile so that it would be difficult to fabricate an espionage charge. These emblems further annoyed the police, who could not accuse the American ambassador of spying while the Stars and Stripes flew over one mudguard and the blue ambassadorial flag over the other.

Not all retorts were equally effective. The Foreign Minister invited me one day to repair with all speed to his office. Other unwelcoming officials were in attendance, plus a stenographer with pencil and paper.

The United States government was accused, said the Minister, of a new and wanton provocation. It had deliberately sent a jet airplane over Prague, scorching the roofs of the city and buzzing Hradcany Castle, for the deliberate and premeditated purpose of threatening the peace-loving government of the People's Republic of Czechoslovakia. This was not to be endured. The People's Republic demanded an apology. It demanded an assurance that the outrage would never be repeated.

The Foreign Minister handed me an official note, which,

61

as I observed from the English translation attached, anticipated a reply within forty-eight hours. The prose, as usual, was as caressing as sandpaper.

By that time regarding myself as something of an authority on self-inflicted Communist indignation, I told Foreign Minister Siroky what he could do with his Ridiculous Charges. American pilots, I said, are *infallible*. American pilots flew around Germany, yes; but their charts showed Czechoslovakia right where the mapmakers left it. Their navigation was perfect. If a stray plane had in fact been over Prague, I said, it was probably some incompetent Soviet pilot mistaking Czechoslovakia for Poland. I suggested to the Minister that he go peddle his complaint to the Kremlin.

When I returned to the chancery I was greeted by a priority message from Air Force headquarters in Wiesbaden. Not one, but *three* American jet planes had inadvertently violated Czechoslovak air space. At thirty-five thousand feet, lost in the February smother, one plane had descended to check position by contact.

The mid-winter overcast that blankets central Europe from November until spring ended at six hundred feet, right over the roofs of Prague. On the ridge overlooking the Vltava River sits Hradcany Castle, which the comrades expropriated as the seat of government, emulating the Hapsburgs. At the sound of the plane, half the Communists present, with wartime experience with Stukas, dived under the table. Not so many commisars' heads had bumped together since the last time Uncle Joe had shuffled his Central Committee.

Next morning I was back in Czernin Palace, the Czech Foreign Office. "Oops, sorry," I said, and left an official note to confirm it. The Minister was so astonished he forgot his invective.

With *Burobin,* we likewise had our moments of frolic. The *Burobin* servants were forever putting microphones around, most of which we uprooted. But now and then we kept one for its mischief potential. A tame microphone made a wonderful pipeline direct to headquarters. We used to invent far-fetched items about American policy and feed them into the apparatus. Several became topics for angry editorials in *Rude Pravo*.

Furthermore, our wretched *Burobin* servants, hostages of the police, could not resign, no matter how hard we worked them. They everlastingly polished the silver; they interminably washed the windows; they indefatigably rolled the tennis court in summer and diligently smoothed the ice wherewith we flooded it for skating in winter; they spent days taking the residence elevator apart and putting that ancient contraption together again.

So although we were harassed and annoyed and threatened daily by editorials in *Rude Pravo,* the coin in which we paid back the comrades was not always counterfeit. We cost the comrades, as when we closed down their consulates in the United States, many thousands of dollars. Although *Burobin* servants sometimes broke plates while washing our dishes, the lawns that they mowed could have been used for a billiard table. And if we could not drink *Prasdroj* Pilsen, at least we could buy Löwenbrau at the army commissary in Nuremberg for fifteen cents a bottle.

And in the broader area of our relations, we had our satisfying revenges.

3. REVENGE

We had three revenges during those years the Communist comrades of Czechoslovakia played spit-in-your-eye with the American embassy. The comrades called the turns — and usually had the first spit — but, like hoodlums wherever you find them, they could dish it out but they could not take it. Our first revenge was against the secret police, toward whom our grudge was substantial. Another was against the Russians, who had treated Embassy Prague with churlish and unco-operative behavior. The last was against the Czech comrades in general.

i. Exit Eneky, Beneky, Kleeky, and Bey

Inasmuch as the hero of our first revenge may one day want to take credit for the episode in his memoirs, we shall call the Latin American Minister concerned, Don Pedro, and the country which he represented, Bolivaguay.

Bolivaguay at the time maintained relations with Soviet Russia, one of whose South American couriers suffered — or imagined he suffered — some slight at the Bolivaguayan airport at Lago Febrero. The Soviet Minister to Bolivaguay wrote a note of protest, full of prickly adjectives. The courier, he complained, had experienced at the hands of the imbecilic Bolivaguayan authorities a baleful and deliberate provocation, not to be endured.

There, if the Soviet diplomat had been more circumspect, the matter might have ended, the Russian note comfortably collecting mildew in the archives of the Bolivaguayan Foreign Office. After all, Soviet couriers are expendable. But the Russian Minister was ambitious; he wanted to chalk up credit with the Kremlin. He demanded an apology from the Bolivaguayan government. More, he demanded an Immediate Apology. Still more recklessly, he sent copies of his note to the newspapers of Lago Febrero, the Bolivaguayan capital.

The Bolivaguayans are a sensitive and proud people. When they read the Russian note over their *café con leche* the next morning, the citizens of Lago Febrero boiled with patriotic indignation. At the ensuing mass meeting in the Plaza de la Constitución, successive orators outdid themselves, and presently a group of university students, augmented as it marched down the principal *avenida* by citizens previously asleep in the shade, or selling lottery tickets, or plotting the next revolution, converged on the Russian legation, where, after singing the Bolivaguayan national anthem, the students dared the Russian Minister to appear on his balcony. And when the Russian Minister prudently did not appear, several Russian legation windows were broken.

Even before the Soviet Minister to Bolivaguay had time to write a new note of protest, the Bolivaguayan government severed diplomatic relations with Russia.

There again the matter might have rested, of interest primarily to Lago Febrero and Moscow, with little more in Prague than a snide editorial in *Rude Pravo* calling attention to the backwardness of Bolivaguay, described by the comrade editor as a malarial satellite of Yankee colonialism. Russia, however, entrusted her interest in Bolivaguay to the Czechoslovak legation in Lago Febrero. The Czech Minister, himself ambitious to chalk up credit with the Kremlin, composed a communication of his own about the Soviet courier.

Instead of limiting himself to notifying the venerable (and hot-tempered) Bolivaguay Foreign Minister that Czechoslovakia was assuming the representation of Russian interests, he explained that his added responsibilities on behalf of Russia were the result of the incomprehensible behavior of the Bolivaguayan government toward his eminent and distinguished Soviet colleague.

Whereupon the venerable (and hot-tempered) Bolivaguayan Foreign Minister severed relations with Czechoslovakia.

All this happened in Lago Febrero almost as fast as the telling. Don Pedro, the Bolivaguayan minister in Prague, was a cheerful young man who possessed a penchant for Paris and at that time the only Cadillac automobile in Czechoslovakia. He had a police siren on his car that was audible from Prague to Hradec Králové; it had more than once attracted the attention of the Communist authorities.

The first Don Pedro knew of the events shaking the palm

65

fronds of his distant South American capital was when Vice Minister Hajdu announced to him that because of the barbaric conduct of the Bolivaguayan Government, Don Pedro, albeit expelled in his turn from Czechoslovakia, would not be permitted to leave Prague until the departing Czech Minister was safely aboard his airplane at Lago Febrero. Until then, said the Minister, the Bolivaguayan envoy would be confined to his Prague legation.

Whence a few minutes later a bewildered Don Pedro telephoned the American embassy. I rallied around. Don Pedro was not much perturbed by the prospect of expulsion; he said he had been thrown out of better places, and anyway it was over a month since his last visit to Paris. But Czechoslovakia had blocked communication with his government. Would the American ambassador kindly cable Washington to find out from Lago Febrero what all this was about? He gathered the Prague version might not coincide with the interpretation of his own government.

Washington obliged with communication facilities. The Bolivaguayan Foreign Minister stated, vehemently, that he was damned if the Czech minister could leave Lago Febrero while his own minister, Don Pedro, was held as a hostage in Communist Czechoslovakia. Simultaneous departure of the two ministers from Lago Febrero and Prague was, after negotiations, fixed for noon on the following Thursday. And in the meantime the Bolivaguayan Foreign Minister confined the Czech Minister to *his* quarters in Lago Febrero and blocked *his* communication facilities.

Honors were temporarily even, and there, once again, the matter might have rested, with Don Pedro happily disappearing among the boulevards of Paris, and the incident of primary interest to Prague and Moscow on the one hand and Lago Febrero on the other. But the Czech Communists wanted the secret police to participate, in order that Don Pedro's deportation might be as humiliating as possible.

The non-Communist members of the Prague diplomatic corps, by then with considerable experience in saying goodbye to expelled colleagues, had developed a farewell procedure. If departure was by train or by air, the non-Communist chiefs of mission congregated at Wilson Station or Ruzyne airport, showering the expelled one with champagne and good wishes. If departure was by highway, as in the case of Don Pedro, we met at the deportee's house an hour before the event, bringing sandwiches and contributions in bottles. These impromptu receptions were galling to the Czechoslovak government and especially to the police, who resented the gaiety, the taking of photographs, and the fact that the participants had diplomatic immunity and could not be arrested. This time it was decided that the police would escort the Bolivaguayan Minister to the border at Rosvadov, one hundred miles away. Eneky, Beneky, Kleeky, and Bey, excused for the day from surveillance over the American embassy, were detailed to accomplish Don Pedro's ejection from the People's Democratic Republic.

Don Pedro, a popular young man among his diplomatic colleagues, had a splendid reception that began at eleven o'clock of a summer morning. The collection outside the Bolivaguayan legation of diplomatic cars, recognizable by their special red and orange license plates, drew a crowd of Prague citizens.

A few minutes before noon a black police Tatra drove up to the Bolivaguayan legation and parked in front of Don Pedro's green and ivory Cadillac roadster. The Tatra was the escort car for the trip to the frontier at Rosvadov. Beneky, having added a snap-brim hat to his brown-belted overcoat, got out of the Tatra and rang the legation doorbell.

Inside Don Pedro's legation a measure of confusion was developing. Successive toasts were being proposed, in several languages: *felix viaje, bon voyage, na zdar, aufwiedersehen, boa viagem, a safe and prosperous journey.* The Latin American colleagues made speeches, which were cheered, and they gave

Don Pedros hearty *abrazos*. Popping of corks punctuated the oratory.

Beneky rang the bell several times before anyone noticed. He was then recognized, ushered in, and invited by the hospitable Don Pedro to join the festivities. Don Pedro declared, to his assembled diplomatic colleagues, glass in hand, that not even a rapist, fleeing from the father of his nine-year-old victim, would be denied the sanctuary of such poor accommodations as Bolivaguay could afford. He said that in Spanish. He inquired, still in Spanish, in what way he might serve this most unsanitary representative of an obnoxious government.

Beneky, standing at attention, announced in Czech that it was time for the Bolivaguayan Minister to be leaving. It was twelve o'clock, the hour fixed by his government for the Minister's departure.

Don Pedro did not speak Czech. He said something in Quechua, the language of the Andean Indians, whereat the Peruvian Minister shouted *"olé,"* and went bottoms-up with his champagne glass.

Beneky stubbornly repeated in Czech that it was twelve noon, the hour specified for the Minister to go; they had better be starting. Don Pedro answered in Guarani, the language of the Chaco, and the Paraguayan Chargé d'Affaires cheered loudly.

Exasperated, but with fine Slavic persistence, Beneky announced once again that he was present to escort the Bolivaguayan Minister to the border.

"You look," said Don Pedro in English, "like a fugitive G-man."

Finally Beneky said his piece in German, which all Czechs understand but few will admit speaking.

Don Pedro had been to school in Germany. He bowed and clicked his heels together. *"Jawohl,"* he replied in German. "Why didn't you say so the first time? But he added, in Span-

68

ish, "Go climb a palm tree, my friend, and throw coconuts at your illegitimate grandmother."

All this was painful to the Dutch Minister, who understood Spanish and had ideas about protocol. He undertook to give Beneky an expurgated account of developments, but before he finished the Brazilian Minister started a speech in Portuguese. Beneky, he said, was a louse, and for two *cruzeiros* he would throw him through the window. Seventy million Brazilians, he concluded, would applaud him. The Dutch Minister gave Beneky a fumigated translation of this patriotic effort, and we eventually all trooped out of the legation to help Don Pedro stow himself and his luggage into the Cadillac.

By now there was a crowd of interested Czechs outside the gate. From editorials in *Rude Pravo* they were privy to what was up, and awaiting the outcome.

The final item installed in the green and ivory chariot was an ice bucket, with the neck of a magnum of Lanson protruding. We all said goodbye again, and the Latin American colleagues gave Don Pedro a final round of *abrazos*. Beneky, looking glum, joined Eneky, Kleeky, and Bey in the black Tatra. Kleeky stepped on the self-starter. The cavalcade would soon be in motion.

A whirring noise, first brisk but diminishing, came from underneath the Tatra. Kleeky tried again; the whirring was repeated, less briskly, and then it died altogether. Kleeky stomped on the starter, but that time nothing responded. At the garage inside Bartolomeska Prison, someone had neglected the battery. By the gate, the crowd murmured as Eneky, Beneky, and Bey got out of the Tatra and Kleeky, scrabbling under the back seat, brought out a long crank handle.

Cranking a dead motor from the forward end, facing the car, is a sufficiently uninspiring activity. But to insert a four-foot metal rod into an engine at the rear end of an automobile, first groping for the aperture, is the epitome of unglamorous frustration — even if conducted decently and in private. While

69

Eneky, Beneky, and Bey took turns savagely twirling the crank, Kleeky twiddled things on the dashboard. Still nothing happened. But outside the gate the murmur of the crowd, abetted by the diplomats, grew in volume and derision.

The three policemen were muscular and stubborn. There is no telling how long the shameful spectacle might have continued if Don Pedro had not become impatient. With champagne under his belt and his eye already yearning toward the Champs Elysées, Don Pedro started his Cadillac motor and suddenly opened the siren. Eager horsepower responded. The noise was shattering. Ten feet in front of the Cadillac, Eneky, Beneky, and Bey fell away from the crank handle, deafened and cursing. Kleeky shot out of the front seat as though propelled by a rocket. The old tiles on Hradcany Castle, two miles down the Vltava River, were possibly loosened.

"Get back into your car," shouted Don Pedro cheerfully, in German. In the silence after the siren his voice was audible to the Czechs gathered outside the legation gate, and all Czechs understand German. "Get back into your car," repeated the departing Bolivaguayan Minister. "I'll push your Tatra all the way to Lago Febrero. But first, my friends, kindly remove your grandmother's enema."

Rude Pravo did not publish a description of Don Pedro's expulsion from Czechoslovakia. It merely announced that the Minister had departed. But outside the American embassy our four secret policemen were replaced by four identical drones. Eneky, Beneky, Kleeky, and Bey were sent — we hoped — to a Communist labor battalion. It was the last any of us saw of them.

ii. Tryst with Comrade Vishinsky

Our next revenge was contrived out of unrelated circumstances, with scant premeditation. We put it together one winter afternoon, without the Communists ever discovering the gimmick.

The first circumstance was an altercation between the *Wagons-Lits* company, which owns the sleeping cars in Europe, and the nationalized Czechoslovak State Railways, which borrowed fifteen *Wagons-Lits* cars and refused to give them back. The cars were useful on the Prague-Warsaw run, and the Communists were so accustomed to stealing property from their own citizens — nationalization, they called it; *narodny podnik* — that they were surprised when the Belgian and French representatives in Prague served notice on behalf of the *Wagons-Lits* stockholders that until the stolen cars were returned, no more sleeping cars from Western Europe would cross the Czech frontier. *Wagons-Lits* cars would continue to run from Paris to Schirnding, but there they would be uncoupled, on the German side. As to what sleeping car passengers ticketed for Prague could do on that windy Bavarian platform, with no porters, no restaurant, and no hotel facilities, the French Ambassador and the Belgian Minister implied that their governments could not care less: passengers could walk to Prague or ride on the wooden benches of the third-class coaches of the nationalized Czechoslovak Railways. When the fifteen stolen cars had been returned, the *Wagons-Lits* company would be pleased to discuss resumption of through sleeping-car service to Czechoslovakia.

The *Wagons-Lits* company has no American stockholders, but we in the embassy found out about the dispute the hard way — as passengers. It was a six-hour trip by train between Prague and Nuremberg, and when our truck was being repaired, or when snow on the Rosvadov highway was too deep to negotiate, we got our supplies over the railroad. The German border station at Schirnding came to know us well, for we had to wrestle diplomatic pouches and cases of food out of the *Wagons-Lits* windows and onto the frozen platform, and then repeat the exercise when the third-class Czech carriage was shunted up the adjoining track. Czech brakemen proved surly and impervious to capitalist tips — only trusted Com-

71

munists were permitted to travel as train crews — so at that border crossing, instead of developing our word power with a popular magazine, we developed diplomatic charley-horses lifting things onto the Schirnding platform.

The second circumstance was the Gray Card requirement. At that time Bavaria and all of Austria to the south of Czechoslovakia were zones of military occupation. Bavaria was American, but Austria was divided. To enter an occupation zone it was necessary to possess, in addition to a passport, a Gray Card issued by the respective occupying power. The cards were oblong pieces of stiff gray paper, specifying destinations for which they were valid. Getting them was a nuisance. Getting them from the Russians was a multiplied vexation.

All of us in Embassy Prague had permanent Gray Cards issued by the United States authorities in Germany for entry into Bavaria as often as we wished. Nuremberg was our usual target. But Vienna was the same distance from Prague; Vienna was less bombed than Nuremberg; Vienna had music and girls and laughter.

To reach Vienna, we had to cross 75 kilometers of the Russian zone of Austria, north of the Danube. And for that we needed Soviet Gray Cards, which for several years after the war were issued by the Russian embassy in Prague. Suddenly they stopped issuing them. No reason was forthcoming. We were told to take our requests to the Russian High Commission in the Imperial Hotel in Vienna. When we asked how we were going to get to the Imperial Hotel in Vienna without Gray Cards to cross Austria with, the Russians shrugged their shoulders.

The only way we could make the trip — and it was a pleasant ride across the Bohemian fields, through the old town of Znojmo, and into the Austrian vineyards — was to send our passports by diplomatic pouch once a month to Vienna, where the American High Commission obtained Gray Cards valid for thirty days from the Soviet High Commission, and then returned our documents to us over the same circuitous route. That was no small inconvenience, because while our passports were out of our hands, no one could make an emergency trip outside Czechoslovakia in any direction.

Therefore we owed no thanks and felt no friendliness toward our Soviet colleagues in Czechoslovakia. Many times we wished for a Russian diplomat, needing a Gray Card for a trip to Bavaria.

The third circumstance had to do with the highways. When the Communists seized Czechoslovakia, there were over thirty roads that connected Bohemia with Austria, Bavaria, and Silesia. Some, like the Rosvadov-Nuremberg route and the highway that leads through Carlsbad to Schirnding, were hard-surfaced. Others were dirt roads through the forests, used time out of mind by farmers less interested in frontiers than they were in moving their mushrooms to market. As soon as the Kremlin seized Czechoslovakia, these back roads proved a boon to anti-Communist Czechs, whose exodus continued for several months after the coup d'état in 1948. But little by little the Communists blocked the exits. Flimsy wooden barriers, like the one at Rosvadov knocked down by the departing Pilsen firetruck, were replaced by steel barriers. Across other highways ditches were dug. A ten mile border zone was established; barbed wire was strung along the frontier. Mines were planted. Unauthorized departure became a precarious hazard.

With all of which — sleeping cars, Gray Cards, and the Bohemian highway system — our embassy in Prague was familiar.

That was the situation when the General Assembly of United Nations, meeting that winter in Paris, concluded its labors. That was the moment when Vishinsky, Soviet Foreign Minister and head of the Russian Delegation, decided to go by train from Paris to Warsaw, via Prague. The Soviet embassy in Paris asked the *Wagons-Lits* company to supply transportation, namely one of those special Pullmans the company main-

73

tained for traveling potentates. They are handsome vehicles, upholstered in satin, with an electric kitchen, vintage wines in the pantry, and silent plumbing that replaces the notice *"Sous le lavabo se trouve une vase"* appearing in proletarian compartments.

The *Wagons-Lits* company replied that Vishinsky could have his special car: the company was honored. But his private Pullman could only go as far as Schirnding, in Bavaria, on the Czech frontier. There was a small matter, said the company, of the fifteen borrowed sleeping cars which the Czechoslovak State Railway refused to give back. A word from the Kremlin would perhaps solve the problem. But until the fifteen cars had been returned, the company regretted that all *Wagons-Lits* cars, including Vishinsky's special satin-upholstered Pullman, would have to be uncoupled at Schirnding.

The first intimation we had of Vishinsky's travel was a call at the American embassy by the Soviet Ambassador himself, a gentleman whose gratuitous impoliteness had previously left little room for cozy relations. On arrival in Czechoslovakia he called on the American Ambassador, who presently called on him. After that, when we wanted Gray Cards to go to Vienna, or any other piece of routine Soviet accommodation, we were told not to bother a busy diplomatic office.

That afternoon the Russian Ambassador exuded sweetness the way a sugar mill oozes blackstrop molasses. We must get to know each other better, he declared. Coexistence was a noble objective. Specifically, he needed some Gray Cards for an urgent trip to Bavaria. Where in Bavaria? Oh, not far; in fact, just over the German border. To Schirnding. A matter of meeting his Foreign Minister, M. Vishinsky, who had asked the Ambassador to drive him by automobile from Schirnding to Prague where M. Vishinsky would take the express to Warsaw. The Ambassador said he would be in Bavaria only a few minutes, meeting M. Vishinsky at Schirnding, then driving back

74

with him to Prague. He would appreciate Gray Cards for entry into Bavaria.

The Russian Ambassador accepted a bourbon and water from his host. *Vashes derolya,* he said. Coexistence is lovely.

At a staff meeting in my office the unexpected Russian request was presently debated. Several members of my official family, including those who brooded most wistfully about laughter and music in Vienna, were in favor of inviting the Soviet Ambassador to jump in the Vltava River, then churning with ice floes. They remembered Russian behavior when the American embassy needed Gray Cards; they recalled the prose that susbtitutes for politeness when a non-Communist asks a Communist for a favor.

Tell the bastard to go to hell, appeared to represent my chancery concensus.

It was a tempting suggestion. We had a score to settle with the raffish Moscovites; this looked like a promising moment to collect an installment.

It was Lex, our First Secretary, who discovered the answer. He produced, and we studied, a Czechoslovak road map, with Lex's inked-in notations. The road to Schirnding was plainly marked; it ran up the valley to Carlsbad, renamed Karlovy Vary by the Communists, then over the Sudeten hills to Cheb, where a monument still stood in honor of General Patton's liberating American forces. From Cheb to Schirnding, the macadam continued for five miles, and then into Germany. An all-weather road, complete with Lex's inked-in notations.

Presently I telephoned my Soviet colleague. "We shall be delighted," I informed him, "to issue Gray Cards so you can enter the American Zone of Occupied Germany at Schirnding to meet M. Vishinsky. What? No, not at all, my dear colleague. Think nothing of it. Happy to oblige. Send around for the Gray Cards at your convenience. Coexistence is dandy."

Foreign Minister Vishinsky was due to reach Schirnding at seven o'clock the following morning. Snow lay on the Schirn-

75

ding station, upon the platform, and upon the flat visor of the cap of the Bavarian station master. Abundantly it lay on the highway beyond the railroad tracks, where the road follows the bend of the east-flowing brook, entering Czechoslovakia. The highway was several inches deep in fresh snow. No track of automobile tires marred the symmetry of its deserted contour, except maybe the track of a rabbit. The Schirnding platform, barring the station master, was equally empty. No welcoming committee. No Soviet ambassador. No shiny black Zurses.

Foreign Minister Vishinsky viewed this gentle winter scene without enthusiasm. Expecting his Prague ambassador, he had instead a German station master. The highway was at hand, but no limousines were waiting. The prospect from the satin-lined Pullman that had brought Vishinsky from Paris might have appealed to a skier, but it held few charms for a corpulent commissar. The station master informed his passenger, politely, that if His Excellency would be so good as to disembark, the Pullman would be pulled back into Germany.

M. Vishinsky, in bedroom slippers, a Moscow zoot suit, and an astrackan hat, descended to the platform at Schirnding. He was the angry man. Snow melted in the pale morning sun, and the platform dripped from one end to the other. The Bavarian station master, not bright but solicitous, pointed the way to the men's room.

Where, demanded Vishinsky, was his escort? Where was the Soviet ambassador to Czechoslovakia? Where were the automobiles of the Soviet embassy in Prague, despatched to Schirnding to meet him?

Where indeed? echoed the station master. But over there, *that* is the men's room.

The Foreign Minister said what the station master could do with that useful facility. The locomotive of the Orient Express, with Vishinsky's Pullman attached, slid westward. Up the track from the opposite direction puffed a Czech locomotive, with a large red star on the front of the boiler. Attached to the locomotive was one third-class railway coach, with wooden benches, belonging to the nationalized Czechoslovak State Railways.

The engineer of the Czech locomotive observed his single Schirnding passenger. He took note of the large pile of luggage. He jumped to the conclusion that the American embassy in Prague, whose supplies the engineer had carried before, was again replenishing its capitalist larder. The engineer was a dedicated comrade. There was enough food on that platform, he estimated, to feed the union of socialized locomotive engineers for a month; the spectacle annoyed him.

The engineer decided that the pot-bellied oaf on the platform could be his own porter. As his locomotive drew alongside, the Czech engineer made an impolite gesture in the face of the Foreign Minister of Soviet Russia. "Welcome aboard," he snarled, "Comrade imperialist warmonger!"

The Soviet ambassador to Prague had dutifully arisen at two o'clock that same morning. The evening before, when our Gray Cards reached him, the Russian ambassador telegraphed the Czech Communist authorities in the frontier zone, instructing them to raise the highway barriers and remove the roadblocks. The Ambassador did not explain why; he gave orders. His three limousines zoomed up the valley past Karlovy Vary. They surged on toward Cheb, approaching the border. His cavalcade of Zurses went through the town before dawn, headlights gleaming on the icy streets; the Russian ambassador entered the frontier zone with throttles wide open.

The Czech comrades were duly alerted. A Soviet ambassador did not visit outlying areas every morning; local comrades could not remember a previous occasion. The barriers and roadblocks between Cheb and the frontier were tidily removed. The headlights showed soldiers and border patrols, standing at attention. They did not know what it was all about; they were obeying their orders. The three black limousines made an im-

77

pressive display with the reddening dawn behind them.

Across the macadam highway, a few yards short of Germany, there was a ditch fifteen feet across and ten feet deep, dug a few weeks before by a battalion of people's volunteers guarded by soldiers. It was the same ditch identified by the inked-in notation on Lex's highway map, which we had happily studied the afternoon before in the American embassy in Prague. Lex had spotted the ditch from the train, on a daytime trip to Nuremberg.

The second and third Zurses, by skidding sidewise in the snow, were able to stop in time. But the leading Zurs, complete with Soviet ambassador to Czechoslovakia, landed right side up on a nest of barbed wire at the bottom of the ditch. His Zurs looked like a folded accordion. From it arose imprecations, in the language of Peter the Great and likewise Ivan the Terrible.

The Czech locomotive with the red star on the front of the boiler, pulling the third-class carriage occupied by the now identified Vishinsky, reduced speed as it approached the severed highway. Things were happening there: gesticulating civilians and Czechoslovak soldiers were present. They were running toward the track, waving. But the engineer, still shaken by recent events at Schirnding, blew a blast on his whistle and went on down the valley.

M. Vishinsky, rummaging in a suitcase for boots, dry socks, and a bottle of capitalist brandy, did not look out of the window.

And on the Prague platform two hours later a satellite Cabinet awaited M. Vishinsky's coming. The Prime Minister of Czechoslovakia was there, also Foreign Minister Siroky attended by Vice Minister Hajdu. They were unanimously apologetic about the third-class carriage and its hard wooden benches. If they had known, they said, they would have sent a *Wagons-Lits* car to await M. Vishinsky at Cheb, where an honor guard would also have been stationed.

78

While Vishinsky's luggage was being transferred to the Warsaw Express, would the Comrade Commissar care to have
slivovitz with the Czechoslovak comrades in the Presidential
Waiting Room of the station? The Cabinet would be honored . . .

There was still no sign of the Russian ambassador to Czechoslovakia. He was shortening the distance between the ditch on
the Schirnding highway and the capital, but the Czech locomotive, lightly burdened, had beaten the Ambassador to
Prague by a margin of minutes.

The Czechoslovak Cabinet, Vishinsky said, could put their
slivovitz exactly where he told the Schirnding station master to
put the men's room. Vishinsky still had no idea what had become of his ambassador; he was not soothed by the train ride
from the border. His invective was scalding. Vishinsky
marched past the Cabinet of the People's Democratic Republic
of Czechoslovakia; he entered the sleeping car headed for Warsaw, slamming the door behind him.

Prague shortly got a new Russian ambassador. The *Wagons-
Lits* company shortly got its fifteen cars back.

iii. The Potato Bug as an Instrument of National Policy

Our final revenge was the most satisfying of the three, because whereas previous retaliatory episodes had involved few
privileged participants, the last one attracted attention beyond
the borders of Czechoslovakia. It reverberated from Buenos
Aires to Tokyo. And the American press was delighted.

There is nothing more galling to the comrades than public
derision — a circumstance too often forgotten by non-Communist statesmen.

Lured by the petty triumphs of their suburban harassment,
the commissars in Czechoslovakia recklessly sought to utilize
the potato bug as an instrument of national policy. Like the
surprise witness in the New York trial who deposed that he

was an eskimo-pie salesman, the Communists didn't know the potato bug was so complicated. By accusing the American government of secretly introducing an insect pest into Czechoslovakia in order to destroy a principal food crop, the Communists led with their chins — once too often.

There had not been an anti-West spy trial for some time, and editorials denouncing the treasonable activities of diplomats had subsided following the expulsion of the Vatican representative, who had been accused of producing a miracle unauthorized by government or party. The miracle had allegedly been abetted by a newspaper correspondent in the pay of the American embassy "as was proved by the confession of the Bohemian seamstress, Heda Veselova." Heda was imprisoned; the Vatican representative was expelled, and the American correspondent reached the border one jump ahead of the deportation order.

After a lull during which *Rude Pravo* and the Red Sancho Panzas tilted at other windmills, the Communists dreamed up the potato bug as the spearhead of a new anti-American offensive.

The potato bug (*leptinotarsa decemlineata*) started his depredations a century ago, when potato planting reached the Rocky Mountains, where *leptinotarsa's* ancestors, time out of mind, had eked out a precarious existence on cactus and sagebrush. *Leptinotarsa* greeted the potato the way a Cripple Creek miner viewed a blonde fresh off the stagecoach from Dodge City. Omitting the technical details, which absorbed savants of that era, it can be reported that by the end of the 1860's *leptinotarsa* had blanketed the United States, wherever a potato was growing.

The potato bug reached Europe shortly thereafter, by ship, through the same unpremeditated carelessness that got the Japanese beetle and the Dutch Elm disease to the New World. And having ascertained that European spuds are just as succulent as those growing in Aroostook County, *leptinotarsa* flour-

80

ished in his new environment. The insect crept persistently east across the European continent, and by World War II he was nibbling Bavarian tubers, close to the Czech frontier. Scientists predicted he would be in Czechoslovakia by 1950. The dauntless durable potato bug became Genghis Khan in reverse; within measurable time he will appear on the plains of China.

While this was going on, European Ministries of Agriculture, then as now staffed by diligent little men with access to pencils, produced treatises which, lacking a more abundant audience, they exchanged with each other. Patient Czech agronomists, long before the Communists got into the act, were aware of the potato-bug peril. In 1947, the last year of freedom in Czechoslovakia, official warnings were posted in the Sudeten area, which, being the closest to infested Bavaria, would be the first Czech territory to suffer potato-bug infestation. Those warnings were still on the trees when I crossed the frontier at Rosvadov: illustrated posters tacked to the spruces along the highway toward Pilsen. They urged Sudeten farmers to purchase Bordeaux mixture and Paris green against the expected invasion.

The comrades neglected, as they readied a new campaign based on the allegation that the United States Air Force was flying over Czechoslovakia at night, dropping cardboard containers filled with potato bug larvae, to remove the pre-Communist potato-bug literature. They ignored the erudite studies of Professor Vlastimil Hrdlika, who predicted, before the Munich Pact, that *leptinotarsa decemlineata* would soon be at the gates of Prague. Posters, warnings, and the works of the professor were filed in the American embassy in Prague, collected by a conscientious Agricultural Attaché and left behind when he departed.

The Communists were likewise unable to resist the temptation — in order, as they saw it, to add verisimilitude to their anti-American fable — to mount a preparatory campaign in

81

Rude Pravo, whereby we were warned of their intention. *Rude Pravo* announced, citing Sudeten farmers, that mysterious sounds of planes by night had been heard in western Czechoslovakia that spring. The planes always came from the direction of Bavaria, and they zoomed around the farmlands, flying low and avoiding the cities.

A moonlight bird watcher hunting for owls was presently quoted: he identified USAF markings. And these sinister night-flying planes, *Rude Pravo* reported, disappeared before dawn, flying back toward Germany where the American Air Force was quartered.

We in Embassy Prague viewed these preliminaries with interest. Since the comrades lack the imagination of free men, their projects are all of a pattern. First the build-up, then the snarling denunciation, finally the execration and abuse.

We studied the files of our departed Agriculture Attaché with admiration and presently with glee. We soon became, in our modest way, authoritative about *leptinotarsa decemlineata,* his appetites, his ambitions, and his unpopularity with the Constituted Authorities. More petinently, we learned of *leptinotarsa's* steady and inexorable march eastward, recognized for years in the knowledgeable brochures of Professor Hrdlika and the pre-Communist Czechoslovak Ministry of Agriculture.

We deduced that the comrades, having recognized the inevitability of potato-bug infestation in Czechoslovakia, had decided to give Uncle Sam the credit. Coexistence again; honest potato bugs coexisting with imperialist warmongers.

Experience likewise having taught us that the impending communication accusing the American government on the basis of evidence "amply confirmed by the testimony of patriotic Sudeten farmers, as proved by reports recently published in the press" would not be sent until the newspaper campaign had reached a crescendo of indignation, we thus had time for the composition of a patriotic potato-bug rebuttal, *before* the accusation was received.

Our potato-bug message was cast in the form of a Third Person Note — as the jargon of diplomacy has it — and we kept the document in the embassy safe until the day when *Rude Pravo* published, along with another ingenious report from the moonlight bird watcher, a photograph of a cardboard container "found at daylight in a field near Strbo." An accompanying photograph, much magnified, showed the container crawling with specks, which the caption identified as potato bug larvae. Beside this repulsive close-up was a cartoon in colors, three columns wide, of a potato bug with a malevolent expression, riding from Bavaria to Czechoslovakia on the Stars and Stripes, as on a magic carpet.

We thereupon delivered the following official communication to the Czechoslovak Foreign Office:

> The American embassy presents its compliments to the Czechoslovak Ministry of Foreign Affairs and has the honor to make the following observations with reference to the potato bug.
>
> To the extent that the potato bug represents a Czechoslovak domestic problem, the potato bug is not a matter of concern to the American embassy, which nevertheless expresses its sympathy over the damage to Czechoslovak agricultural production caused by the insect in question.
>
> To the extent, however, that efforts have been made in Czechoslovakia to connect the United States with the presence of the potato bug in this country, the matter is of legitimate interest to the American embassy, which declares that allegations to the effect that the United States encourages the depredations of the potato bug in Czechoslovakia, or that the United States has sought clandestinely to introduce the potato bug into Czechoslovakia, are false and preposterous.
>
> The Embassy, in availing itself of this opportunity to renew to the Ministry the assurance of its highest consideration, ventures to suggest the inherent unsuitability of the potato bug (*leptinotarsa decemlineata*) as an instrument of national policy.

Copies of this solemn communication were handed to the delighted American correspondents, who had it on their telegraph wires within minutes. It was published from Aleppo to Zanzibar. The embassy sent the text to Washington, slugged for the Voice of America, and the Voice broadcast it back again, in Czech and in Slovak. Follow-up broadcasts quoted official Czechoslovak bulletins, including those of the excellent Professor Hrdlica. They reminded Sudeten farmers, not forgetting the nocturnal birdwatcher, of the warning posters tacked to the spruce trees on the Rosvadov-Pilsen highway — which posters the Communists then belatedly confiscated.

By the time the Czech Foreign Office got around to accusing the American government of introducing the potato bug into Czechoslovakia "with the intent of provoking a food crisis in order to starve workers' wives and children," practically everybody in Czechoslovakia was laughing. Everybody, that is, except the commissars and the editors of *Rude Pravo*.

The reflexes of the Communists, geared to the meat ax, are vulnerable to the rapier of ridicule. On our thin skewer the comrades squirmed with furious anguish. The Voice of America kept the potato-bug story tauntingly alive for days, and presently we had an unexpected assist from a new ally — the Bohemian hop aphid.

The hop aphid is also known as the hop louse. Possibly because of the concentration of the comrades on the potato bug and the disproportionate amount of time they spent in bird watching, the hop louse (with no assist from anyone) suddenly menaced the immemorial ingredient of Bohemian beer — that wonderful *Prasdroj* Pilsen that diplomats could obtain from *Burobin* at a dollar a bottle.

The Voice of America was encouraged to take note of the hop louse. The Voice reminded the Communists of the shortcomings of *leptinotarsa decemlineata* as a tool of proletarian expansion: it urged the comrades to try again, with the hop louse carrying the banner.

84

Don't-let-the-hop-louse-louse-up-the-hop-crop, was suggested by Voice of America as a suitable slogan, to be chanted in unison by Communist farmers, assisted by a chorus of bird watchers.

That our potato-bug triumph in Czechslovakia taught the Communists anything worthwhile is doubtful. Although the Communists were repulsed in Czechoslovakia and backed away from *leptinotarsa decemlineata,* Communists on the other side of the world were presently at it again, the next year in Korea.

During the Korean War, germ warfare was the accusation. Sure enough, mysterious planes were reported over the Yalu River. Manchurian bird watchers reported USAF markings. And soon the party newspaper in the North Korean capital of Pyongyang published photographs of cardboard containers "dropped outside Wonsan by planes of the Fifth Air Force."

It was the same campaign we had witnessed in Czechoslovakia — with one modification. In North Korea the Communists tortured captured American pilots, hoping thereby to obtain "voluntary confessions."

But back in Prague, in Hradcany Castle where the commissars gathered to rivet new shackles on their helpless Czech victims, it was a long time before a comrade could see a baked potato on the dinner table without wanting to throw it out of the window.

V.

It Cost the Communists Fifty Million Dollars

to Imprison Bill Oatis

Tᴴɪs describes the arrest, imprisonment, and release two years later of the Associated Press correspondent in Prague, William N. Oatis, a case that at the time attracted widespread attention and indignation. It tells how this outrage was planned, what the Communists hoped to accomplish by it, and some of the mechanics of an espionage trial, Communist version.

And lest anyone think that with "peaceful coexistence" those days are over, let him be reminded of the case in Moscow in 1963 of the visiting Yale professor, and of his release that was obtained only after direct Presidential intervention.

A consular convention with Russia has since provided for notification of arrest and for prompt consular access to an accused American citizen. Assuming the Senate approves the agreement, it remains to be seen how this worthy effort works out in practice, and whether the price — granting diplomatic immunity to Russian consular officers — proves exhorbitant. If the agreement is satisfactory, it will doubtless be followed by comparable conventions with other Communist countries.

On July 4, 1951, a day chosen by the Communists for the added offense it would give the American people to be insulted on their own Independence Day, a Communist court in Czechoslovakia sentenced Bill Oatis, Associated Press correspondent in Prague, to ten years' "deprivation of liberty" for alleged espionage against the People's Democratic Republic.

On May 16, 1953, twenty-five months after Bill's arrest and not quite two years after the sentencing, the Communists pardoned Bill Oatis and expelled him from Czechoslovakia.

During those two years the Communists were penalized by the American government approximately fifty million dollars for abusing an innocent American citizen, not to mention other discomforts visited upon them, as is presently recounted. At a time when the complaint of appeasement sometimes echoes across the land, I note with satisfaction that in the Oatis case the Communists took an expensive beating.

Near the turn of the century President Theodore Roosevelt, seeking to free an American citizen named Perdicaris, demanded "Perdicaris alive, or Raisuli dead," whereupon Roosevelt sent American gunboats to Morocco. Raisuli, an unlaundered Moor living in vulnerable proximity to the Mediterranean coast, relinquished Perdicaris — and the episode became part of the American heritage, to the edification of upholders of the national honor.

Since USS *Missouri* could not be despatched to Bohemia, the Communists were able to hold Oatis longer than Raisuli held Perdicaris. But whereas Raisuli closed the incident without loss of anything more expensive than his prestige, which was not high in the first place, the American embassy in Prague was able to charge the Communists seventy-five thousand dollars for every day they held Bill Oatis in prison.

Oatis was arrested on April 23, 1951. Lengthening shadows across his trail had already been cast by the seizure earlier that month of all the Czech employees of the Associated Press bureau in Prague, which Oatis headed, and by the expulsion during the previous year of seven foreign correspondents. Those expelled were accused of "unobjective reporting." That is, they had delved too closely into the workings of the Communist utopia. Or they had failed to show sufficient respect for the publications of *Ceteka*, the official news agency of Czechoslovakia, whose fantasies the correspondents were supposed to export intact, with no side glances toward the unmade Communist bed or the untidy Communist closet.

For failing to titillate the self-appointed successors of Masaryk and Beneš, foreign reporters had, previous to Oatis, been declared *persona non grata,* and escorted to Ruzyne to take an airplane for Frankfurt or Vienna. Bill's predecessors on the expulsion circuit included an AP colleague and Jack Higgins of United Press, plus another correspondent who, when his name was mentioned at a propaganda spy trial the year before, fled across the frontier so fast the customs inspectors mistook him for a flying saucer.

Bill Oatis himself had been harassed since his arrival by mousetrap plays by the Foreign Office and the Ministry of Public Information; his accreditation as a correspondent was taken from him "for scrutiny," and his residence permit was extended for only brief periods. In the meantime he was allowed to file stories as a "private person." Ironically, both documents were finally validated in mid-April, 1951, one week before his arrest.

We saw Bill Oatis often, in the early months of 1951, attending embassy press conferences. That institution was modified in Prague to meetings in the office of the ambassador, on an informal basis. Rumors, impressions, and reports were assembled and set beside the official *Ceteka* pronouncements. The sessions were off-the-record, and we tried to distill a possible truth from the distorted legends that pass for information among the comrades. *Rude Pravo* was the official organ of the Communist Party of Czechoslovakia, and we referred to it as Rude-and-Depraved, which gave it the benefit of all possible doubts.

Bill Oatis came to these sessions wearing a bow tie and an expression of zealous concentration. We talked about the disappearance of Noel Field and his family, the whereabouts of Archbishop Beran, and whether Stalin's failure to send birthday greetings to Rudolf Slansky, then head of the Czech Communist hierarchy, presaged a forthcoming fall from grace. And we wondered about Clementis, former Foreign Minister, whose denunciation in 1939 of the Molotov-Ribbentrop pact might not be overlooked indefinitely by the Kremlin.*

Once away from Communist jurisdiction, it is hard to remember how complicated it becomes to find and identify a kernel of truth. In Nazi days the rule was, "everything not prohibited is compulsory." In Communist Czechoslovakia, everything not published by the government was secret, obtained by the inquirer at his peril and transmitted abroad at a risk considerably greater.

Furthermore, the word espionage in the Communist dictionary is so broad and elastic that it covers almost every possible manifestation of human behavior. For example, if a correspondent sought to obtain data on beet production in Moravia, he was automatically engaged in "economic espionage." And if an official of the Ministry of Agriculture recklessly imparted the desired information, he could be charged with treason.

Thus all manner of innocent statistics, published freely in non-Communist countries, are guarded in the Communist wonderland as the most top-secret of top secrets, with ferocious penalties for dissemination. One reason is that Communist economic operators are generally so incompetent that a revelation of the facts would humiliate the commissar concerned and quite possibly lead to his early extermination.

Before the Oatis case, offending foreign correspondents had been admonished or expelled from the country. By keeping brisk the turn-over of reporters by successive expulsions, no foreign correspondent could become embarrassingly familiar with the local scene. By tossing out a reporter now and then, those remaining (or replacing the ones expelled) were sup-

---

* The Fields, after over ten years, are still behind the Curtain. The Archbishop is still in a Bohemian prison, and Slansky and Clementis were hanged in 1952, side by side on the Pankrac Prison gallows.

posed to understand that the way to effective newspaper performance lay in accepting the aforesaid official *Ceteka* emanations, and then eagerly regurgitating them in cables to Paris, Washington, Rio de Janeiro, and other "reactionary centers," exactly as the local comrades laid the information on the party platter.

To the credit of American correspondents, they rejected the *Ceteka* garbage. Our embassy press conferences were relaxed affairs, with the Counselor of Embassy, Tyler Thompson,* in attendance with the latest political gleanings, and the atmosphere one of skepticism and good humor. At one of those meetings I remember Oatis suggested that the Voice of America recommend the abandonment of the Communist slogan, "Workers of the world, unite; you have nothing to lose but your chains." The Voice would propose it be replaced by, "Suckers of the Steppes, relax; you have nothing to show for your pains." That would have looked wonderful, we thought, as an editorial in *Rude Pravo*.

Those same days that elevated our press conferences to an irreverent but close pursuit of the facts of Communist behavior also saw the establishment, outside our chancery at Trziste 15 in old Mala Strana, of surveillance by the secret police. From time to time these unattractive characters popped out of their automobiles to seize departing embassy callers, whom they dragged away for questioning. The volume of our Czechoslovak callers dwindled, and by the time Bill Oatis was arrested, Czech visitors were limited to documented messengers of the various *narodny podnik* enterprises — Communist monopolies selling glass, costume jewelry and velour Bohemian hats — calling to present to the embassy for certification, consular invoices without which those commodities could not be shipped to the United States to be exchanged for coveted American dollars; to diplomats, who were immune to seizure by the po-

---

* Since 1960, Ambassador Thompson.

lice; and to newspaper correspondents, who we thought were immune.

When Bill disappeared, the initial cables of the embassy to Washington reflected our uncertainty. Could Oatis be a possible defector? The record gave no support for that assumption. Had Bill perhaps left Prague unannounced, to scout the Bohemian plain for former Foreign Minister Clementis or for clues to the whereabouts of the missing Noel Field family? We doubted whether Bill would have embarked on such an expedition without word to friends, or notifying the embassy.

The embassy concluded that seizure by the police was the likeliest explanation. We despatched a note to the Foreign Office, expressing our concern over Bill's disappearance and requesting an investigation.

By generally accepted standards of international conduct, when an American citizen is arrested abroad, he is entitled to communicate with his consul, who then calls on the prisoner by arrangement with the local authorities, ascertains what the charges are against him, what treatment he is getting, and when the trial will be held. Depending on the circumstances, the consul may aid in obtaining an attorney, seek to facilitate release on bail, and communicate with relatives in the United States. In the absence of a treaty detailing these rights of access and assistance, most countries recognize that it is legitimate for a consular officer to interest himself in the welfare of a fellow citizen abroad, and to take steps on an arrested citizen's behalf.

Three days after Bill's arrest, after the note of inquiry and numerous phone calls to the Czech Foreign Office, the embassy was informed that Oatis was in fact in custody, accused of espionage against the Czechoslovak Republic. An official message to that effect was received the next day, April 27. Our request to see Oatis was rejected in a note of April 30.

Initial demands having been rebuffed, our government's efforts for the next two months were concentrated on trying to

91

obtain access to the prisoner, and on trying to expedite his trial.

Since no treaty provisions on the subject existed between United States and Czechoslovakia, our representations were based on comity and on the aforesaid "generally accepted standards." Our arguments were probably useful for the record, but they had no appreciable effect on a Communist regime that had already embarked on a course of action — pressing a framed-up case against an American newspaper correspondent.

During the two months before Bill's trial, I had numerous meetings with Vilém Siroky, then Foreign Minister and later Premier of Czechoslovakia, on the right of an American citizen to the protection of his government — treaty or no treaty — and also on the right of the receiving government (Czechoslovakia) to expel an accredited correspondent if it objected to his activities, but not to arrest him for activities directly connected with his profession as a newspaperman. Siroky, a tough Communist who came up through the ranks in the railroad labor movement in Slovakia, always looked out of place in Jan Masaryk's office in Czernin Palace, with its atmosphere of graciousness and leisure and its magnificent view over the roofs and spires of the old city. I was to come to know that room well during the months of Oatis' imprisonment, and I rarely entered it without thinking of Jan Masaryk, and wondering whether he jumped from his window or was pushed.

Siroky conceded that there might be some shadow of a right, or at least a claim to a shadow of a right, recognized perhaps among warmongering reactionary imperialist countries if not among the forward-looking progressive people's democracies, to have a consul interview an accused felon awaiting trial. This alleged right could perhaps be applied, provided the accused was guilty of some common crime like burglary or manslaughter or embezzlement. Furthermore, Siroky continued, there might be something in favor of expulsion as the

92

proper government remedy in the case of activities directly connected with the profession of journalism, when those activities ran counter to the generous hospitality of the receiving state. In fact, that was precisely the view of the Czechoslovak government which, as I had reminded him, had, over the past year, invited a number of foreign newspapermen who had shown regrettable tendencies toward unobjective reporting to leave Czechoslovakia. But all that, declared the Minister, has nothing to do with the case of William Oatis, whose crime was espionage. Espionage was a different matter altogether. Espionage was the gravest of crimes against the state. Those committing espionage automatically placed themselves in a separate category, divorced from any right that might perhaps pertain to those guilty of lesser crimes, including the alleged right to be visited by a representative of the American government. Therefore no embassy representative would be permitted to see Oatis until after his trial. On another occasion, before the trial, Siroky made the illuminating observation that Oatis could be visited "after his conviction."

When I produced the Czech law on espionage (which closely follows the Kremlin version) and pointed out that under it practically any action could be construed as plotting against the state, so all-inclusive and at the same time so imprecise is the language, Siroky reminded me that in the United States a foreigner accused of espionage is not made immediately accessible to the representative of his government. That is true, but it had nothing to do with the facts, as distinct from the false charges, of the Oatis case. It is also true that the United States statute on espionage clearly defines the offense, which the Communist law does not.

I was to have many hours of this sterile interchange during the months that followed. In addition to sessions with subordinates, I had upwards of fifteen meetings with Foreign Minister Siroky about Bill Oatis, and several of them lasted between two and three hours at a stretch, while Siroky smoked innu-

93

merable acrid Czech cigarettes, and the twin photographs of Gottwald and Stalin stared down from the walls of Jan Masaryk's study.

Communists rarely lack for a formal pretext in support of action they have taken. One of the distinguishing features of even the most preposterous Communist argument is the existence, ready to hand, of some ostensibly supporting citation which is then brought out again and again and reiterated interminably, even though it has only the most tenuous connection with the subject at issue. Communist diplomatic notes pant and heave with these irrelevant citations, often set forth with considerable skill and imagination. Their purpose is to confuse the issue, not to clarify it.

Calling again on Siroky about four weeks after Bill's arrest, I found the Minister, normally cold and impassive, full of raffish geniality. "The spy Oatis," he informed me, "has confessed. Now we shall see what can be done to expedite his trial."

I looked at the Minister, smug in his Communist effrontery, and I looked out across the spring hillside to the park fresh with lilac and pear blossoms. I thought of Cardinal Mindszenty in Hungary, and of Kostov in Bulgaria, and of all the Moscow "confessions" in the 1930's. And I thought, sick at heart, of the way those confessions had been obtained.

That Bill had in fact "confessed" the Communists were not slow in exploiting. A day or two after that conversation, Siroky sent me a letter from Bill to his wife, Laurabelle Oatis, with the request that the embassy in Prague forward it to her home in Minnesota. That the letter was in Bill's handwriting seemed evident, for we had samples in the embassy. But if the writing was Bill's, the words — with equal certainty — were the words of Bill's jailers. Bill's letter to his wife, after nearly one month as a prisoner of the People's Democratic Republic of Czechoslovakia, read as follows:

94

Dear Laurabelle:

My wish has been granted and so I may write you a few lines to stop your worrying. Surely you must be surprised that I have been arrested. In explanation, all I will tell you now is that I have been caught in espionage activity against Czechoslovakia. I am very sorry that I allowed myself to be drawn into this, but I hadn't enough experience, and so when I got orders to carry out espionage I fulfilled them very zealously. Today I know very well how I harmed the interests of the Czech nation, which honestly works for keeping world peace. I know you can accuse me, but I should like to tell you that the guilty ones are those who led me into espionage and who used my abilities in this espionage work. I see quite clearly that the truth is on the Czech side. I want to understand this truth much more and by means of telling the truth about my activity I want at least a little to make up for all the damage I did to the Czech nation. I want to return to a new life as a clean and new man.

You must not worry about my welfare. I have become convinced that all reports about the circumstances in these prisons are lies and are the opposite of reality. I am well treated here. The prison is clean — the food is decent. I have medical care whenever I want it. My health is the same as before. Don't worry about me at all and trust in the goodness and justice of this state, as I do. I hope this letter will find you in Minnesota and that you haven't left for New York yet. Personally I don't need anything. I have enough money. But please send some English language novels, plays and poems and also some cigarettes from there — airmail.

I send my regards to my parents, to your mother, to Aunt Velma and Aunt Flo and my cousins Bob, Annamae, Dorothy, Barbara Nell and Beverley and others. I love you. I shall be glad to see you again. I live in hope and I believe that I shall meet you again and that we shall spend our lives together as honest people. You will surely understand that I am ashamed and that I am most deeply grieved and do not want to see anybody of ours. I share my grief only with you, my dear.

Write me at this address: American Consulate, Prague, for Mr. William Oatis (personal).

I am sure I shall immediately get your letter. The Czechs are granting my wishes and I shall be able to answer your letter immediately.

All my love forever,

(Signed) Bill

The handwriting, I repeat, was Bill's. It was recognized at once by loyal Laurabelle Oatis. But the letter was a translation out of Czech; that text could never have been written in the first instance in English. And the tone of self-abasing apology. That "trust in the goodness and justice of this state, as I do." Words that would hardly come naturally to an American reporter.

The letter was a Communist effort at once naïve and vicious. Looking back on that message Bill was forced by the police to send to Laurabelle Oatis renews the pleasure I still derive from considering how costly we were able to make the imprisonment of Oatis for the Czechoslovak government. Two million dollars a month; to have played some part in plucking such expensive tailfeathers from the gaudy Communist dove that burped like a Zapotocky remains to this day a splendid satisfaction.

After the "confession" Bill's trial went into rehearsal.

Bill's "confession" to charges of espionage was squeezed out of him by the Communist police within a month of his arrest. Weariness and insomnia rather than physical abuse were the weapons used to obtain it, for the Communists wanted an unmarked body for their courtroom spy trial. The period between confession and trial was spent preparing for the spectacle that was to culminate on our Independence Day in the sentence of ten years' imprisonment. The waiting period was infinitely depressing for all of us. The Communists had informed the embassy of Bill's "confession," and we could imagine what was probably happening behind the gray walls of his prison, where Bill was being groomed for his appearance as a stellar attraction.

I selected two members of my staff to attend the trial: Dick Johnson, an exceptionally competent Vice Consul who was familiar with the case, and Mary Horak, a trained American secretary and interpreter. Dick had been in Czechoslovakia since 1949. He had worked hard on the language and now was quite fluent. Mary's parents emigrated from Bohemia to the United States before she was born, and Mary grew up bilingual. She was an American college graduate and an exceptionally proficient secretary. She and Dick made an effective team, and the job they did at the trial was outstanding. Mary made a verbatim record of Bill's testimony and of all the questions asked by the judge, together with a full summary of the testimony of Bill's Czech colleagues in the Prague Associated Press bureau, who were tried with him. Dick Johnson concentrated on the proceedings themselves and on making notes for the American press, which he telephoned after each session to the American High Commission at Frankfurt, which made them available to American correspondents.

That was an important service to American newspapers, for by the time Bill's trial opened, the three foreign correspondents remaining in Czechoslovakia at the time of his arrest (Russ Jones of U.P., Bobby Bigio of Reuters, and Jacques Fournier of Agence France Presse) had all left the country. That meant that with the indignant eyes of the United States on the trial, no colleague of Bill's was in court to take down the story; it was recorded entirely, from start to finish, by the two junior members of the staff of our embassy in Prague.

The purpose of a Communist political trial has little to do with determining the guilt or innocence of the accused. The prisoner is present to serve a purpose of the state, which conditions him for one appearance, not given until the star has

97

been brought to the peak of his training — that is to say, not until the accused has learned his part as thoroughly as any other actor prepared for the footlights. The Communist management plays only a single performance, but it plays that for keeps. No encores. A two-line obituary maybe, but no encores.

The objectives behind the Oatis spy trial were not difficult to identify. Communist leaders, individually tough and durable characters, collectively are often timid and nervous. Public criticism, including criticism in the free-world press, can effect the digestion of an entire Politburo. Hence the angry hullabaloo over "unobjective reparting" that led to the expulsion of various foreign correspondents before Bill was arrested.

It was only when the expulsions failed to produce acceptance by correspondents of Party propaganda handouts that the Communist hierarchy decided on stronger measures. It was only when the Communists failed to convert the foreign reporters into instruments of Communist policy that the decision was made to frame an American correspondent, extort a confession, and publicly try him.

A principal purpose was to attack the United States by humiliating an American citizen. It is not a pretty spectacle when a beaten man, declaring his guilt, is held up to public ridicule. Well do the Communists know it.

Another objective was to intimidate the Czech people by demonstrating that Westerners are evil, that American reporters are especially evil, and that any Czech who had dealings with Americans, specifically including diplomats and newspaper reporters, is not likely to prosper in a People's Democracy. The trial was also a part of the program to isolate our embassy from any sort of contact or relationship with the Czechoslovak people.

The Pankrac Prison courtroom was accordingly floodlit and rigged for sound. Invitations were issued by key Communist officials and to *stakhanovites* still rosy and warm from exceeding their norms and thereby proving the validity of Communist emulation. Selected "progressive" writers all the way from East Berlin and Pilsen to Lake Baikal and Vladivostok converged on Prague in a column of squads, still wearing their winter underwear.

One result was unventilated congestion (without which no Communist gathering is complete), and another was that Dick Johnson and Mary Horak, the embassy representatives accredited to witness the proceedings, were assigned rear seats, where lonely and near-sighted Bill Oatis, who surely would have been heartened to know of their presence, could not possibly see them. To make certain Bill would miss his friends, the Communists brought him to court without his glasses, and then required him, a guard on either side, to face directly forward into the light.

Bill's trial began with the reading of the indictment, a document publicly unveiled two days before at a special Ministry of Information press conference, and already widely published under indignant headlines. The indictment was a rambling, fantastic tale to the effect that Oatis was only incidentally a reporter, his real vocation being espionage on behalf of the American Secret Service, pictured as a huge, malignant caterpillar with one hundred poisonous feet and scores of moist and sticky tentacles. Serving this monster with ecstatic devotion, Bill was pictured as plotting to overthrow the People's Democratic Republic of Czechoslovakia, a project foiled by the almost superhuman sagacity and patriotic alertness of the ever-watchful servants of the people, who at the final moment sprung the fateful trap, captured the archenemy of the nation, and exposed his imperialist treachery.

No proof of any of this nonsense was submitted. Examination of comparable proceedings in other Communist jurisdictions indicates that few people's courts waste time inspecting evidence. Why go to the bother of studying evidence when the prisoner himself declares he is guilty? Why waste the court's energy when the prisoner himself says his crime was even

99

more heinous than the offenses described by the public prosecutor, and that there were no extenuating circumstances.

The role of the so-called defense attorney in this hocus-pocus is usually limited to acting as prompter during the detailed testimony that follows the plea of "guilty," and to remarking piously just before sentence is pronounced that his miserable client must have been tempted by imperialist warmongers, beyond his powers of resistance.

The verbatim story of Bill Oatis' trial was recorded by Mary Horak in the Pankrac Prison courtroom. Let any doubter refer to the *Department of State Bulletin* of August 20, 1951, available today in American libraries.

After Bill's plea of "guilty" there ensued two days of carefully rehearsed testimony, likewise recorded by Miss Horak, excerpts from which appear in the same issue of the *Bulletin*. It contains a fascinating description of a Japanese "spy school" Oatis was supposed to have attended during World War II, in company with the Army Attaché of the American embassy in Prague (who saw Oatis for the first time when Bill reached Prague in 1950). This imaginary association between Oatis and the Attaché was supposed to supply the link between the "espionage apparatus of the embassy" and the comparable network of Associated Press.

In addition there was a lengthy digression about Oatis' "secret telephone" which he was accused of maintaining for clandestine conversations with his agents, and with his contacts in the American embassy. This phone was in the office adjoining the AP premises in downtown Prague. It belonged to a Czech architect who had rented the extra room to the AP, months before Bill's arrival. Inasmuch as after the advent of Communist government in Czechoslovakia the publication of telephone directories fell farther and farther behind the listings, this second AP phone remained in the name of the architect, a circumstance the sinister implications of which occupied several paragraphs of testimony. The architect got a rough going-over by the police and was lucky not to follow Bill into prison as an accomplice.

Practically anybody who was anybody in the Prague diplomatic corps was mentioned at one place or another in espionage trial testimony, and we considered adopting the initials "M.I.T.," standing for "mentioned-in-trial" to tell which friends had been on the receiving end of spy-trial brickbats. (For example: "The Honorable Geoffrey Kirk, M.I.T., His Britannic Majesty's Chargé d'Affaires ad interim.") We abandoned the project when it became apparent that nearly the entire roster of non-Communist diplomats were candidates for identical distinction. The Communist reason for this lavish name-calling was to build up cases of record against "unfriendly diplomats," in order to embarrass their governments and to provide ready-made pretexts should it later be decided to ask for an individual's recall. The Czech Foreign Office note would then read: ". . . as was conclusively proved during the trial of the spy Oatis in July 1951 . . . ," followed by the official demand for the departure of the representative in question. Dossiers against most of the members of my staff were constructed in this fashion during my service in Czechoslovakia.

To all of the questioning based on the indictment, Bill Oatis responded mechanically, without pause or hesitation. Five weeks of rehearsals with his jailers had rendered Bill's responses almost perfect. To each prepared question Bill's incriminating reply came automatically. First the question in Czech, then the translation into English, then Bill's testimony in English, and finally the translation of Bill's testimony into Czech, proclaimed by the court interpreter.

There was only one catch in the courtroom performance: the interpreter, with the prepared script of the testimony before him, and with several acts and scenes safely performed, at one point lost the thread of Bill's testimony. Instead of waiting for Bill's next reply in English and then translating it into

101

Czech, the interpreter ran several sentences *ahead* of Bill's testimony. The positions were thus reversed and Bill's answers in English were delivered *after* the court interpreter had already delivered them in Czech.

This was duly recorded by Mary Horak, to the indignation of the comrades when the State Department published the text of the proceedings.

So Bill Oatis was declared guilty, and at half past nine on the morning of the Fourth of July, 1951, he was sentenced to ten years' "deprivation of liberty," which the court explained might be reduced by good behavior, followed by expulsion from Czechoslovakia. Asked whether he accepted the sentence, Bill replied that he did, and he was led away between two policemen.

No summary of these proceedings would be complete without emphasizing that nothing in the foregoing description of Bill's ordeal is set forth without both understanding and sympathy — understanding of that ordeal, and sympathy extended to a friend in his time of trouble. No one who has not himself been in the hands of the Communist police — no one who has not himself descended into the pit of Communist "justice" — is entitled to entertain a judgment toward those who do, and who survive the experience.

Here follows the text of the press release of the Department of State, commenting on the Oatis trial:

OATIS TRIAL

The mock trial of the Associated Press representative at Prague, Mr. William N. Oatis, has now been brought to a conclusion. The sentencing is but an epilogue to this ludicrous travesty of justice in which the victim was required to speak his prefabricated "confession" as a part of a public spectacle exhibiting all the usual Communist trial techniques. This was prepared and rehearsed in advance under police auspices and by customary Communist police procedures when Oatis was held incommunicado for seventy days between his arrest and presentation in court.

The proceedings revealed the flimsiest kind of alleged "evidence," even more insubstantial than the Communists are accustomed to produce in trumped-up trials of this type. For example, the normal routine requests of the Associated Press for news reports openly transmitted by wire were distorted into "espionage missions on orders from centers in New York and London."

The Czechoslovak regime has clearly demonstrated that it considers legitimate and normal news gathering and reporting as "espionage." As the prosecutor publicly stated, Oatis was held to be a particularly dangerous "espionage" agent because he insisted on obtaining accurate, correct and verified information. To do this is "a crime," according to the concepts of the present Czechoslovak authorities, who find any press activity except the transmission of official propaganda to be "espionage." The Czechoslovak government thus rejects completely the principle of freedom of information. It is presumed that the press of the free world will so view this turning back of the clock.

The proceedings of this especially arranged spectacle also included a number of groundless accusations against the American ambassador and other members of the United States embassy staff. These were invented as a part of the entire propaganda performance in attacking the United States.

If further evidence were needed, the arrest, the detention for months without access to friend, embassy representative, or trusted legal counsel, the forced "confession" to fabricated charges, the shabby "conviction" of William N. Oatis shows that the present regime in Czechoslovakia fears truth, hates liberty, and knows no justice.

When Bill Oatis was marched out of the Prague courtroom between two SNB Communist guards, condemned to ten years' imprisonment for having committed no crime, the American government was faced with a problem more difficult than the expression of indignation. Indignation, yes. But what were we going to do about it?

For seventy-five days the Communists had been marching up and down the propaganda field, virtually unopposed, because they possessed the breathing body of Bill Oatis, which they proceeded to exhibit in a public spectacle. The accusations were false and preposterous, but nevertheless there was Oatis confessing to espionage before microphone and camera. There were his words of guilt and there were the details of crimes he never committed, gleefully broadcast by Radio Prague to every continent.

Communist satisfaction was substantial, but of brief duration. The remainder of my story has to do with the steps the American government took to bring about Bill Oatis' freedom, and what our government was able to charge the Communist commissars of Czechoslovakia for abusing an American citizen. Bill's case engaged the personal attention of two successive Presidents of the United States and two Secretaries of State. It was the principal preoccupation of the American embassy in Prague for every day that Oatis was a prisoner.

The American position had elements of strength which the Communist leaders, basking happily in the sunshine of American Independence Day humiliation, either overlooked or ignored.

In the first place, Bill Oatis was innocent. He was an honest newspaper reporter, honestly seeking facts and honestly engaged in following his profession. No amount of distortion, no amount of "confession," no amount of propaganda had been able to hide the true character of the proceedings in the Pankrac Prison courtroom. That an innocent man by the fact of his innocence can constitute a hazard to those who have wronged him is a lesson the Communists are often slow in learning.

In the second place, Bill's value to the Communists rapidly declined as soon as the trial was over. The Communists could declare that the court proceedings had been a triumphant and spectacular show, but what use is a convicted reporter once the courtroom floodlights are darkened, the courtroom radio silenced, and the reporter led away to his prison? And those pages from *Rude Pravo,* with their lava-hot editorials denouncing imperialist espionage, what good are they then to the comrades? The day after Bill's trial ended, Prague housewives were using *Rude Pravo* to wrap up their rationed potatoes — indifferent to the trial but perhaps remembering that before the Communists came, potatoes were unrationed.

In the third place, the Communists miscalculated the durability of the indignation of the American people. They expected some publicity to follow Bill's arrest, possibly accompanied by official notes of protest and demands for the prisoner's release. They perhaps anticipated angry editorials for a few days in American newspapers and even protracted grumbling on the part of the Department of State.

If the Czech government had had the sense to expel Oatis as soon as the trial was over, they could have banked their dividends and clipped their coupons, with scarcely an entry on the debit side of the ledger.

When, instead, Oatis was sentenced to prison, his government set about reviewing the possibilities. Our choices included breaking relations with the Czechoslovak government, which might have provided short-lived satisfaction for the American people, without, however, helping to get Bill Oatis out of jail. Or we could have lodged "an indignant and emphatic protest" (to borrow an overworked phrase from the comrades, whose prose habitually hiccoughs), and we could then have sat back, glowering, but again without much prospect that a note of protest alone would help Bill Oatis.

We could likewise have offered to pay ransom, which might perhaps have solved the immediate problem of Oatis, but it would simultaneously have exposed every American citizen within the range of the Communist claw to the hazards generated by appeasement. (It should be added that, notwithstanding their distress, neither Laurabelle Oatis, Bill's wife, nor the Associated Press, his employer, ever suggested that ransom be paid to obtain his freedom. That attitude is relevant to a development hereafter.)

Or we could make it so uncomfortable and expensive for Czechoslovakia to hold Oatis that the Communists themselves would eventually be glad, before the expiration of his sentence, to release the prisoner on their own initiative.

The first step was taken within a week of the trial, when I called on Foreign Minister Siroky under instructions from Washington. I told Siroky what my government thought of the courtroom proceedings. In return, Siroky quoted from the indictment and from Bill's testimony. Siroky declared the sentence stood. It was an unproductive meeting.

Two weeks later there was a second opportunity, in circumstances more gratifying. Dr. Prochaska, the new Czechoslovak ambassador to the United States, called at the embassy to pay his respects, as required by protocol, before his departure for Washington. Not only was I able to tell Dr. Prochaska about the Oatis case, but I was able immediately thereafter to witness from the safe haven of my diplomatic doorway, the arrest of Ambassador Prochaska by the Secret Police, as described in the previous chapter. To see the freshly appointed Communist envoy dragged away by his own policemen was an uplifting experience, which I savor to this day with pleasure.

Prochaska, if he survives, probably wishes he had not been chosen for that Washington assignment, which began in humiliation and ended with an inglorious fizzle. The Ambassador established his identity with the police in time to catch the *Queen Mary* two days later at Cherbourg, but when his ship reached West 50th Street, angry crowds were deployed, banners and placards demanding Bill Oatis' release. In the White House, where Prochaska was promptly received, President

106

Truman accepted his credentials and then gave the Ambassador the rough side of his Missouri tongue.

At the State Department whither the new envoy repaired in disorder after his call on the President, the Secretary of State was equally abrasive. And after Dean Acheson came the American press — Bill's colleagues and friends — who ambushed Ambassador Prochaska outside the Secretary's office.

Prochaska fled to his embassy at 2349 Massachusetts Avenue and locked the door. He never returned to the State Department. His first visit was the only call he ever made there. Six weeks later he was ordered to Paris as a member of a Czech delegation to a United Nations meeting. From there he was recalled to Prague. Ambassador Prochaska disappeared.

Meanwhile, having had its say for the record, the American government was translating the indignation of the American people into tangible measures. Czechoslovakia was declared out-of-bounds to American citizens, and passports were stamped "Not valid for travel to Czechoslovakia." That put a stop to the ooze of fellow travelers and "progressives" who had been using Prague as a sounding board for hostile propaganda.

Next, the wings were pulled off CSA, the Czechoslovak National Airline. CSA ran a daily service between Prague and West Europe, with flights to London, Paris, and Amsterdam. For the comrades it was an important operation — at that time almost the only Red airline outside Communist territory. But to reach West Europe, CSA had to fly over West Germany, for which the line required a permit. In a joint endeavor to assist their nationals in prison in Czechoslovakia, the occupying powers in West Germany suspended the permit, thereby grounding CSA. For many months thereafter the only Czech airplanes reaching the West were machines seized by anti-Communists and flown out of Czechoslovakia clandestinely, their pilots seeking freedom.

Grounding CSA really hurt, and the Communists were furious.

Our third penalty was the most effective. It, too, drew bright, angry blood from the Communist artery. At the time of Bill Oatis' arrest, Czechoslovakia was selling to the United States merchandise valued at over two million dollars per month, or about thirty million dollars per year. At the same time, Czechoslovakia was buying nothing from the United States, so this trade represented a net inflow of dollars to almost the full amount of Czech exports to the United States — dollars available for all manner of fascinating Communist enterprises, from fomenting unrest among banana workers to printing *The Daily Worker*.

Not long after Bill was marched away from the Pankrac Prison courtroom, I was able to report to the State Department that Czech exports had been reduced from $2,500,000 per month to almost zero. The embassy accomplished this by being too busy to certify any more consular invoices, without which Czech merchandise could not be shipped to the United States.

I had the pleasure of reminding Foreign Minister Siroky of his vanished trade, at the end of another long Oatis session. "Mr. Minister," I said, pointing to the clock on the wall of Jan Masaryk's study, "since I arrived here this morning, it has cost your government seven thousand dollars to keep William Oatis in prison."

This was translated to Siroky by the interpreter. "How come?" growled the Minister.

"Two and a half million dollars per month is seventy-five thousand dollars a day," I told him. "And seventy-five thousand dollars a day is fifty dollars a minute. Fifty dollars a minute," I repeated. "Two hours and twenty minutes. Seven thousand dollars, Mr. Minister."

To watch this arithmetic add up, inside the Communist

skull, was something to set beside the indignities which the comrades had visited upon Oatis.

Nevertheless, it took time to get Bill out of prison. The barrage against Czechoslovakia in the American press continued unabated. That was good as a demonstration that when a foreign government wrongs an American citizen, the American people do not forget it, but it also kept the Czech government on the defensive and in a position in which the release of Oatis, except on payment of ransom or some comparable consideration, could be interpreted as "yielding to foreign pressure." No government, Communist or free, wants to do that.

Ransom was accordingly what the Foreign Minister tried to collect; ransom in the shape of a steel mill. The steel mill was in the United States. It had originally been designed for Czechoslovakia, in the days when Czechoslovakia was independent. After the Communist seizure of power, the deal was canceled. Siroky sought to revive it. He believed he had the ideal formula: one steel mill for one Oatis; one Oatis in exchange for one steel mill.

When Washington declined, Siroky monotonously reiterated his proposal.

At that juncture an unrelated event, unhelpful to all our efforts in behalf of Otis, occurred almost within sight of Czechoslovakia. Down the Danube from Bratislava was another Communist paradise, and in Hungary the comrades succeeded in impounding an American C-47 airplane and four American fliers. While Siroky for the fifth or sixth time was repeating: "One Oatis, one steel mill; one steel mill, one Oatis," and I was replying: "No steel mill, no ransom," the United States Air Force suddenly pulled the rug out from under my feet. The Air Force paid the Hungarian Communists one hundred and twenty thousand dollars to release the four captured fliers.

That deal, made public by the happy Hungarians, complicated the efforts in Prague to help Oatis. The cost of appeasement can rarely be computed, but that payment, coupled with our refusal to pay ransom for Oatis, probably lengthened Bill's stay in Ruzyne prison. It certainly added to our difficulties.

So 1951 became 1952, and although conversations with the Czechoslovak government continued, we were making little perceptible progress. It had become a waiting game, with stagnation on both sides. Economic sanctions were taking their toll, and Communist hopes of obtaining a ransom were probably fading; I was convinced it was only a question of time, but how much time was the unanswered question.

I flew to Washington, and the situation was discussed with President Truman and Secretary Acheson (who enjoyed the story about Prochaska and the Secret Police), and with all the State Department officials who had worked on my cables and drafted the Washington instructions. At the suggestion of the General Manager of Associated Press, Oatis' able and understanding boss, Laurabelle Oatis came east from Minnesota to receive first-hand news of what we were doing. It was agreed on all sides that the line laid down would continue to be followed.

In Prague, a visit to Oatis in prison was finally arranged, although with a prearranged agenda and with a police officer and two interpreters present, few confidences were possible. Bill seemed, however, to be in reasonably good health, and I gathered that once his "confession" had been obtained, he had not been ill-treated. The "confession" was apparently reached through a combination of exhaustion, duress, insomnia, and endless repetition of questions.

Bill's condition, and the relative courtesy of the authorities in handling the interview, encouraged the hope of an early release. At the end of the visit I told Oatis that efforts had been made continuously on his behalf, beginning on the day of his disappearance. I declared that neither the American people nor the American government would allow his case to be forgotten.

The State Department having given out my cabled report of the interview, proof of American sympathy was not long in coming. From the London office of Associated Press came a handsome edition of Shakespeare. A publisher in New York furnished a Bible, with large print for a near-sighted reader. Anonymous well-wishers sent books on music, musicology, and harmonics. These and other offerings were forwarded by the embassy via the Czech Foreign Office, which scrutinized them for capitalist subterfuges, but eventually permitted most of them to reach Ruzyne prison. Meanwhile the Overseas Press Club awarded the Polk Memorial Prize to William N. Oatis, *in absentia.*

I myself left Prague before Bill was freed. The news of his release reached me in Korea, during the war against that country by the Communists. Korea is on the opposite side of the earth, but as the war correspondents in Seoul brought me the cables from Europe with the report of the Oatis "pardon," the scene ten thousand miles away took shape and came alive for me, almost as though I were standing with Bill in Bohemia.

From the last Czech village the road dips toward the German frontier, through a forest of spruces. On the right side, the customs building, with barbed wire behind it; on the left, the frontier police office. The police would have been alerted from Prague about the impending expulsion. Around the lowered gate would be soldiers in brown uniforms, with sub-machine guns slung from their shoulders. There would be police dogs on leashes. An inspector would be examining Bill's passport, freshly validated by the American embassy in Prague. He would return the passport. He would signal the soldiers to raise the barrier.

A few yards beyond the barrier there is a brook at the foot of the slope, with a meadow on the western side of it. That brook is the actual frontier: embassy travelers used to set our file of empty Löwenbräu bottles on the narrow bridge, just inside Czechoslovakia, while we waited for the comrades to finish examining our papers. Today the May sunshine would be warm on the clover and buttercups in that Bavarian meadow. There would be American soldiers on the free side of the bridge over the brook, between there and the black-and-white traffic sign listing in German, Czech, and English the speed limits in Germany. Frontier guards in green uniforms and peaked caps would salute. And there would be welcoming American correspondents and photographers, trying to make Bill Oatis, a free man, feel what the American people meant him to feel, after two years in a Communist prison.

When I was sure that Bill Oatis had crossed that frontier, I issued, from Korea, the following statement:

> There is no gratitude, I wrote, due to the Communist masters of Czechoslovakia for releasing an innocent man after two years of wrongful imprisonment. The free world should never forget that Bill Oatis was falsely accused, shamefully exhibited in a public spectacle in Prague, and on July Fourth — American Independence Day — sentenced to ten years' imprisonment.
>
> Oatis' crime was that he conscientiously carried out his duties as a newspaper correspondent, seeking behind the Communist façade of self-praise to ascertain the truth about Czechoslovakia.

The knowledge that Czechoslovakia was assessed fifty million dollars for injuries inflicted on an American newspaper correspondent should be as gratifying to Bill Oatis as it ought to be sobering to the Prague comrades who inherited, half a century after Theodore Roosevelt rescued Perdicaris, the soiled mantle of their predecessor Raisuli.

112

VI.

Nocturne in Buenos Aires

PATRIOTIC Argentines proclaim in Buenos Aires that their beloved Teatro Colon has the best acoustics in the world — and they offer to bet you a steak two inches thick against a thin arpeggio to prove it. Argentines may concede that *La Scala* in Milan is worth listening to, if you have time on your hands and no pressing business elsewhere in Italy. The old Metropolitan in New York they dismiss as a draughty barn, *mal ventilado,* which gave Caruso laryngitis.

But Teatro Colon, on brave nights when *estancieros* crowd the boxes with their ladies under cascades of mink; Teatro Colon, bursting with three thousand patrons of music, a *gaucho* in every other balcony seat and each *gaucho* with his *chinita* beside him; Teatro Colon, where the faintest crackle on stage is as loud as breaking the shinbone of a steer at an *asado con cuero*: there, at Teatro Colon, you find true lovers of music.

And music, *Señor,* is a business not lightly to be interrupted. No, *Señor.* Not if you value your own *cuero.* Not in Buenos Aires.

All of which, and especially the acoustics, I learned about the hard way, while the music lovers of Teatro Colon howled for my scalp and consigned me, a chord at a time, to the red billows of the River Plate that flows past their city.

It was before Dunkirk in 1940, in the ebbing days of the phony war, when Sumner Welles sent me down the east coast of South America, scouting for likely sites for wartime American consulates. From Belém, at the mouth of the Amazon, I prowled south to Rio Grande do Sul in planes of Panair do Brasil, a couple of hundred miles a day in Sikorsky amphibians.

Having cabled the Under Secretary of State from Montevideo that Natal, on the bulge of the continent, would make a good hopping-off place for a military air route to Africa and hence for an American consulate — a conclusion we could also have reached by remaining beside the Potomac and consulting an atlas — I visited the fresh wreckage of the *Graf von Spee,* still a collector's item among naval attachés accredited to Uruguay, and I came at last, worn with travel, to Buenos Aires.

In the vast house on Avenida Alvear, which is the only embassy in the world with a bronze plaque saying, "The President of the United States of America slept here" — meaning President Roosevelt in 1936 — the American ambassador gave me hospitable refuge, while his household staff undertook to catch up on my laundry. And presently the Ambassadress said that if her husband and his State Department guest had nothing more profitable to do that evening than heckling the Argentine Foreign Office, we were invited to join her at a concert in Teatro Colon. It would be the debut, in Argentina, of a famous violin maestro.

The Ambassador remarked that, what with wartime prices for Argentine beef and Patagonian mutton, Argentina was hiring, and Teatro Colon was hearing, the finest musical talent in the world. We would make every effort to finish our Foreign Office business and get there.

The Ambassadress warned us that the management of Teatro Colon is schooled in an austere tradition. No disturbance from tardy ones, not even from a late-blooming American ambassador and his Washington guest, was likely to be condoned. Not in Teatro Colon. So we had better be prompt, or risk not being admitted.

Our Foreign Office appointment was at six. We could hardly make a seven o'clock curtain. It was left that the Ambassadress and her three accompanying Argentine ladies would occupy the box, which seated six, and that the Ambassador and I would join them, provided the management would let us in, when we got there.

What the Ambassador and I talked about with the Foreign Minister I no longer remember. Something about the war, for Argentina had just given asylum to over one thousand Nazi survivors of *Graf von Spee,* when that proud ship committed suicide outside the Montevideo breakwater. Hitler's sailors were all over Buenos Aires, honored guests of Colonel Juan Domingo Perón, about whom the continent was to hear more. Ours was certainly wartime business, but it made less impression upon me than the decibels that followed.

It was after seven — too late for the maestro's first gleaning — when the Ambassador and I left the Foreign Office. At the Jockey Club I scribbled notes of our conversation on the back of an embossed menu that listed *mejillones,* and squid, and meatballs in seventeen different dimensions. By now, said the Ambassador, the maestro ought to be well into his program. We'd see if the management would let us into his wife's box.

Relinquishing a *rosbif* sandwich the color of a barn door in Maine, and almost as large, I drained my glass and we resumed our odyssey.

The Teatro Colon is an enormous establishment. *Aïda* is played there without crowding the Pyramids. The bull in *Carmen* could wander around in it for days, looking for Ernest Hemingway. In the deserted foyer the American ambassador flushed an ancient usher wearing maroon breeches, white silk stockings, and pumps with square silver buckles. The usher was not enthusiastic, but pesos changed hands, and after a pause the usher produced an assistant manager.

Everyone else was inside, listening to the maestro's music.

115

The assistant manager said the second half of the program had already started. Rules were rules. He was sorry. My host said he was sorry, too. He and his distinguished colleague had been detained at the Foreign Office. We came as soon as we could. We were lovers of music. The assistant manager said rules were rules, and also that regulations were regulations. He was still sorry.

"In Box One," the Ambassador persisted, "my wife awaits us. She will be disappointed . . ."

"Ah. *Palco Numéro Uno*. Box One," exclaimed the assistant manager. "Then you, *Señor,* must be the new American ambassador."

My host turned on the charm. He is an imposing man, and his Spanish was adequate. Our dedication to music was reviewed, and our respect for the venerable traditions of Teatro Colon was emphasized. His colleague, went on the Ambassador, pointing at me, his colleague with whom we had been transacting important business with His Excellency the Foreign Minister, had come all the way from Washington. And again — in Box One his wife was expecting us.

The assistant manager conceded defeat. He spoke to the ancient usher. He turned to us. "You may enter, *Señores,*" he said. "But, please — very quietly."

The usher led us away, and we tiptoed after him. We came to the long carpeted arc that runs behind the doors to the boxes. All were closed. The sound of a violin penetrated to us, faintly, and there was the smell theaters have when they are opened for gala nights, when costly French perfume mingles with the more earthly emanations of the distant balcony patrons. We reached the door of Box One, the front of which overlooked the stage and the grand piano of the maestro's accompanist, as well as the maestro himself and his violin.

By the closed door we halted, still chaperoned by the usher, whose expression recorded how little he thought of our breach of Teatro Colon protocol.

116

"Sweet are the abuses of ambassadorial privilege," whispered my host cheerfully.

"Shush!" ordered the usher. He addressed us in refined *platense* Spanish. "Soon there will come a pause in the number." Not the *end* of a number, he continued, but a pause of some seconds at the end of a movement, during which — not in accordance with the traditions of Teatro Colon, nor yet again in accordance with his own good judgment — we might silently enter the box.

"*Pero, Señor Embajador,*" he pleaded unhappily, "enter carefully. *Sin el mas minimo ruido.* Without the slightest of noise. *Por Dios. Señor Embajador.*"

The usher was a lovely little man. The Ambassador patted him on the shoulder. He said we would be as silent as mice walking on cotton.

The pause in whatever the maestro was doing, came. The usher unlocked the door of Box One. "Go now, *Señores.* But softly. . . ."

Four hats were dimly visible in silhouette; the hats of the Ambassadress and her three Argentine ladies. But the passageway itself was as dark as a pocket. The Ambassador stepped back. I was his guest. "After you," he whispered.

"After you, Mr. Ambassador," I responded automatically, for no officer of the Foreign Service precedes the personal representative of the President of the United States in the country to which the Ambassador is accredited. "After you, sir!" I repeated.

It was a poor time for a dialogue over precedence. Precious seconds were passing. The usher popped up and down on the toes of his pumps, in a frenzy of anguish. "*Señores,*" he pleaded, "*Por Dios.*"

Gently the American ambassador propelled me. I remember, as I dashed forward, that I planned to pause at the end of the passage, squeezing myself against the wall, so that the American ambassador could be seated before me. I sped into

117

the darkness, conscious of the great silence that exists in a disciplined theater, when the dust motes, caught by the spotlight, hang motionless and expectant in the air. Not a *gaucho* in the balcony moved; not a *chinita* breathed beside him.

Box One holds six. Before the concert began, there were six little gold chairs in readiness. Four of them were now occupied by the Ambassadress and her three Argentine ladies. But to give themselves more room to enjoy the maestro's music, they had moved two of those chairs out of the box. They parked them, one behind the other, in that dark-as-a-pocket passage.

At the moment when the next round note floated out of the maestro's music box, beautiful as a shining bubble, I upended myself over the first spindle-legged gold chair and, spread-eagled, crashed down upon the second.

On the open Argentine *pampas,* the noise might have shaken the leaves off a distant *ombu* tree; it might have attracted the startled attention of armadillos half way to the Chilean border. In Teatro Colon, with its oversexed acoustics capable of converting the faintest Wagnerian twitter to the magnitude of a blast in a tunnel, it was the most devastating sound since General San Martín returned from the revolutionary wars with the independence of Argentina in his knapsack.

A surviving American vice consul, thriftily perched in the balcony among the *gauchos* and *chinitas,* reported that his teeth rattled and the inlays fell out of his molars. The American ambassadress said the look directed by the maestro at Box One set fire to four afternoon bonnets.

The maestro slammed his violin on the top of the grand piano. He marched off the stage. After him, looking like a disheveled mongoose, pattered the stricken accompanist.

And in the ensuing pandemonium, three thousand music-loving patrons of Teatro Colon howled for the blood of the disturber of the peace. They acted like Salome demanding the head of John the Baptist.

The next day I left for Washington. No W. H. Hudson, stealing his bride from the *estancia,* got out of Buenos Aires any quicker. The last I saw of my hostess, she was reading a note from the maestro, declining an invitation from the American ambassadress to take tea in the embassy that afternoon, there to receive my apologies. The maestro was evidently a man who enjoyed perpetuating his lacerated feelings. Not the type who forgives readily. I gave the Ambassador a check payable to Teatro Colon, to buy two spindle-legged gold chairs, and he put me on the northbound plane, with plaster covering my contusions.

It was two years before I had an opportunity to apologize to the maestro. By then, I assumed he would have written off the incident as one of the hazards of his exacting profession, and be amused by it.

We were at war by that time, and I was chargé d'affaires in Cuba. My wife was with me, and she knows about music. She was elected a director of *Orquestra Filharmonica,* which rated us seats, once a week, in a Vedado theater. The Cuban Orchestra was little bothered by acoustics, and the *aficionados* of Teatro Colon would probably have sneered, but there were compensations. You could smoke a cigar during the performance. They had a bar in the theater, where between numbers Pablo made daiquiris almost as well as Constantino made them at the Floridita. There was a pregnant cellist, who before the baby was born had to play her instrument almost horizontally; we used to bet on the date, and whether they were twins or triplets. It was all very relaxed and carefree.

In Havana we also enjoyed an occasional guest artist whose wartime airplane priority used to deposit him in the Pearl of the Antilles. The members of the board of directors of *Orquestra Filharmonica* took turns giving after-concert suppers to these stranded celebrities, and it was my turn

119

to be host, after the violin maestro's Cuban performance.
The maestro was booked for supper the same way he was booked for the concert, except he was paid for playing whereas the supper was on the representational tab of an American diplomat. The idea was to give the Patrons of Music in Cuba, who are not necessarily identical with the Patrons of Cuban Music, an opportunity for their wives, who are among the loveliest women in the world, to wear their Paris and Fifth Avenue dresses. Their husbands, busy helping the war effort by building distilleries to make Cuban gin out of cane juice, thereby evading the ceiling price on raw sugar, would have settled for a couple of maraca players and a hot rumba number; instead they made respectful remarks to the guest of honor and depleted my dwindling stock of pre-Pearl Harbor Scotch whiskey.

I had reached the maestro's concert on time that night, and my conduct during the musical proceedings was exemplary. While the maestro performed his magic, I perspired gently through my sharkskin dinner jacket, wondering whether it was the same violin slammed on the grand piano back in Buenos Aires when the world was two years younger.

And so, around midnight, under the soft Cuban sky, music lovers and diplomats and wives of Cubans making gin out of *miel de cañas,* converged on our garden, where there was Chilean champagne for the maestro, because champagne is the only drink maestros will consume after the rigors of a concert, and also because the last of my French champagne had been consumed by one of the maestro's predecessors.

The guest of honor was tired, perhaps, from fiddling his way through those Vedado acoustics. He had no small talk. Or possibly he was brooding about the baby, or babies, of the pregnant cellist. Not even the efforts of the gracious Cuban wives elicited a favorable response from the maestro. He yawned, against the time when his suite at the Hotel Nacional might contain him. His burps, inadequately suppressed, put

120

my *Valdivieso extra sec* on notice with the Good Neighbor Policy.

Culture fluttered in the bougainvillea vines, the audience was captive, and the maestro more and more resembled President Coolidge posing for the pickle advertisement. Nor was the maestro cheered by the tardy arrival of the accompanist, still looking like a disheveled mongoose, who reported that although they had tickets, no airplane priority was available for the maestro's flight to Puerto Rico in the morning.

It was the moment, clearly, to try to cheer things up and to brighten the guest of honor. His scowl was poisoning the evening. Possibly an anecdote of his profession might do it. Fortunately, his host had just such an anecdote — a cherished recitation.

"Maestro," I said, "it's a privilege for all lovers of music to have you here in Havana, and I'm sorry you haven't a priority for San Juan tomorrow morning."

The maestro continued to scowl. Someone filled his glass with greenish *Valdivieso extra sec.* He sipped it without enthusiasm.

"Also," I continued brightly, uptilting my own glass to show I could take Chilean champagne without burping, "your being in Havana gives me a chance to tell you how sorry I was to spoil your concert in Teatro Colon two years ago."

The guest of honor looked puzzled, and not friendly.

I plunged on, recklessly. "To the fine old River Plate and Teatro Colon," I cried, waving my champagne glass. "From Teatro Colon to Morro Castle. Here's to you and your stalwart violin, Maestro."

The maestro screwed up his eyebrows until he looked like something out of the Carpathians, which was where he originally came from.

"Teatro Colon? Buenos Aires? My concert?"

His attention, I was gratified to see, was now properly focused. It had been a long evening for a tired diplomat allergic

121

to music. I had waited two years to tell my story to the maestro, and to make my apologies. If he didn't like them, the hell with it. Launched on my adventures, with my Cuban guests now clustered around me, I led the maestro down the east coast of South America, all the way to the American embassy on Avenida Alvear in Buenos Aires. I escorted him from the Foreign Office to Teatro Colon. I described how my host the Ambassador had handled the assistant manager and the unwilling usher.

"Teatro Colon," I declared. "Best acoustics in the world, way the Argentines tell it. The assistant manager tried to keep us out because we were late. But we foxed him. . . ." And I described how nimbly I had dashed into that dark passageway that led to Box One, where the American ambassadress was waiting.

"Best acoustics in the world," I repeated. "I'm the man who tripped over those spindle-legged gold chairs. Booby trap if I ever saw one. Damn near broke my neck. Been waiting two years to tell you how sorry I was to interrupt your program."

A vein was throbbing in the maestro's temple, and I suppose it should have warned me. The glass in his hand trembled. "Vas you!" he suddenly shouted. All the rage that had possessed him, there in the spotlight in the center of the stage in Buenos Aires, boiled up anew, lava-hot, in Havana. "I remember it puffikly." He choked with hatred. "Teatro Colon. My debut. Interrupted my concert . . . you *ruined* my concert!"

I faced an audience diminished by two. The maestro slammed his glass on the garden table the way he had slammed his violin on the grand piano. He marched out of my garden, precisely as he had marched off the stage in Buenos Aires. His disheveled accompanist pattered after him.

As the representative of the United States in Cuba, I had access to communications. The maestro got off the next day

122

without incident from Rancho Boyeros, south of Havana. With satisfaction I learned that he was off-loaded four hours later at Port-au-Prince, in Haiti, to make room for an Air Force sergeant in a hurry to reach Recife with a magneto for a B-17 bomber. I didn't think the maestro would care for Port-au-Prince. I rather hoped he wouldn't. In Haiti they don't bother much about the acoustics. There, it's all in the drum beat.

VII.

Musical Chairs Is Hard on the Furniture

THE next chapters have to do with various operational problems and ways in which the conduct of foreign affairs could be improved, to the enhancement of efficiency and the relief of the taxpayers. The first innovation would be to leave an ambassador at his post long enough for him to approach maximum efficiency.

Having survived seven ambassadorships in sixteen years, with corresponding wear on liver, luggage, and loved ones, my testimony is that although such abbreviated tours of duty at each post constitute a stimulating career for the individual, they emphatically do not produce the most efficient diplomatic service.

Of all the ways in which the conduct of our foreign affairs could be improved, the most important as well as the easiest would be to leave each ambassador at his post long enough for him to become fully effective. That means five or more years at a post, instead of one or two as at present. Moreover, the superiority of the professional over the amateur is often blurred by these too frequent transfers, which sacrifice competence to the inevitable requirements of orientation. The Constitution gives the President the right to shuffle diplomatic representatives around; successive Chief Executives, often egged on by the politicians, have succumed to the temptation to play musical chairs with their envoys, regardless of the effect on the furniture.

Take our recent representation in Brazil, for example. We

went to Rio de Janeiro after only one year in Peru — an important country that was not flattered by being used as a railway station for an itinerant American representative. Having moved into that lovely tropical residence at Rua São Clemente 388, we dedicated ourselves to Portuguese and set ourselves to traveling within the vast country, which shares frontiers with every one of the other twelve countries of the continent except Ecuador and Chile.

In due course we visited each of Brazil's twenty-two states and the governors thereof, plus innumerable mayors, legislators, generals, bishops, consuls, and even a couple of cardinals. Wherever we went, Brazilians inveighed against the rapid turnover in American representations. Oldtimers remembered Edwin Morgan, who served from 1912 to 1933 (by far the longest ambassadorial tour of duty ever recorded in the American diplomatic service), and they spoke warmly of the seven years of Jefferson Caffery. But the rest of my predecessors were a blur of envoys who scarcely had time to meet the Brazilian cabinet before they were gone like carnival confetti, leaving as little impression.

Our Brazilian acquaintances said politely that they hoped we might be around somewhat longer. We answered, by now in pretty good Portuguese, that we hoped so, too. Shortly thereafter, however, Secretary Dulles sent me word that my successor would be a distinguished Republican lady, and almost before I knew it I was on my way to Greece.

And when the lady, following her confirmation by the Senate, decided she did not want to go to Brazil after all,* the State Department tore up *twenty-two* sets of travel orders that would have transferred eleven senior officers from Embassy Rio and replaced them by eleven Foreign Service Officers of the new Ambassadress' choosing. Apparently Mrs. Luce had not for nothing kept a scrapbook during her Roman holiday.

* As recorded in the chapter entitled "Here Today, Gone Tomorrow."

Secretary Herter, who by then had taken over from the ailing Foster Dulles, plucked from Bogota the able and experienced Jack Cabot, who had been ambassador to Colombia for only one year, and sent *him* to Rio. Cabot was in turn succeeded two years later by a Frontiersman professor, now busy with inflation and the Alliance for Progress cornucopia — the latter an instrument even larger than the one the Brazilians hoped Clare Boothe Luce would bring them. The professor is the tenth American representative appointed to Brazil, our most important South American neighbor, since the end of World War II.

By moving our ambassadors around every year or two, the American government not only fritters away their talents but also gives other governments the impression that we lack serious or consistent purpose. American representation is weakened, and the agents of the American Government are handicapped in their dealings with colleagues and competitors.

Our behavior toward Chile, another proud and sensitive member of the inter-American family, further illustrates what our friends can only regard as frivolous representational activity. In 1955 we sent Cecil Lyon to Santiago, a popular choice, for the Lyons had been in Chile as junior members of the staff of the well-remembered Norman Armour. Cecil and his wife had scores of Chilean friends who rejoiced at his assignment and hoped for long years for the couple in the shadow of Aconcagua.

I first knew of their transfer, a few months later, when my Chilean colleague in Rio de Janeiro telephoned me in distress: *"Qué cosa terrible ha hecho Cecil?* . . . What terrible thing has Cecil done?" the Ambassador asked. "Your government is sending him to France, demoted to Counselor."

The story as I had it later from Washington was that the incumbent deputy in our Paris embassy could no longer survive the inescapable expenses of the post and had made an urgent plea to be moved before he became bankrupt. The State Department, searching for a replacement, propositioned Lyon, assuring him that if he would step down to ministerial rank and take the number two spot in Paris, he would be re-appointed ambassador as soon as a suitable opening occurred. Meanwhile the State Department would seek an appropriation sufficient to underwrite the inevitable expense of the job in Paris.

To the Chileans this transfer was a double irritation. First we removed an effective and popular representative, just as he was getting started, and secondly we created the impression that we considered the deputy position in France more important than the ambassadorial grade in Chile. Whether it is or not may be debatable, but rather than accept such a belittling admission, the *chilenos* preferred, like my friend their ambassador in Brazil, to assume that the displaced ambassador might have been caught defacing the Great Seal of the United States, or at the very least feeding tainted sunflower seeds to the macaw in the patio of the Pan American Union. The same transfer attracted almost equally unfavorable attention in other countries of Latin America, where it supported the contention of our critics that we regard the Southern Hemisphere as a second-class area.

As this is written, Lyon is still in Paris,* still serving as deputy to short-term ambassadors to France, and still waiting for an adequate allowance to cover representational expenses.

And in the meantime, the Kennedy administration in 1962 kicked the Chileans on the same bruised shin by appointing another ambassador to Santiago and then removing him to be Assistant Secretary of State, only *four weeks* after his arrival in Chile.

These rapid transfers are not confined to the New World. While few appointments result in the free-wheeling hoopla

* As the book goes to press, Lyon has just been appointed Ambassador to Ceylon.

127

that followed the Luce nomination in Brazil, each one of them jettisons the experience acquired at his post by a chief of mission who may have reached his ambassadorship after long years of highly competitive service. Moreover, it takes at least one year in a new country for even the most diligent and experienced professional to dominate the immensely complicated job of a modern ambassador. Performance results from confidence in the character, intentions, and ability of the new American envoy; and confidence cannot be achieved without developing personal relationships with the key foreign officials concerned: president, prime minister, industrialist, monarch, labor leader, prelate — with whomever the leaders of the country may be. Even the smallest country has a complete set of officials both national and local, whom the new foreign representative must meet and know before he can operate efficiently.

That takes time. There is no substitute for time-at-a-post, a circumstance which is, of course, well known within the operating areas of the Department of State — the geographic bureaus where nine-tenths of the substantive work in foreign affairs is accomplished in Washington. It is equally well known in foreign chanceries, which find it excessively tedious to break in new American envoys and then to have each one — on the verge of reaching useful performance — packed off to his next assignment.

Several years ago, in a European capital, I had occasion to remark on the activities of my Soviet colleague, who was throwing his weight around and apparently getting away with it. The Russian representative was neither prepossessing nor personally attractive. Quite the contrary. A ridge of fat bulged over the back of his collar, and his eyes — shiny as moist currants — were set close together. He was a noisy and untidy eater. The Ambassador was not, but for other reasons, a popular table companion among the ladies of the capital.

128

And yet, in some raffish, unlaundered way, the Soviet representative seemed to have an influence that bore little or no relation to his behavior. I asked a fellow ambassador who had served with me before and who had been at my new post much longer than I how he accounted for this.

My friend replied with a quotation from the gaucho poem we used to recite in our youth: "The devil is smart as the devil, but what makes him really smart is experience."

"Our Yuri," explained my friend, "may not be smart as all that, but he has been here so long that automatically he does not make mistakes. He knows this country, and he knows the people in it. Under the table, Comrade Yuri may pinch the wife of the Minister of Posts and Telegraphs, but you will notice he does not pinch the wife of the Minister of National Defense. *Mon jeune collègue,* in diplomacy there is no substitute for experience."

It was a sound observation, reminding me of an amateur ambassadorial career blighted by disregard for the pitfalls of inexperience that I had observed when I was a junior officer in Latin America. My boss, who had never been ambassador before, became charmed with the notion that a display of interest in indigenous culture would flatter the citizens of the country and hence serve as a key to local popularity. On the advice of a professor friend in the United States, the Ambassador decided to collect *huacos,* which are Indian artifacts, often in the form of drinking vessels, which the conquering Spaniards largely ignored because there was no gold or silver in them.

But like the shrunken heads of the Jivaros in neighboring Ecuador, which the Quito craftsmen learned to manufacture from the heads of monkeys and dogs as soon as a cosmopolitan market developed, the *huacos* of the pre-Columbian civilization became subject to fraudulent enterprise on the part of Atahualpa's descendants. Behind the scenes, the word got around that the American embassy housed an uncritical and

129

enthusiastic buyer. A houseboy got into the act, and before long the Ambassador imagined he was making rapid progress toward the acquisition of a substantial private collection.

So he might have, at that, except that the Indian houseboy was passing the Ambassador's purchases out the window to a confederate, who was able to sell the same *huacos* to the Ambassador again, two or three days later.

When the Ambassador finally caught on, he ought to have fired the houseboy, pocketed his losses, and charged the incident to Learning About Indigenous Culture. Instead, he indignantly summoned the local police, and the story was all over town in no time. Several of the *huacos,* including a couple of pornographic ones the houseboy had planted to confuse pursuit, were found to be counterfeits. The houseboy prudently vanished, but the opposition press had a field day: it accused the Ambassador of deliberately failing to register his purchases with the *Comisión Nacional de Arqueología,* and even of scheming to smuggle the *huacos* out of the country, under the shield of his diplomatic immunity.

Pretty soon practically everybody in the country was laughing at the American ambassador, and no one can be an effective representative if he allows himself to become a subject of ridicule.

All of which might have been avoided if the Ambassador had not tried to rush into popularity and leave his mark on history before he had enough experience at his post to back up his judgments.

Since the American Foreign Service was reorganized in 1924 under the Rogers Act, only a small scattering of envoys have served long enough to be truly at home in the countries of their assignment. Joe Grew in Tokyo, his contemporary Nelson Johnson in China, Hugh Wilson and his successor Leland Harrison in Switzerland, plus such men as Myron Herrick in Paris, Claude Bowers in Chile, and Lincoln MacVeagh in Greece, are all remembered not only for what they did but also for the fact that they remained long enough to have an intelligible impact on their environments.

But among the literally hundreds of American representatives who have gone abroad in the past forty years, those mentioned above — each of whom served a decade or more at his post — are in almost microscopic proportion to the short-order cooks (and fireless cookers), many of whom never stayed in their diplomatic kitchens long enough to identify the ingredients of foreign affairs, let alone cook anything worthy of historical record. And some have not been permitted to remain long enough to light the stove or warm the oven.

American Presidents ought to be reminded of the importance of time-at-a-post by contemplating the foreign diplomatic corps in Washington, where country after country facilitates its operations and multiplies its influence by leaving its representative beside the Potomac long enough to join the Metropolitan Club and post a modest golf handicap at Chevy Chase, and sometimes even long enough to learn how the American government operates and who therein can be helpful to a foreign envoy in the performance of his duties.

There are, for example, sixteen foreign ambassadors who have been in Washington for five years or more. The Dean of the Corps has been there for nearly twenty years. His Peruvian colleague, with fourteen years, witnessed the swearing in at the State Department of no less than seven American ambassadors to Peru.

In contrast, since the departure of Llewellyn Thompson from Moscow, only one American ambassador in the entire world has been at his post for as long as five years. Practically no one has been in his country of assignment for as long as four years. The average tenure of the fifty-six professionals serving as ambassadors on June 30, 1962, was just over seventeen months — not quite a year and a half.

This phenomenon is not an aberration of the present administration. Previous administrations have been equally profli-

131

gate with manpower. Twelve years ago, toward the end of the Truman administration, the comparable figures for the forty-six officers of career then serving as chief of mission was under nineteen months, and for the twenty-five political appointees not quite twenty-two months. Five years later, in 1957, it was 21.4 months for ambassadors of career, and 24 months for the politicians.

That is to say, American diplomats have always been uprooted and transplanted, and replanted and uprooted again, more rapidly by far than the representatives of any other country. Each ambassador serves at the pleasure of the President of the United States, and his commission clearly so states. Each, nevertheless, is required to submit his resignation after every presidential election, even when an incumbent President is re-elected. The same usually holds when a President dies in office. Thus the moving of our envoys is not only facilitated; it is encouraged.

This never-ending shuffling of American representatives (and also of senior Foreign Service personnel assigned as deputy chief of mission or as ministers and counselors) often makes for a fascinating career in the diplomatic service. It also puts a premium on durability as an officer is bounced from snowdrifts and ski-lifts to monsoons and tropical mildew, or from sea level to high altitude and back again. But in terms of the effectiveness of our representation abroad, transfers after only a few months at a post represent a frivolous and wasteful misuse of trained manpower. Exceptions are the so-called unhealthy or hardship posts — capitals in Central Africa, Southeast Asia, et cetera — where the maximum tour of duty is properly two years.

Assuredly there are factors other than longevity that contribute to the success or failure of an American diplomatic mission. Knowledge of a foreign country's history, its culture, and (sometimes) its language, may be important. A flair for inconspicuous operations is nearly always useful. Since they

132

now travel abroad at the rate of several hundred per year, a deft hand at the care and feeding of Congressmen is becoming essential. So is the ambassadorial fortitude necessary to ride herd on the Great American Double-Breasted Do-Gooder, as well as on the multifarious and persistent retainers of agencies other than the Department of State, with which every American embassy in the world is now afflicted.

All these and many other ingredients are relevant to diplomatic performance, but not all of them taken together can equal in importance the experience gained at a post, which comes only from having lived and worked there. Moreover, familiarity with a post represents knowledge that is difficult to transmit to a successor, and it cannot possibly be compressed into a few months of service at a foreign capital, no matter how talented an ambassador may be.

The game of diplomatic musical chairs has always been more popular with the Pennsylvania Avenue master of ceremonies than it has with the players, who comprehend the effect of the play on the furniture, and who know what it costs to replace and repair it. That the game continues, at a time when we should be seeking to extract maximum efficiency and performance from our diplomats, seems as childish as it does incomprehensible.

When this argument was first advanced, sounds of approval were heard in the land. The press expressed itself. A Senate subcommittee, mentioned in Chapter I, took testimony on the subject. The consensus appears to be that, except for hardship posts, four to five years ought to be a normal tour of duty for an American ambassador.

The present abbreviated tenure is irrational and expensive, but it is sanctioned by the Constitution and firmly established. The public, and Congress, should continue to be heard from.

133

VIII.

Here Today, Gone Tomorrow

As a companion chapter to "Musical Chairs," I have likewise examined the reasons why ambassadors are moved. The most common one is that an envoy is wanted for another, and sometimes more important, job. But there are other reasons, less encouraging, including those that involve twitching the rug out from under the incumbent ambassador. The twitcher is often a politician, or the protegé of a politician, who covets the ambassadorial office. The twitchee is often a career civil servant. Here is the fruit of my investigation.

A master of ceremonies once introduced me as the ambassador who had served in more different countries than any American envoy of record. Later he explained to me that his introduction was intended to impress the customers as well as to flatter the guest of honor. Here, he implied, is a Statesman Rich in Years and Wisdom, who has known not only friendly democracies but malevolent dictatorships; industrial powers and banana republics; the Occident and the Orient, with the Levant and Africa and the Good Neighborhood thrown in for good measure.

Heady prose, and for a while I almost believed it.

Then one day I resolved to examine the saga of the much-traveled ambassador. Is it true, I wondered, that service in *x* countries in *y* years denotes a gifted and exemplary public servant? Or is somebody merely thinking of the Secretary of State and his airplane? Do that many transfers in so short a time predicate a competent diplomacy, or a frivolous system

— if there is a system, or indeed any intelligible reason for all this international huffing and puffing and coming and going. Transfers, after all, are made one at a time and in individual cases. If some pattern could be discovered, its existence might illuminate the problem. How, in brief, do the President and the Secretary of State go about establishing the placement of American ambassadors?

Official documentation about foreign affairs runs to thousands of pages per administration, an almost overwhelming freshet of government material. Little of it, however, sheds light on the treatment of ambassadors. The bureaucratic emanations range all the way from the plush Madison Avenue "News Letter" of the State Department, which the Foggy Bottom scribes produce once a month in the spirit of Narcissus admiring his reflection, to the formidable precepts of the promotion panels assembled annually to examine the personnel dossiers of approaching four thousand Foreign Service officers. Take, for example, the qualifications for career minister, the rank held by a majority of professional ambassadors when appointed to be chief of mission.

> A career minister (goes the precept) is expected to possess the exceptional experience, ability and personal characteristics which qualify him to serve in key executive and policy positions in Washington and abroad. . . . Typically he will have demonstrated unusual leadership and command talent, a penetrating insight into the foreign affairs process, a high degree of executive proficiency, superior competence in planning and conducting negotiations, and well-developed skill in oral and written expression. . . .

And so on and so forth, for nine lilting paragraphs. Note that the successful candidate is not limited to "insight into foreign affairs" (apparently an astigmatic sort of perspicacity) but to *penetrating* insight into the foreign affairs *process,*" which is presumably the difference between a two-cart emporium in an eastern Maine village and a two-hundred-cart supermarket combined with shopping center on the approaches to Boston.

It is accordingly reassuring to read that of approximately seventy-five career ministers now on duty, no less than thirty-six are serving as ambassadors. But if they are so talented and experienced, reaching by merit the top of an exacting competitive service, why are they constantly shifted around, like football players whenever the ball changes hands in the stadium? Why are they not left in one capital long enough to do the job for which they were selected?

Next to promotions, transfers are the most compelling things that can happen to a professional diplomat. Not only is the family uprooted, after a period of intense dedication to the affairs of the host country, but it is then transported clear across the globe, or between north and south, to an entirely different climate, language, and environment, in circumstances often varying as greatly from the last capital as milk from molasses. On the subject of ambassadorial transfers, alas, the spokesmen of succeeding administrations are strangely silent, for that activity approaches those constitutional provisions that are applicable to the President's conduct of foreign relations. And who is prepared to tread on presidential toes, or to paint a moustache on the Chief Executive's Mona Lisa?

My inquiry into the transfer of ambassadors thus became an exercise in pure research, buttressed by observation of the treatment of ambassadorial colleagues, but fortified primarily by my own lengthy and varied experience.

Assuming that an ambassador does not resign or become what the underwriters describe as a claim, there appear to be five principal reasons that govern an initial appointment or a subsequent transfer. In the process of being hedge-hopped over the world from my first embassy in 1944 to my eighth one in 1962, I was involved, one way or another, with all five of these reasons. After nineteen years as an apprentice, I went from

Santo Domingo to China to Washington, and then from Uruguay to Czechoslovakia, Korea, Peru, Brazil, Greece, and Spain. In Washington I headed a State Department bureau, and in China I was minister, the deputy position; but to the remaining eight countries I was appointed ambassador. There was even a ninth — Indonesia — an assignment that evaporated before it reached the boiling point, but not before I had been notified by the Secretary of State and spent the next three months re-reading, in our luxurious embassy in Prague, the works of Joseph Conrad. Then the Djakarta incumbent turned out to be more tenacious than anticipated, and Dean Acheson abandoned the project.

I had nothing to do with my appointment in 1944 as ambassador to the Dominican Republic, my first post as chief of mission. The State Department recommended me to President Roosevelt on the basis of dossier and record, including service in neighboring Cuba and a knowledge of Spanish. That is the way the majority of career appointments are made. The most important reason for a professional assignment is past achievement and assessed promise. Nothing could be fairer.

So off I went to Santo Domingo, or Ciudad Trujillo as the capital was then called, in the image of its infamous *Benefactor de la Patria*. And there, less than one year later, I experienced the second reason for moving a diplomat: dissatisfaction with his performance. In short, I was fired.

Being dismissed from a job as chief of mission is often fatal to a diplomatic career, and it rarely builds it up any. In my case there was the factor of Secretary Hull policy, to which I warmly subscribed, and successor-to-Hull policy, for lack of sympathy with which I was bounced. The Hull policy was to treat the odious tyrant of Santo Domingo with chilly formality and to touch his bloodstained paw as infrequently as possible; the successor policy was to stroke the *Benefactor* and woo him with cozy phrases. As I had no stomach for the new emetic, my franchise was revoked, and presently I was shipped off to

137

China, demoted to deputy chief of mission, with the rank of minister instead of ambassador.

In Chungking I served with the ornate and eloquent Patrick Hurley, whose favorite comment was: "If it's a day old, or an inch high, I'll fight it!" Because Ambassador Hurley and I saw eye to eye on the "agrarian reformers," whose leaders Pat invariably referred to as Mouse Dung and Joe N. Lie, we got on well on the Yangtze River: two bulls, as some described it, in FDR's China shop. And soon after World War II was over, I was summoned to Washington, pragmatism having momentarily replaced *boyscoutismo* in Latin American policy.

Thus my career suffered no great damage as a result of my expulsion from the Dominican Republic, ignominious though it seemed to me at the time. On the contrary, the experience supplied perspective on the impermanence of public service, as well as giving me a reputation for wanting no part in a policy designed to butter up a disreputable despot.

So much for the second reason for diplomatic transfer.

My next post, Montevideo, was the only one I deliberately sought — a third reason for having a transfer.

On the day President Truman announced he was selecting a general to be Secretary of State, I was lunching with an important official, an admirer of the nominee, who deplored the appointment.

"The military tradition," he said, "is a poor introduction to the insoluble problems of foreign affairs. The rigidity that makes a good soldier is the inflexibility that prevents diplomatic agreement. The General will bring to the State Department all those admirable and outstanding qualifications which enabled him as Chief of Staff to shorten World War II, and they will get him nowhere in diplomacy."

We ordered a second brace of martinis and my companion continued: "The General will summon his aides and ask what is the most compelling problem facing the American people. Having identified the problem, he will demand the formulation

138

of a plan, and in due course a plan will be adopted. Let us call it Operation World Saviour. And just as in those vast enterprises during the war, the resources of the United States government and its allies will be mobilized to promote that operation. Diplomats will be deployed like task forces, and Foreign Ministers will do setting-up exercises.

"Finally the great moment arrives. The Secretary of State having secured — so he thinks — the last contingency between Antwerp and Zanzibar, presses the button that puts Operation World Saviour in motion. Mankind, unanimous at last, is supposed to march forward.

"And what happens then?" my friend demanded, brandishing his olive on the end of a toothpick. "Nothing happens! San Marino and Monte Carlo say the hell with it. Operation World Saviour is a shambles . . ."

Not long after that conversation, in the year 1947, the embassy in Uruguay became vacant through the death of the incumbent ambassador. Deciding that I, too, was perhaps allergic to soldier-statesmen, I moved to Montevideo. As head of the Latin American section, it was not too difficult to do so. I take credit, however, for the fact that no colleague of mine was bumped to make way for my appointment.

Although his tour of duty as Secretary of State is in no further respect germane to my investigations, it may be mentioned in passing that the soldier-statesman fared better than our luncheon judgment predicted.

A fourth reason for the transfer of an ambassador is that he ceases to be acceptable to the country to which he is accredited: in contrast to being fired by his own government, the host government fires him. "Handing the ambassador his passport," was the euphemism for this gambit, in the days when an ambassador's passport remained on deposit with the Foreign Office. If the passport was given back, the envoy was expected to use it to cross the frontier with. Because rejecting an ambassador is an attribute of sovereignty, there is no appeal by the sending state, which can, however, retaliate by packing off the ambassador of the other country, leaving each diplomatic mission in the hands of a chargé d'affaires.

Since the next move is often the breaking of diplomatic relations, a step associated in years past with going to war, declaring a diplomatic representative *persona non grata* used to be indulged in rather seldom, and rarely without considerable provocation. But in the half century since Communism has afflicted the world, gross behavior by a government has achieved the status of policy, and the expulsion of diplomats has become more common. In our own hemisphere the dismissal of the American ambassador to Haiti in 1963 may be mentioned; he was declared unwelcome in answer to rude remarks aimed at the dictator by a crusading State Department.

No country I served in ever threw me out, although I suspect that the Benefactor of Santo Domingo may privately have abetted my departure from Ciudad Trujillo in 1945. I did, however, experience the uncommon sensation of having the president of the country *next door* to the one I served in try to have me expelled. It is one of the few occasions when the chief executive of one country attempted to force from office the diplomatic representative of a second country, serving as ambassador in a third country.

It was while I was in Uruguay, and the complaining president was Juan Domingo Perón, the shirtless wonder of Argentina, a nation that has done more public screaming about American intervention than all the rest of the Good Neighbors combined, while simultaneously intervening itself in as many of them as possible. I knew Perón only by reputation, but the dictator, as innately suspicious as most tyrants, conceived the notion that, as a friend of his enemy Spruille Braden, I had been sent to Uruguay not only to represent the American government, but also to spy on Perón and stir up trouble for him. The fact that I often visited Buenos Aires was cited to prove that the American ambassador to Uruguay was up to no good on the south side of the River Plate. Also, Montevideo at that time was crowded with dissident Argentines, fugitives from the perónista utopia, who were represented as plotting with the American envoy against Juan Domingo and his bride, Evita.

Or so went the fable peddled on Perón's orders by the Argentine ambassador in Washington, who tiptoed uneasily into the State Department, apparently expecting to be thrown out of the premises. Instead, "Tell us more," was the substance of the Washington response, where selling its own agent short is not an unknown phenomenon. The State Department likewise neglected to report Perón's accusation to its own ambassadors in Montevideo and Buenos Aires.

Few things stay secret for very long in Latin America, and while Washington was still brooding about Perón's demand for my scalp, the President of Uruguay was tipped off by the Uruguayan ambassador in Washington. In Montevideo, President Battle Berres sent for me; Don Luis showed me the despatch from Washington, and his astonishment knew no bounds when I told him that was the first I had heard of Perón's attempt to have me expelled from Uruguay.

Returning to my chancery on Avenida Agraciada, I fired an angry telegram at the Department of State.

In 1949 the case caused a brief flurry among the Foreign Offices of South America, where international lawyers were fascinated by the triple-play aspects of President Perón's maneuver. Various chiefs of state were likewise alert to determine the extent to which Let's-Appease-Perón dominated the Potomac statesmanship of the moment. The excitement was punctured by the President of Uruguay, who sent word to Washington that the American ambassador enjoyed his confidence, and also by the American ambassador to Argentina.

Hearing of Perón's move even more belatedly than I, Ambassador Bruce laid it forcefully on the line in Washington (a) that the American ambassador to Argentina had been in

Uruguay as often as the American ambassador to Uruguay had been in Argentina; (b) that each ambassador had invariably been the guest of the other in Buenos Aires and Montevideo; (c) that the purpose of our respective expeditions was not to shoot poisoned darts into each other's official dartboards, but to shoot *perdiz, patos,* and *martineta* with our double-barreled shotguns; and (d) that when it came to Argentine-American relations he, the American ambassador to Argentina, was quite capable, thank-you-very-much, of looking after his own responsibilities.

Thus belabored, the State Department stiffened its spine, the Argentine ambassador in Washington was told to go climb an *ombu* tree, and that was the end of the incident.

The fifth and final reason for transferring an ambassador is that someone else wants his job. That happened to me after I had been posted to Rio de Janeiro. At the end of two years in Brazil I came home on leave, and John Foster Dulles genially volunteered that no change in American representation was contemplated by the Eisenhower administration, which still had two years to run. On the strength of that prospect I bought an air-conditioned automobile, drove it to New Orleans at the end of my vacation, and sailed back to my post, where shortly I had a personal letter from the Secretary of State. He was sorry, but . . .

The net of the message was that my successor as ambassador to Brazil was a well-known lady, who would probably be reaching Rio de Janeiro in April.

It was then February, and I was just leaving for the mouth of the Amazon, two thousand miles away from Rio, there to receive the merchant marine school ship of my state of Maine. A frozen salmon, a peck of clams, and a bushel of Aroostook County potatoes were to be presented by the Captain of the ship to the Mayor of Belém, who would then attend a dance in honor of the cadets. As American ambassador I was scheduled to be host at that party.

142

Scarcely had I reached Belém, with Foster Dulles' eviction notice in my pocket, when the local radio picked up a White House leak reporting the lady's impending assignment. The Brazilian press converged on the Hotel Grande: Is this true, *Senhor Embaixador?* When is the lady coming? Why are you being thrown out, *Senhor Embaixador,* when you have learned to speak our language and know our country?

The initial response on the part of the Brazilians was one of bewilderment. Woman's Place is the Bed may not be an exclusively Brazilian adage, but it conveys an idea. The notion of an *Embaixatriz* running the vast American chancery on Guanabara Bay was at the beginning difficult for the *cariocans* to assimilate. The more the Brazilians thought about it, however, the more intrigued they became. And before long they were enthusiastic about the appointment.

As soon as Mrs. Luce's nomination was sent to the Senate, making the situation official, the publicity kettle started to boil. Rich, intoxicating emanations shortly enveloped Sugar Loaf and Corcovado; they covered Copacabana Beach like a mist. Pictures and prose and sound effects describing dona Clara, as she was promptly named by the Brazilian press, throughout her colorful and distinguished career: The appointee attending the opening of a play in New York; the appointee presenting credentials to the President of Italy; the appointee lecturing the Pontiff and, later, attending His Holiness' funeral; the appointee skin diving in the Bahamas; the appointee making mosaics; and, currently, the appointee in Arizona studying Portuguese.

By the time the word got around Rio that the lady's husband was renting an entire floor in the Gloria Hotel, whence to direct the destinies of his magazine empire, it occurred to the Brazilians that publicity for the country was going to be little short of terrific. Research among the Italian archives confirmed that wherever dona Clara was, there also were klieg lights and a camera, with reporters in attendance.

Pictures of the American embassy in Rome were published in Brazil, and in Rio we received telephone calls asking how the paint on the ceiling of the master bedroom at Rua São Clemente 388 compared with that of Villa Taverna beside the Tiber.

Brazilians love the spotlight. Here, they reasoned, was a beacon capable of illuminating everything from Arroyo do Chuy on the Uruguayan frontier to the summit of Roraima overlooking Venezuela. Before long all Brazil was basking happily in the reflection of that alluring prospect.

The second reason that turned Brazilian skepticism to welcoming warmth concerned policy, United States policy toward Brazil, and the proposition that a new envoy automatically means a new approach to political and economic problems. The simple explanation — that the lady wanted to be American ambassador to Brazil — was too uncomplicated for the Brazilian mind to accept. It was more diverting to assume that since the outgoing representative stood for such notions as Curb Inflation, Don't Borrow More Than You Can Afford to Pay Back, and Don't Expropriate Your Neighbor's Property, the incoming envoy would repudiate those tiresome and archaic tenets, replacing them with Advanced Thought and Liberal Lending. Especially Liberal Lending.

Thus was planted by the Brazilian specialists in political necromancy the legend of the Lady with the Cornucopia. In the warm tropical soil, the legend grew like a giant fern at Os Esquilos. In a few days practically everyone in Brazil believed that dona Clara had been selected by President Eisenhower for the specific purpose of playing Lady Bountiful on behalf of the American government.

The next development bearing on her appointment was an unscheduled explosion in Bolivia, with immediate Brazilian repercussions. The footloose Rio correspondent of *Time,* possibly concluding that once his boss' wife reached Brazil his days of independent travel might be numbered, had gone sniffing about on the Bolivian *antiplano,* where he encountered an ancient story that the inhabitants of that backward land might be better off if Bolivian territory were divided among Chile, Peru, Argentina, and Brazil. This shopworn observation was first heard on the rooftop of the Andes soon after Pizarro conquered the Inca Empire in 1532, but the *Time* man, exhilarated at thirteen thousand feet above sea level, lightheartedly attributed it to the American embassy in La Paz in 1959, some four hundred and twenty-seven years later.

That was something else again. *That* practically made it official. Scarcely had the offending issue of *Time* reached Lake Titicaca than the demon of nationalism took possession of Bolivia. Illimani belched molten lava. The local Communists happily stoked the Aymará Indians with *pisco* and *pulque,* so that presently they converged on the American embassy, brickbats in hand.

"Yah, yah!" they shouted. "Down with *Time* and *imperialismo yanqui!*" And for good measure, "Yah, yah! *¡Abajo Doña Clara!*"

Embassy wives and children were hastily evacuated from La Paz, and in Washington there was even talk of curtailing the millions of dollars of handouts wherewith the Bolivian politicians were accustomed to go through the motions of balancing their precarious budget. Instead, Washington patiently explained to the Bolivian authorities that *Time* was not the American government, and would the Bolivian government please be so kind as to explain *that* to the Aymará Indians. The Bolivian government, continuing to pocket American largesse, explained to the American government that trying to explain anything to an Aymará Indian never got anybody anywhere.

In faraway Russia, *Pravda* explained that the American government and *Time* were in fact indistinguishable: if that were not so, declared *Pravda* reasonably, what was *Time's* owner's wife doing with an appointment to be American ambassador to

145

Brazil? The American press, taking note of these portents, wondered whether they constituted the happiest augury for the representational activities of a lady diplomat in the most important country in South America. The State Department, apprehensions aroused, nervously queried Embassy Rio.

By that time the legend of the Lady of the Cornucopia had become standard folklore all the way from Mato Grosso to Manaus. Not for anything would Brazil have damaged the chances of dona Clara's coming to their country.

"We know perfectly well," declared the Brazilian Foreign Minister, "that Madame is not responsible for what is published in *Time*. The warmth of her welcome in Brazil is unaffected by incidents in Bolivia."

Embassy Rio telegraphed that to Washington, and Washington relaxed.

But not for long. The next report to alert Rio de Janeiro was a rumor that Brazil had not, after all, been the first choice of the lady. That story had it that while on a special mission with Secretary Dulles to attend the Pope's funeral, she had propositioned the Secretary for London, pointing out that since the British people have a Queen, it would not be inappropriate for the American people to have an ambassadress to represent them in the Queen's capital.

Foster Dulles was described as applauding the idea, although he was constrained to remark that Jock Whitney had rented Embassy London for the duration of the Republican administration, so the Thames diplomatic establishment was not on the market. The Secretary was reported to have promised that if the lady would spin the globe again, and spear it with an index finger, wherever she willed, that post would be hers.

The Brazilians did not care for that story. It irritated them far more than the *Time* incident with Bolivia, and I was charged privately to obtain a denial. Busy by that time with my own preparations to go as ambassador to Greece, I made no such inquiry. And when I returned to Washington a short time before Secretary Dulles' death, he was too ill to be questioned about it.

By now April was at hand. The lady abandoned her winter headquarters and came east for a State Department briefing, and for hearings about her nomination before the Foreign Relations Committee of the Senate. About her State Department activity we heard little, except that wholesale personnel changes in Rio would shortly be in order. The Senate hearings, on the other hand, produced immediate fireworks. These delighted the Brazilians, who understood the process well enough, their own confirmation procedure parallelling the American one and their candidates not infrequently emerging with little skin on their backs. The impression in Rio was that the lady gave the Senators as good as she got, and presently she was confirmed by the comfortable margin of 79 to 11.

There remained only the formal oath-taking for her to become American ambassador to Brazil, a diplomatic passport in one hand and a southbound ticket in the other. For the sixteenth time since Vice Consular days, the evicted ambassador finished folding his tents for departure. That, in the normal course of events, should have been the end of the story.

But not this time. The nomination having been confirmed, two more events, spectacular in nature, immediately occurred. The first was generated by the Ambassadress, the second by the Ambassadress' husband. As soon as the nomination was approved, the lady remarked that one of her senatorial questioners had been kicked in the head by a horse; this was accompanied by explanatory prose not calculated to soothe the recipient.

Instantly the Upper Chamber was in an uproar. There was debate whether, a colleague having been attacked, the whole august body had not been insulted. The question arose if confirmation of a presidential nomination, once given, could not for cause be withdrawn. "Why beat an old bag of bones?" inquired a Republican Senator, ostensibly in the nominee's defense.

The Brazilians loved it, especially the horse and the bones. The lady's husband picked that breathless moment to enter the act, flourishing a public statement addressed to his wife. He warned his wife that senatorial vengeance could frustrate the prospects for a successful diplomatic mission. To escape this persecution, he asked that she tender her resignation.

"You made your bed; don't lie in it" appeared to be the gist of the advice of the publisher to his lady.

Rio was pop-eyed. Having taken practically everything else in stride, including the nominee's effort to extract an advance ruling from the Brazilian Foreign Office that as an ambassador in her own right she outranked all the wives of the diplomatic corps, the easy-going but volatile Brazilian public was shattered by this unintimate message from a spouse to his consort. Here was a development beyond Brazilian comprehension.

Now no one in Rio de Janeiro could divine whether the lady was coming, thereby defying her husband (which no wife in Brazil is encouraged by her husband to do); or whether the lady was not coming (which left all the bewildered promoters of the Legend of the Lady with the Cornucopia on the beach with no *jangada* to ride in).

Having an appointment to make my farewell call on the President of Brazil, I telephoned the State Department in Washington. "Is the lady coming, or is she not coming?" I demanded. "What answer shall I make to President Kubitschek?"

The Deputy Under Secretary of State emitted a sigh audible across five thousand miles of telecommunications equipment; few sighs have been heaved a longer distance. "Say we don't know," he advised me. "Tell the President of Brazil the lady is seeing President Eisenhower tomorrow."

The telephone call cost the American taxpayers twelve dollars. I'm not sure President Kubitschek thought it was worth it.

As historians and a few Senators may recall, dona Clara

never did get to Rio de Janeiro. She saw President Eisenhower, handed him a letter of resignation, tossed a couple of horseshoes in the direction of her favorite Senator, and retired from public view.

And I, Acropolis bound, sailed away from Pão de Açúcar two years, nine months, and fourteen days after my arrival in Brazil as American ambassador.

By this count there are therefore five principal reasons why American ambassadors are moved out of one place and sent to another.

The first and most frequently invoked reason is that a man is wanted for a certain job. That reason accounted for five of my eight assignments as ambassador. For instance, not long after Perón's unsuccessful bid for my dismissal from Uruguay, I was told that President Truman had demanded for Czechoslovakia, recently subverted by Moscow, "a tough s.o.b. who would stand up to the Communists." In Prague for the next three years I tried to do precisely that, and there followed the important embassies in Korea, Peru and Brazil — posts that I accepted with equal interest but which I had no part in choosing.

From Brazil I went to Greece for the complicated reason that the official whom President Eisenhower wanted to appoint to head a Washington agency turned out once to have voted for a Democrat in Connecticut, an aberration which disqualified him in the eyes of a politician in a position to veto the assignment. That left a large hole urgently needing to be filled by a competent non-controversial executive who was also a first-rate economist, a description which fitted my friend Jimmy Riddleberger, then serving as ambassador to Greece. Soon after dona Clara lowered the curtain on my Rio performance, Jimmy was dragooned from Athens for the Potomac position. I was queried by telephone, Washington to Rio de Janeiro, whether I would accept Greece as my next responsibility, and I made the predictable answer.

Incidentally, I have always admired the generosity with which I was welcomed by my colleagues of the Near and Middle East, who have for distribution, heaven knows, few enough posts more attractive than Iraq or Saudi Arabia or the Hashimite Kingdom of Jordan. Athens is their showpiece, toward which worthy and industrious wretches yearn for decades as they perform their tasks in insalubrious places, hoping that some day (if the gods are propitiated and the politicos dozing) it may be their supreme good fortune to serve in the shadow of Lycabettus. And here was Greece being awarded to a candidate from Brazil, who had done no penance whatever in Kuwait or New Delhi. To this day I view those tolerant colleagues with affection.

The next most frequent reason for moving an ambassador is that someone outside the diplomatic service covets his embassy, and has enough political power to make the covet stick. Statistics indicate that losing one's post in that fashion is infinitely more likely to happen to a professional ambassador than to a political appointee, and that the hazard varies in proportion to the prestige of the capital and the reported pleasures of living there. Few envoys serving in Laos or the Ivory Coast or Paraguay are ousted by acquisitive outsiders, whereas a career diplomat serving as chief of mission in Rome, Rio de Janeiro, Copenhagen, or Athens is vulnerable twenty-four hours a day.

As I myself shortly found out. I reached Greece in 1959, and, sure enough, during the first year of the New Frontier, Embassy Athens was needed to meet a political exigency. Once again I had no personal complaint, for I was offered Spain — the post that throughout all my years in the diplomatic service I had hoped someday to occupy.

The fact remains that the greatest weakness in the conduct of American government business abroad results from the White House penchant for giving diplomatic missions to non-career applicants, or of using them as depositories for officials ousted from positions in Washington. Nine times out of ten this is done at the expense of a professional officer, who will have had twenty to thirty-five years of experience. The efforts to find new posts for displaced ambassadors disrupt the management of the Foreign Service, rendering it impossible to maintain in the upper echelons an orderly personnel program, not to mention its effect on morale.

Worse is the effect abroad. Few embassy grabs may duplicate the hilarious pandemonium that reigned for two months before I left Rio de Janeiro, but each one destroys continuity, disrupts pending negotiations, and generally paralyzes government business for a period varying from several weeks to several months, between the first rumor that an ambassador is going to be replaced and the arrival of his successor.

The remaining reasons for ambassadorial transfer that my researches unearthed present no very great problem. So brisk is the competition within the Foreign Service that few duds are chosen to be chief of mission, and almost none are dropped for not measuring up to requirements. Most career ambassadors make good. They would undoubtedly make better if they were able to proceed from one accomplished mission to the next, without being constantly uprooted.

Similarly, seeking a post for oneself is not a frequent reason for transfer. Senior officers ending an assignment in Washington, as I was before I went to Montevideo, or ambassadors completing their measured stint in a hardship post, may be in a somewhat different category. Moreover, the State Department encourages officers to express area or functional preference, and that often points if not to a specific post then toward a specific zone or geographical region.

The final reason for transfer, expulsion by the host government, does not happen often enough to affect calculations, even though the practice seems to be growing, with "open diplomacy" and diplomacy by communiqué inflaming national passions. The case of President Perón of *Argentina* trying to get rid of the American envoy to *Uruguay* is recounted be-

151

cause of the initial failure of the State Department to back up its own representative — a tendency that, if extended, would do little to promote esprit de corps among Foreign Service Officers.

I was more fortunate than many of my brethren in that although I was ejected from three of my eight ambassadorial posts — once fired, and twice with the bathroom rug pulled out from under me — my destinations turned out to be China, Greece, and Spain.

I repeat, I was lucky. Today, the corridors of the Department of State are crowded with dispossessed professionals who are awaiting another assignment. With one third of our diplomatic posts still being awarded to politicians, amateurs, and other outsiders, the confusion in American embassies is bound to continue, to the impairment of United States representation and the frequent frustration of our foreign policy objectives.

Here-today-gone-tomorrow may be a good slogan for an airplane pilot, but it is a poor motto for American ambassadors.

IX.

How to Tell a Bureaucrat from the Bouillabaisse

THIS explains how an ambassador goes about buying a set of gold-embossed crested crockery — timely advice on a practical subject. The moral of the story is that a clerk, factotum, or administrator in government service almost always tries to become a Repository of Policy; if he is permitted to succeed, he becomes an intolerable nuisance, and the best way to prevent that from happening is to beat him over the head with a precedent.

Once upon a time, after the Korean War, my wife and I dined with a retired general, and we greatly admired his four-star crockery, with the emblem of his rank in army red on the white background of each plate. Our host confirmed that once-a-general, always-a-general, as far as the prerogatives of retirement go, and it seemed a pleasant thing, after all the years the General had served his country, for him to be allowed to continue to eat off the china of his exalted position.

I determined to seek for retired diplomacy what was approved procedure for the military brethren. I would fix it, I said to myself, so a retired diplomatic officer could go on using ambassadorial china.

When I returned to my embassy abroad I summoned my administrative officer. I directed him to requisition from the appropriate section of the State Department — whatever that office might be — a set of china for twelve, for my personal account. I told the administrative officer that he could if necessary explain that I wanted the china to use after I myself had

153

turned in my uniform and retired from the Foreign Service.

The officer said, "Yes, Mr. Ambassador. I'll order the china right away, Mr. Ambasador."

Embassy china is a relatively new phenomenon. It dates from a few years ago when the State Department, then as now grudgingly underwritten by a suspicious and parsimonious Congress, began equipping its legations and embassies with official table services. The theory was that few persons who are appointed ambassadors already possess, in their private capacities, dinner sets for the forty or fifty persons who have to be invited from time to time to embassy dinner parties. Therefore our government, a century and a half after the first American envoy went abroad, finally began supplying our diplomatic missions with plates and cups and saucers.

Embassy crockery is white, gold-bordered with a design of stars. The shield of the United States, with the eagle clutching his arrows and olives, appears in gold relief on each piece — hence crested china. Whoever chose the design did well. The sets are dignified and impressive.

At the time of my request to be permitted to buy a personal set to use after I retired from the Foreign Service, I had no idea what branch of the State Department was the watchdog of the crockery stockpile, and it would have made little difference if I had. My proposition seemed reasonable. There was precedent for it in the military sphere. And precedent, as I myself well knew from over three decades as a bureaucrat, is the safe haven of the termites that live in the bureaucratic woodwork.

So I told the administrative officer in Embassy Athens to get on about my private crockery business, and to let me know when he received the bill for this, my projected first retirement present for my ambassadress.

Some weeks later the administrative officer handed me a memorandum received from Washington. It was typed on a pale blue piece of paper called in the Foreign Service an Operations Memorandum. I read this document with mounting blood pressure, for it was couched in the snide and abrasive prose I had come to recognize, after many years and innumerable altercations, as emanating from the Service of Buildings Section,* of the Department of State, the unit that builds embassies for the Foreign Service abroad and then, likely as not, neglects to maintain them. The fact that Congress neglected to pass an appropriation is often cited to account for the leaky roof, the paralyzed air conditioning, or the rebellious plumbing, which is, however, rarely repaired at any given capital within the incumbency of a single chief of mission.

Since I was then on my seventh embassy, the relations between the American ambassador to Greece and the Service of Buildings Section were approximately seven times as brisk as those of a freshman ambassador.

It is contrary to the policy of the Service of Buildings Section (declared the Service of Buildings Section in its Operations Memorandum) to permit the acquisition of official crockery for personal use. Embassy crockery is exclusively for embassy use, said the Service of Buildings Section, and therefore embassy crockery is not for personal use.

The request of the American ambassador to Greece to be allowed to establish a private cache of crested crockery was accordingly rejected by the Service of Buildings Section.

There are few things that I find more provocative than the lofty dissent of the minor bureaucrat. Whereas it takes an egg twice as long to boil beside Lake Titicaca, over twelve thousand feet above sea level, as it does on the Pacific shoreline at Mollendo, it only takes an atom-split-second for my ambassadorial reactor to take note of the sort of smug display of patriotic logic with which the Service of Buildings Section sought to demolish my crested crockery project. Whereupon blue

* The Service of Buildings Section is a fictitious designation. Any resemblance to an existing bureau or bureaucrat is purely coincidental.

lights played over the Acropolis, the ancient Parthenon smoked, and my subordinates in Embassy Athens dove for their earmuffs and dark glasses.

As soon as the chancery typewriter was cool enough to touch, I set about confecting a message in reply. I did not, of course, address myself to the Service of Buildings Section; that would merely have added to the self-importance of the termites by presenting them a second time with the same ambassadorial target. Nor did I write to my titular chief, the Secretary of State; that official was occupied then as now with atomic problems and NATO. I wrote instead to the Deputy Under Secretary of State for Administration, himself a former ambassador and hence (so I hoped) sympathetic toward my campaign for crested crockery.

Since when, I inquired rudely, are janitors and housekeepers in the State Department empowered to drink the heady nectar of policy? Policy, I asserted, is the prerogative of the President of the United States, and I haven't heard of his delegating it to the Service of Buildings Section. By what right, I demanded, has the Service of Buildings Section installed a pipeline into the policy barrel? If that keeps up, I warned, those same policy gremlins will soon be telling ambassadors who can occupy space in embassy office buildings. Why, they may even try to dictate who can eat off that crested crockery they are paid by the taxpayers to keep on hand in embassy pantries. Don't laugh, I said. The appetite for power of the wood weevil of bureaucracy is ravenous; it becomes insatiable if you let him eat policy.

Leaving that field covered with broken termites and mangled metaphors, I turned to my crockery proposal. I acknowledged that after many years in the Foreign Service, the last fifteen of them as ambassador, I had grown attached to the chinaware of successive embassy residences. I said that one of these days, rachitic and full of bile, I planned to retire to my New Hampshire cottage by the village green, and that if I wished to invite the governor of the state or the president of the college to share a crust of dry bread with a former ambassador, it seemed a harmless conceit on the part of a pensioned public servant to be permitted to honor his guests with ambassadorial china.

And in conclusion I told the Deputy Under Secretary of State for Administration that I would settle for the withdrawal of the Operations Memorandum of the Service of Buildings Section, plus a finger off the right hand of the author, the latter to be forwarded to me by diplomatic pouch within twenty-four hours of the receipt of my message.

Somewhat startled by this essay, the Deputy Under Secretary of State sent me a pacific reply. He indicated he would be glad to look into the matter of official china for retired ambassadors, and he implied that since my own retirement did not then appear imminent, my crockery problem might not be the most urgent item of business facing the Department of State in the waning years of the 1950's.

And there, for a considerable period, the matter rested. I can only surmise, albeit with satisfaction, the fury which my letter to the Deputy Under Secretary of State must have produced when it trickled its unclassified way down to the Service of Buildings Section, which on the strength of it hired still more mastiffs to protect the threatened crested crockery stockpile.

In a bureaucracy it is easier for a determined termite to *block* a proposed action than it is for anyone else to *force* something to happen. Thus my blueprint friends of the slide rule and meccano sets found strong allies in procrastination and attrition, and I myself was soon forced to consider additional tactics. It promised to be a long campaign, for which nevertheless I was not altogether without resources.

Years earlier, not wanting to be a Vice Consul caught out with an unanswered letter from a Congressman in his pocket, I had invented a wonderful system whereby no unresolved case

157

was permitted, like unrequited love, to languish. Every so often, under my formula, the pending case popped up, waving a little colored flag and making a noise like Donald Duck with bronchitis. My scheme for reminding myself of unfinished business was the despair of visiting IBM technicians, who struggled in vain to devise a computer that would keep track of my unzippered mnemonics. They finally gave it up when they discovered, poking about in my archives, that during my service in Liberia I had once filed "Mining" under the letter T. "Why 'Mining' under T?" they asked me.

"*Thar's* gold in *Them Thar* hills," I answered.

Thus the wretched Deputy Under Secretary of State, if not prodded every hour on the hour about my china, at least had his elbow jiggled so often that he began to flinch whenever he saw a Foreign Service envelope marked "Embassy Athens." As my messages arrived, he used wearily to ask his administrative assistant to ask the Assistant Secretary of State for Administration to ask the Deputy Acting Assistant Secretary of State for Foreign Buildings to ask *his* administrative assistant what was the status of the Ambassador's request to be allowed to purchase, at his own expense, a dinner set for twelve of embassy crested china.

The reply that as regularly climbed its inexorable way back up the ladder from the Service of Buildings Section to the office of the Deputy Under Secretary of State for Administration was nothing if it was not consistent. That is to say, it was consistently obstructive. And as Christmas followed Christmas, there was no crested china in the ambassadorial stocking.

So time passed, and so matters rocked along, with the advantage for the most part on the side of the termites, until after a Presidential election. Then, suddenly, a new team was operating in Washington. The patient Deputy Under Secretary of State retired; he informed me, on the eve of his departure, that my crockery problem, with unspecified accumulated dilemmas, was being referred for decision to his successor.

158

Before I knew it, I found myself addressing the freshly appointed Director General of the Foreign Service, while New Frontiersmen hooted like owls in the chimneys, and others raced up and down the fire escapes like exhilarated squirrels. Meanwhile, the question of my own retirement moved without warning from the theoretical to the accomplished. Mine was an affliction unprofitable to dwell upon, except to say that it permitted me to review at leisure my gay and fascinating career, and to meditate upon how much easier it was to accomplish something in the Foreign Service in 1925 — in fact, to accomplish *anything* in 1925 — than it became after World War II, when the State Department was evicted from its home beside the White House, and diplomacy itself was sold down the Potomac to the experts, the managers, and the administrators.

No population explosion, I reflected, could surpass the philoprogenitive prowess of the bureaucratic wood weevil (*Rhynchophora publica*), which discovered in Foggy Bottom the ideal environment in which to propagate. The staff aide of yesterday sheds his larval title overnight, blossoming forth the next day as Executive Director, with wall-to-wall carpet and a blonde with an electric typewriter. Abroad, the administrative assistant is miserable unless he can soon call himself Minister for Administrative Affairs, with dozens of indigenous beavers to chew on his pencils. And all over government bureaucracy, the mechanic hired to fix the carburetor jumps instead behind the steering wheel, shouting over his shoulder as he takes off for the nearest turnpike that the car was his in the first place.

Those were somber meditations, as I assembled my file on crested crockery. It was by now a formidable documentation, possibly not yet so famous as the file on Mrs. Gillespie's piano, but certainly approaching its equal in volume. Mine were gloomy meditations, and they turned out, all at once, to be unduly pessimistic.

While I was out of circulation, and my patented reminder

159

system correspondingly shackled, the new Director General of the Foreign Service had been bestirring himself on my behalf. Enlisting New Frontiersmen, who turned out to be willing to try anything once, he had mounted an assault in strength against the hitherto impregnable ramparts of the Service of Buildings Section. The ramparts crumbled.

Scarcely had I reached the retired list when I received word that the crested crockery citadel had finally capitulated. I was informed, and in writing, that as a retired ambassador I would now be permitted to purchase the set of china that I had been trying since the year 1959 to requisition through the American embassy in Athens.

While I was still admiring this miracle, certification of which I contemplated having mounted between the Declaration of Independence and the Constitution of the United States for the edification of future generations, the rumor reached me that a former mainstay of the Service of Buildings Section had been exiled from Washington to Zamboanga, where he was set to stacking coconuts for the village elders of Mindanao to throw at volunteers of the Peace Corps. That rumor, it turned out, was merely my own wishful thinking. One cannot have everything, as I found out again when the bill for my crested crockery arrived; it knocked a large chunk of the granite of New Hampshire off the summit of Mount Washington.

Mine was nonetheless a notable triumph. The fadeout is a happy picture of the now-pensioned public servant. He is smiling with senile glee as he unwraps saucers and soup plates from their protecting layers of tissue paper. There is a place of honor for each one in his cupboard. A jug of north country applejack sits at the ambassador's elbow, and presently he will dream benevolent dreams about the Service of Buildings Section of the Department of State. He will be wishing that Section well as it moves from foreign capital to foreign capital, building miniature Mount Vernons in Mogadiscio, and life-size Grand Central Terminals in New Delhi.

All of which I have meticulously reported, in the expectation that there may exist in the Foreign Service other ambassadors who, harkening to the sound of crested crockery shattering against a precedent, may themselves desire to embellish their autumn years with the richly glazed fruits of my bureaucratic victory.

As an American Vice Consul once bravely telegraphed the State Department in another but not dissimilar context: "Flag up. Precedent established."

Following the appearance of this story, there was a demand for the parable of the flag, and since it is one of the two or three most valuable lessons I learned about the relations between a Foreign Service Officer and the Department of State, here it is:

Saint Petersburg, now Petrograd, was the capital of Russia in World War I, and the offices of the American Consulate General occupied a floor in a building owned by a private American company. When the revolution broke out in 1917 and public order began to disintegrate, the ambassador and most of the embassy staff departed, and the Consulate General was left in charge of an enterprising young Vice Consul called Imbrie, who was presently importuned to fly the official American flag from the main flagpole on the roof of the building, instead of from the less conspicuous staff projecting from the windowsill of the consular office.

The American flag over the building itself, it was represented to Imbrie by the American owners, would be an added measure of protection in a situation that was rapidly coming to pieces.

Imbrie, having in mind that the American company was technically a Russian operation, and also that there were additional firms occupying other parts of the building, prudently decided to query the State Department. He explained the situation in a cable to Washington. He pointed out that, technicalities aside, there was no question of the American ownership of the building, nor of the mounting danger. He referred to the disorder fomented by the Bolsheviks, he urged that he be authorized to fly the Stars and Stripes from the roof, and he respectfully requested an urgent telegraphic reply.

Imbrie's cable was routed to the legal adviser, a cautious individual who retired behind his treatises on international law, emerging several days later with the draft of a telegram which was duly despatched to Saint Petersburg. The gist of the message was that there was no precedent for the action recommended by the Vice Consul. Although the State Department said it sympathized with the predicament described, it was confident that oral representations to the *de facto* authorities would be sufficient to ensure the protection of the building. There was no precedent, Washington repeated, for flying the American flag except from the consular staff mounted over the consular shield, outside the consulate window.

It took Vice Consul Imbrie four words to acknowledge this message. "Flag up," he cabled the State Department. "Precedent established."

X.

Everybody Wants to Play Diplomacy

THE American Embassy in Rio de Janeiro needs a science attaché," I telegraphed the State Department, "the way a cigarstore Indian needs a brassiere."

This was unwelcome comment in Washington, and the reply was frosty. "Your telegram," wrote an official, "did *not* amuse the White House, which is personally interested in the rapid development of the science attaché program abroad. . . ." For this was one year after Russia had startled the world with the first sputnik, and Washington was determined to impress our allies with the earnestness of our late-blooming orbital preoccupations.

Thus my dissent postponed only briefly the assignment of a science attaché to the embassy over which I presided in Brazil. The candidate originally tagged for Rio was sent to Buenos Aires instead, but as soon as the Brazilians heard about him, they wanted a science attaché too, so they would not appear to lag behind Argentina.

At no time were the merits of assigning science attachés to Latin America investigated. If our ambassadors had been called upon to show cause why such an attaché would be a useful addition to their staffs, only a handful, serving in highly industrialized countries, could have presented a sensible affirmative argument. As it was, the program was pre-fabricated in Washington, recipient ambassadors were notified, and only a brash or uncooperative representative — so my correspondent implied — would cock a skeptical eyebrow at having a Ph.D. in physics join his official family.

If it is difficult, serving abroad, to avoid having superfluous personnel thrust upon one by Washington, it is ten times as difficult to dislodge supernumerary personnel who are already there, and dug in, before the arrival of an ambassador.

At my last post I discovered soon after presenting credentials that the Coast Guard maintained an office in Athens. After over thirty years in the diplomatic service, this was something new to me. I admired the open-air achievements of the Coast Guard, from spotting North Atlantic icebergs to chasing poachers from the Pribilof Islands, but I had never pictured the organization as an adjunct to diplomacy. And here in the shadow of the Parthenon I found a lieutenant commander, a lieutenant, and a supporting cast of enlisted men, all with families and family possessions. I decided to investigate.

My Consul General, in whose section of the embassy the Coast Guard operated, was unable to explain their presence. He said they were there when he came. Something, he thought, about their use in the event of an accident involving an American merchant ship in the Aegean Sea. This explanation appeared to ignore the fact that consular officers in the regular performance of their duties have time out of mind coped with just such situations, without Coast Guard participation. When I asked how long it had been since an American ship had had an accident in Greek waters, no one could tell me.

Inquiring further, I learned that the Coast Guard maintained another and larger office in Naples, less than two hours from Athens by air. In the event of an emergency in the Aegean Sea it would have been possible to fly a Coast Guard representative from Italy to Greece on very short notice.

Inquiring still further, I was informed that likewise within my jurisdiction was a Coast Guard vessel, the *Courier*, anchored off the island of Rhodes, rebroadcasting Voice of America programs. Rhodes is Greek territory, and services on

164

behalf of the *Courier* were being performed by the Coast Guard unit in Embassy Athens — housekeeping and supply services, requiring the attention of one enlisted man for approximately one hour a day. They could just as well have been performed by one Greek clerk in the embassy administrative section, hired at a fraction of the cost of maintaining the Coast Guard establishment in Athens.

And so, after a suitable pause during which I assembled all this fascinating data, the net of which was that there was no conceivable need, reason, or excuse for United States Coast Guard personnel to be stationed in Greece, I sent a message to the State Department requesting that they be removed.

Today there is still a Coast Guard Unit in the American embassy in Athens.

These two incidents, from Brazil to Greece, illustrate why practically every United States diplomatic mission in the world is so stuffed with unnecessary personnel that the handful of State Department officials trying to perform substantive diplomatic functions can scarcely find a chair to sit down on or a desk on which to stack their papers.

Of over one hundred American embassies in the world today, a majority could perform *twice* as effectively with *half* the persons now cluttering up the premises.

In addition to the propaganda, handout, and skullduggery agencies, all abundantly staffed, practically every executive department in Washington is now represented abroad. Many of the bureaus within departments, and even offices within bureaus, have established foreign operations. So have the commissions and boards and independent agencies.

The list includes the Department of Commerce, whose Bureau of Foreign and Domestic Commerce is forever exhorting the State Department for bigger and better reports on the market for roller skates in Antofagasta; of Agriculture, whose long-handled spoon dips into so many foreign nooks and crannies that a computing machine could scarcely keep track of their

165

operations; of Treasury, whose aforesaid Coast Guard is a relative newcomer abroad, compared to Financial Attachés and to the peripatetic agents of Customs, Internal Revenue, and Narcotics; of Justice, whose Immigration and Naturalization Service is trying to duplicate consular visa functions, and whose spooks from the Federal Bureau of Investigation adorn several foreign capitals; of Interior, which supplies Minerals and Petroleum Attachés; and of Labor, with representatives in nearly every Embassy, promoting trade union movements.

The Tariff Commission, the Public Health Service, the Federal Communications Commission, the Civil Aeronautics Board, the Bureau of Public Roads, the Peace Corps . . . to compile a full roster of Washington agencies abroad would require months of research beside the Potomac. The offices mentioned are merely some of those with whose overseas operatives I myself have been regaled or afflicted during service as Ambassador to seven countries, plus two decades in the Foreign Service before my first ambassadorial appointment.

In theory each ambassador is responsible for all government operations conducted within his jurisdiction. That is a good thing, but in practice it would be manifestly impossible for a chief of mission to accomplish, as ambassador, anything in the way of business with the government to which he is accredited, if in addition he tried personally to supervise all the programs operated in the name of the American government within his bailiwick. Liaison with other agencies is customarily delegated to the ambassador's overworked deputy, who in turn must rely on the senior members of the embassy staff, an appreciable part of whose time is devoted to preventing the representatives of other agencies, who invariably regard themselves as diplomats, from damaging the delicate machinery of international relations.

This is not to imply that the representatives of other agencies are lacking in patriotism, or even in energy. On the contrary! And therein lies much of the trouble, for ambition and energy in conjunction with inexperience can be a dangerous combination in foreign affairs.

There are various reasons for the bewildering prolifieration of American officials abroad, of which the most significant is the failure of the State Department — through inertia, indifference, timidity, or whatever — to exercise its authority. Moreover, across the years the State Department has paid little attention to the recommendations of its Embassies when those views have been unwelcome to aggressive parent agencies in Washington (e.g., the Treasury Department when I tried to dislodge the Coast Guard from Greece).

Americans love to go abroad. Furthermore, Americans are generous. We are sympathetic with the struggles and difficulties of others. As a nation we are not accustomed to closing our eyes, or to going by on the other side of the street. Admirable qualities. We are also inveterate volunteers to fix anybody else's carburetor, especially if it is the differential that is out of order.

Witness the instant success, in the United States, of the Peace Corps, an undertaking essentially irrational but wrapped in the irresistible pinafore of romantic endeavor.

"Yoo-hoo! Let's go out and wreak good on some natives."

Born reciting a credo of austerity, the Peace Corps soon hatched its own larval bureaucracy, panting for diplomatic privileges and immunities.

In all this, the example of the American military has not been beneficial. Since the war, the Pentagon has introduced tens of thousands of impressionable young Americans to the PX way of life, identifying service abroad with ten-cent gasoline, fifteen-cent cigarettes, two-dollar bourbon, and a host of special privileges not enjoyed by what the military term the Indigenous Personnel of the host country.

This has added to the pressure on the State Department for the establishment of irrelevant and unnecessary privileges for the representatives of civilian agencies, who should not,

167

so the argument goes, have to serve abroad as "second class citizens." The real question is not whether a sanitary engineer attached to a consulate needs diplomatic immunity, but whether the American soldier, nearly twenty years after World War II, needs the PX way of life.

A further reason for the swarming of bureaucratic bumblebees abroad is that no President since Theodore Roosevelt and no Secretary of State since Charles Evans Hughes has taken any sustained personal interest in the *mechanics* of our foreign operations. And no Secretary of State has been willing, except in rare specific instances, to throw the weight and prestige of his office against the invasion of his foreign affairs bailiwick.

Thus the Foreign Service, with few grassroots constituents in the United States, has been handicapped in coping with agencies capable of mobilizing Congressional support. As a result, those agencies have imposed "treaties" on the State Department, dictating what rights their representatives abroad shall enjoy, regardless of the effect on our overseas operations.

Much of what we are doing abroad is blowing expensive soap bubbles, the principal admirers of which are the bureaucrats who are doing the blowing. That involves manpower. In fact, to respond to the whims of all the amateurs in foreign affairs now based on the Potomac might require several times as many people as those already afield. But at any given "moment of truth" — whether it be Berlin crisis, Cuban crisis, NATO crisis, or just the King of Cambodia having mislaid his clarinet — the number of officials required to take cognizance of a single situation and to act upon it is invariably limited. And at such times the rest of the cast is superfluous, and often a nuisance.

I learned about this the hard way, as we say in Maine, a good many years ago. Not long after the Communist seizure of Czechoslovakia, I was assigned to Prague as Ambassador. The State Department asked me to survey the staffing needs

168

of the Embassy "in the light of the changed situation" — meaning the Communist coup d'état of 1948, which had converted one of the friendliest of European governments into one of the most glowering and hostile.

Quickly ascertaining that in the Communist utopia the normal sources of diplomatic information are either cut off or polluted and that everything not published by the state is classified secret, there seemed to be little reason to maintain a large staff in our embassy in Prague. I recommended to Washington that my inherited complement of eighty Americans (almost microscopic by today's embassy standards) be reduced, as a start, by one half. That is to say, that the roster be cut from eighty to forty, with the major part of the reduction to be from agencies other than the State Department, since those agencies were the ones supplying the soap-bubble blowers.

Pentagon personnel, for instance, accounted for thirty-three of my eighty colleagues. I suggested to Washington that ten soldiers ought henceforth to be sufficient to advise one Ambassador about military developments in Czechoslovakia. I also suggested that since Czechoslovakia was a landlocked country, lacking seacoast or navy, my naval attaché might just as well be assigned to Switzerland or Bolivia.

The State Department, after meditation, informed me that my recommendations were "interesting" and that there was "agreement in principle" that they ought to be implemented.

I was thus encouraged to embark on a campaign of the utmost frustration. The outraged squawks of my American colleagues in Prague quickly reverberated beside the Potomac, where every agency represented in my embassy demanded of the State Department that the proposed reductions be borne by every other agency.

The State Department, which had instigated my investigation, and encouraged my recommendations, promptly went into a tailspin. After six months, and an expenditure of effort on my part sufficient to have built, singlehanded, a bridge across the Vltava River, I had managed to reduce my overblown staff by two persons — from eighty to seventy-eight.

At which point, the Communists, ignorant of my hassle with Washington over personnel, and believing that they were doing the American government in general and the American ambassador in particular the greatest possible disservice, suddenly declared five-sixths of the embassy personnel *persona non grata*. That is to say, unwelcome people. Czechoslovakia gave the embassy two weeks in which to evacuate sixty-six of my seventy-eight colleagues, together with all their families, pets, and belongings.

A *persona non grata* declaration is not debatable, and the State Department had no choice but to comply. We got the sixty-sixth member of the staff across the border at Rosvadov within the prescribed time limit, and I sat back to enjoy the first unobstructed view from my chancery since reaching Czechoslovakia the previous autumn.

The American embassy in Prague then consisted of thirteen people, including the ambassador. There was one deputy, a senior foreign officer who acted as general manager of the mission and as chargé d'affaires whenever the ambassador was absent from Czechoslovakia. Something of a linguist, he used to drive the Czech monitors crazy by holding conversations in Eskimo over the tapped telephone line with our Danish colleague, who had also seen service in Greenland. The deputy, I am happy to report, has long since become an ambassador in his own right.

We had one first secretary, with analytical talents in Communist demonology. He doubled as an economist and in his spare time composed material for the Voice of America to broadcast from New York.

We had one administrative officer, who tidied up after the departure of the sixty-six expelled colleagues and thereafter did housekeeping chores, which included driving a two-ton truck to Nuremberg every two weeks for supplies. We had three wonderful girls, all volunteers, the pick of our secretarial resources. One spoke Czech fluently, and all three were wizards with archives and papers.

A consul, a vice consul and one code clerk completed our State Department complement.

The Pentagon had three persons on my reduced staff, instead of the ten they had earlier insisted upon. Two colonels, one from the Army and one from the Air Force, competed unhappily for the services of one sergeant.

It was an efficient embassy. It was probably the most efficient embassy I ever headed. Our operation was compact. Our personnel were alert. We kept Washington accurately informed of what was going on. Our work was accomplished with a minimum of friction and delay. No longer was it necessary to refer everything to an inter-agency committee or a "country team" for decision. Our morale, challenged by Communist malevolence, was the highest of the seventeen posts that I served in. Our entire operation was conducted by a staff smaller than I found in many of the separate units and sections and even sub-sections of the embassies over which I presided after I left Czechoslovakia.

There is no optimum number of officials required to handle essential American interests in a given country. What is appropriate for Paraguay is not necessarily relevant to Pakistan or Peru. The key word is not geographic but what is meant by *essential,* and the number needed to take care of essential operations, in whatever country, is surprisingly modest.

It may take a few more officials to operate an embassy in a friendly country than it does in a Communist one, but the number it takes — anywhere — is only a fraction of the number we have in our diplomatic missions scattered over the globe. And we have new countries — and more embassies — hatching at every United Nations Assembly.

The average size of a mission a generation ago was about a dozen Americans, including clerks, stenographers and at-

171

tachés. In smaller countries, not yet identified as underdeveloped by the harbingers of the abundant life, our legations operated with only five or six persons.

Today, everybody wants to play diplomacy.

Today, almost everybody *is* playing diplomacy, and by permitting all these extraneous participants to invade the field, we have made it difficult to tell who has the ball, and even impossible at times to tell what team is defending what goal line. Everybody-playing-diplomacy is playing havoc with our international relations.

The only American official who can rescue the conduct of our foreign affairs from the expensive confusion created by un-needed personnel abroad is the President himself, by directing the Secretary of State to take action. The President must then be prepared, when the hurricane of protest arises from the Potomac patrons of supernumeraries, to stand firmly behind his Foreign Secretary.

Fortunately there are a number of practical steps that would arrest the multiplication of barnacles on the ship of state, and even remove a few of them, provided the President is determined to act.

The first thing is to reestablish the primacy of the State Department in the conduct of foreign relations. The military, after paddling in the pond of diplomacy for nearly a quarter century, should be invited to go dry their feet. All civilian agencies that maintain personnel outside the United States should likewise be alerted.

The next thing is to separate the diplomats from the hordes of volunteer competitors. The distinction should not be difficult to establish. A second secretary, calling on his opposite number in the Foreign Office to discuss a rumor that Greece is about to establish diplomatic relations with Albania, is performing a diplomatic function. An artificial inseminator, working with West African veterinary colleagues to improve the quality of water buffalo, is not performing a diplomatic function. No question of relative merit arises. Conceivably the inseminator, provided he is kept off the Ouagadougou diplomatic list, could facilitate the tasks of American diplomacy in Upper Volta.

It follows that all the so-called treaties imposed on the State Department by other departments and agencies in Washington ought to be abrogated. They should then be revised in terms that accept the proposition that it is the State Department, under the President, that is responsible for foreign affairs. State should then determine, on the basis of recommendations elicited from ambassadors, how many — if any — representatives of another agency can profitably be accommodated in a given foreign country, and what the circumstances of such service shall be.

Since no one goes abroad on official business without the corresponding passport, control by the State Department should present no insuperable problem.

Again, civilian personnel of other agencies on regular assignment to embassies — e.g., financial attachés of the Treasury Department, minerals attachés from Interior, etc. — should be commissioned in the Foreign Service Reserve, for which legislation is already in existence. They would thus become responsible to the ambassador in the regular chain of command, and it would become possible more effectively to control their activities and to curtail their independent reporting, often at variance with what is being submitted officially under Embassy aegis. Similarly, clerical and supporting personnel of other agencies should be integrated into the Foreign Service Staff Corps for the period of their foreign duty.

The establishment of separate foreign services by other agencies should be resisted by the President. Our government struggled with this problem for twenty years after World War I, and sought to settle it by the amalgamation of the then independent Commerce and Agriculture services in 1939. At that time the State Department accepted upwards of one

173

hundred officers of those Departments for lateral entry into the Foreign Service. That should have ended the matter. After World War II, however, the Department of Agriculture lured Congress into reestablishing a separate foreign service of agricultural attachés, and this has once again stimulated other agencies to lust after the dark side of the diplomatic moon.

The Department of Justice is now attempting to take over consular visa functions. It is not alleged that consuls, as visa officers, have been incompetent public servants. It is merely that the Immigration and Naturalization Service is ambitious to go abroad. If this proposal is not headed off, a brand new army of bureaucrats will soon march into foreign lands, and the houseflag of the Attorney General will then be displayed in consulates and embassies.

A significant saving would be to combine under embassy jurisdiction all administrative and housekeeping functions on behalf of civilian government personnel abroad, as well as those of all military personnel attached to our diplomatic missions (Army, Navy and Air attachés, plus military missions). Facilities could thus be made intelligible and uniform. That would terminate situations, corrosive to morale and disicipline, in which employees of one Washington agency receive free transportation, while employees of another agency, working in the same embassy building, have to pay their own transportation to and from the office.

In some capitals, merely combining the numerous motor pools would save thousands of dollars.

Centralizing adminstrative operations should be undertaken, however, along with a determination to ride herd on the administrators. That would be a reversal of post-war trends, which have been to inflate the housekeeper at the expense of the householder. Embassy administrators, hired to press pants, have been encouraged by the fluffed-up bureaucrats of the State Department to wear them.

As for the Foreign Service itself, this has grown from

around fifteen hundred officers at the end of the war to approximately four thousand today. The bulk of the increase resulted, however, from the so-called Wriston integration program of a decade ago, whereby hundreds of uneager State Department employees were dragooned into the Foreign Service. This program nearly wrecked the Foreign Service. It also resulted in a dilution of competence. The Herter Report would apparently encourage another Reorganization in Depth, the consequences of which could be equally lugubrious.

Foreign affairs would prosper if the 1960's could become known as the decade in which the American Foreign Service was *not* reorganized.

While we are at it, each ambassador should be encouraged to fumigate the American section of the foreign diplomatic list in his capital, so that only those officials the performance of whose functions is significantly facilitated by being on the list, are included. In nearly every country, the American chapter of the diplomatic list is conspicuously larger than that of any other country. In some, the American embassy section runs to a third of the total volume. This renders us ridiculous. We cheapen the profession of diplomacy by listing janitors, groundwater hydrologists, and social welfare advisers as diplomats, estimable though those individuals may be in their respective spheres of activity.

The foregoing program is recognized to be revolutionary in character. It reasserts the authority of the President in foreign affairs. It calls on the President to direct the Secretary of State, to whom the responsibility for operations abroad is delegated, to exercise that responsibility, instead of sharing it cozily with every agency within sight of the Washington Monument whose personnel are ambitious for travel. It is designed to shake loose thousands of superfluous employees now serving abroad, thus contributing to stopping what is euphemistically referred to as the Drain on the American Dollar.

175

No easy victory is foreseen. The paralysis resulting from the uninhibited operation of Parkinson's Law within the Department of State itself is already far advanced. Housecleaning at home should accompany housekeeping abroad.

Obviously this is not a one-shot operation but a continuing campaign. There may be setbacks and disappointments. No tick clings with greater tenacity than the threatened civil servant, especially the supernumerary civil servant. Moreover, the military have conditioned us to the notion that whenever a ten-man job is to be tackled, one hundred men must be mobilized to undertake it.

Nevertheless each American ambassador should be required by the President to submit an annual report showing how many useless positions were abolished, how many soap-bubble blowers were evacuated, and at what savings to the American taxpayers.

The White House might offer a suitable prize to the most successful United States envoy. No matter how expensive, from the point of view of the taxpayers the prize would be worth it!

Everybody-wants-to-play-diplomacy is thus an understatement. Practically everybody is *already* playing diplomacy, at times almost paralyzing the operations of the American government abroad.

The scope of this continuing problem is indicated by a volume of over one hundred pages recently issued by one of the semi-autonomous nooks and crannies of the State Department.* According to the introduction, the compendium was assembled "for the purpose of providing useful information regarding activities of the U. S. government in international educational and cultural affairs," a worthy area of activity, without which, however, the nation was able to get along

* "Some U. S. Government Agencies Engaged in International Activities." Policy Review and Research Staff, Bureau of Educational and Cultural Affairs, Department of State, November 1963.

fairly well during the first 160 years of its independent existence. Remarking that the need for such information "has long been evident," the introduction adds that "the increasing involvement of several government agencies underscores the growing complexities of U. S. foreign relations."

It does indeed. It truly does.

To certify the aforesaid involvement, and presumably also the complexity, the publication then lists twenty-five separate government agencies which are today carrying a spear for education and culture alone. In fact the purpose of the book appears to be the laudable one of helping the Department of State chart a path through the Indians and totem poles of this far from petrified forest.

And since international education and cultural affairs cover, one may safely surmise, only a relatively small area of total government activity, it can be imagined what the congestion of agencies must be when it comes to such far more popular operations as economics, welfare, taxidermy, finance, trade, bird-watching, defense, science, or agriculture — in fact almost any conceivable activity that can be pursued abroad at the expense of the American taxpayers — except diplomacy.

Only the President is capable of reducing this chaos to an endurable confusion.

XI.

A Hair Shirt Ill Becomes the Eagle

Part 1

For three long decades Uncle Sam has been punctuating his observations about Latin America with: "Oops, sorry! My fault. I apologize."

The *latinos* have seized upon the American guilt complex with glee. "Keep 'em rolling," they cried, meaning the golden eggs concealed in Uncle Sam's coattails.

Presently the *latinos* invented a more efficient arrangement. They devised a hair shirt for Uncle Sam's eagle, with a special built-in mechanism: kick the eagle and the bird molts beautiful golden negotiable feathers.

This phenomenon has been going on for a long time, but never so abundantly as in these days of *Alianza para el Progreso*.

Back in 1933 President Roosevelt concluded that armed intervention in Latin America had become unpopular with the American people — a conclusion already reached by the outgoing administration of President Hoover — and that the hemisphere might accordingly be ripe for a revelation. Roosevelt proceeded to reveal:

"I would dedicate this nation," he announced in his inaugural address, "to the policy of the Good Neighbor, the neighbor who resolutely respects himself and, because he does so, respects the rights of others. . . ."

Those words read well today. By stressing *reciprocal* respect, a sound charter for hemispheric relations should have resulted.

But just as President Theodore Roosevelt shortly after the turn of the century added a colophon to the Monroe Doctrine, transforming it from one of *non-intervention* by European powers to one of *intervention* by the United States, so the eager cohorts of Franklin Roosevelt invented the corollary of the Guilt Complex and added that to the Good Neighbor Policy.

The Guilt Complex involves two equally pernicious propositions. The first is that everything that *latinos* don't like about their situation — low coffee or sugar prices, galloping inflation, or the absence of a Marshall Plan for Latin America — is the fault of the United States. Wherefore each Neighbor is entitled to kick Uncle Sam's Eagle from Acapulco to Tierra del Fuego.

The second proposition, deriving from the first, is that the Underdog is Always Right. And inasmuch as Pablo Descamisado and Mario Pelado are both Underdogs, whenever they bark at some established American interest, it would be un-neighborly of the United States to bark back or to try to defend that interest.

Thus the nation which built a great canal through a fever-ridden jungle and operated it for fifty years for the benefit of all nations is suddenly guilty of colonialism, and the men who operate the locks are all sub-standard Americans.

Thus the self-accusing phrase: "We were friendly with Batista — that was very, very wrong of us," paralyzed for months American response to the progressive theft of one billion dollars in United States property in Cuba.

The Guilt Complex underlies much of the philosophy of those who have aspired on behalf of the American government to accomplish good in the hemisphere during the past generation. That most of the practitioners have been earnest and well-meaning is beside the point.

To this day the propagation of the myth of Uncle Sam's alleged responsibility for whatever is distasteful engages the

179

attention of *latino* politicians. Their appetite was whetted at the outset by a congeries of do-gooders from within our own borders. Among the early birds titillated by these mysteries were Sumner Welles as Assistant Secretary and later as Under Secretary of State, and his colleague Laurence Duggan, who headed the Latin American Division for the first decade of the New Deal. The then youthful Nelson Rockefeller and Adolf Berle, to mention two who years and years later are still carrying lighted *macumba* candles, were likewise attracted.

The same voodoo almost fetched so otherwise sagacious a performer as Cordell Hull, who during the 1930's loved to attend hemisphere conferences and expatiate on this and that, looking benign as he gestured with a pince-nez attached to a black silk ribbon. At Montevideo in 1933, Hull dutifully promised that the United States would intervene no more. And three years later, at Buenos Aires, the words "directly or indirectly" were added to that promise, by way of rubbing the eagle's beak in it.*

Meanwhile, as an earnest of our penitence, we relinquished our treaty rights to intervene in Cuba under the Platt Amendment. Albeit the hair shirt of the eagle was nowhere so triumphantly displayed a generation ago as in the Pearl of the Antilles, it was waved elsewhere in Latin America, often with New Deal oratory describing the United States as sinful until 1933, but thereafter fragrant with honest sweat and the juices of salvation.

* There is, of course, no such thing as U. S. non-intervention in Latin America because what the American government refrains from doing may, because of our preponderant power in the hemisphere, constitute an exercise of influence almost as weighty as intervention itself.

It can also be represented that the various American interventions in the first third of the century did the countries concerned little but good. Along with valuable lessons in deportment and administration, much tidying-up was accomplished in the Caribbean. Roads and schools were built. Mosquitoes were exterminated. Uncle Sam left each campsite cleaner than he found it.

Private American enterprises during the same period were often assumed to be guilty of one tort or another.

Secretary Hull never went all the way with the apologizers. When in 1938 Mexico dispossessed the oil companies, Hull called for "adequate, effective, and prompt" compensation. Expropriation without compensation was, to his way of thinking, no different from stealing.

With the outbreak of World War II, Hull was able to devote less attention to the New World. He nevertheless rallied the Neighbors around after Dunkirk and even succeeded in implanting among them the proposition that "an attack on one is an attack on all" — a formula which was later to make possible the NATO alliance. Hull appeared reluctant, however, to discipline the freewheeling Coordinator of Inter-American Affairs, a wartime official who with uninfectious enthusiasm operated a duplicate Washington Latin American Bureau, peddling the taxpayer's largesse and generating confusion.

At the end of the war there occurred almost the only challenge in thirty years to the proposition that the kicked American eagle ought to molt golden feathers and that the Good Neighbors, regardless of their conduct, ought to retrieve them. It was led by Spruille Braden, and for two years the Latin Americans sat up and took notice. The Good Neighbor Policy, they were politely reminded, was originally laid out as a two-way street of respect. Henceforth, *Señores*, traffic is going to be in *ambos sentidos*. In both directions.

These worthy efforts soon petered out, and for almost twenty years thereafter the amateurs and the do-gooders have been in the ascendant. Chit-chat by conference was substituted for diplomacy. There was a meeting at Quitandinha, loudly applauded by the participants, which produced an elaborate treaty theoretically governing the relations of the Neighbors with each other; it is more vividly remembered because the gate was crashed by Evita Perón, the mink-upholstered consort of the Argentine dictator.

Another conference, at Bogotá, blew up in riots and bloodshed — those events obscuring a Cuban effort (ten years before Fidel Castro) to obtain hemispheric endorsement of the proposition that a move on the part of the United States to relate its treatment of a given country to that country's treatment of American interests constitutes "economic aggression" by the United States. Thus the Guilt Complex came close in 1948 to being sanctified by treaty.

During these post-war years the twenty republics of Latin America were diligently spending the profits accumulated between 1939 and 1945. Soon many of them had little left above or below ground to hock, and they were resentful about it.

The United States was at the same time pouring money in unprecedented volume over Western and Central Europe and even over little Greece. Viewing this, it occurred to the Neighbors that what was needed was a Marshall Plan for Latin America. Without a Marshall Plan for Latin America, Uncle Sam had clearly been derelict in his duty. Uncle Sam was guilty of "taking Latin America for granted."

For a dozen years thereafter that was to be the substance of hemispheric chanting. Until, that is, *Alianza para el Progreso.*

In vain was it explained to the Neighbors that what the United States invested in the free world's freedom, anywhere, benefited all parts of the free world, including Latin America. Also that by rebuilding the shattered economies of Europe, the United States was simultaneously restoring the European market for Latin American goods. And finally that the Marshall Plan was designed to repair the devastations of war, which Latin America had happily escaped.

The *latinos,* having marched out of the Truman classroom to the tune of these unwelcome sonnets, marched back again in 1953 to greet the Republican administration. By now they had crossed out the word undevastated and written *underdeveloped* in its place. The Neighbors explained that by being underdeveloped, a nation has the right to thrust a hand into Uncle Sam's pocket.

In the beginning the Eisenhower mentors were unimpressed. Work harder, *amigos,* they suggested. Balance your budgets. Create a favorable climate for private investment.

When the *amigos* said what they intended to do with those pages out of Poor Richard's Almanac, the Republicans decided to travel. Out of office for twenty years, they wanted to see for themselves. They organized expeditions, culminating in the Cavalcade of Nixon around South America.

But before Nixon came Brother Milton, not yet fermenting bitter wine but working hard at being a harbinger of his relation to come. Sure enough, Milton was shortly followed by the President himself, who promoted a conclave of presidents in Panama in 1956. Since no one was able to invent a plausible reason for holding this elaborate barbecue, it was given out that the reunion would commemorate a meeting on the Isthmus summoned by Bolívar, one hundred and thirty years before 1956. A declaration to that effect was solemnly inscribed on twentieth-century parchment, and the American ambassador to Panama fell heir to an electric go-cart that had done presidential duty on the isthmian golf course.

Finally Vice President Nixon bought a new suitcase. Having already visited Brazil, he knew about *favelas* and *feijoadas* and *festas,* but on the west coast of South America he ran into trouble.

The American people were profoundly shocked by the treatment of their Vice President, first in Peru and then outside the capital of Venezuela. But so conditioned were they by a quarter century of guilt and self-blame that almost before the unconquering hero returned to Washington, Americans were proclaiming that the Nixon Ordeal could not possibly have occurred if the Neighbors had not been so shabbily treated by the United States.

183

To the *latinos,* that was stimulating music. It was the prelude, in fact, to *Alianza para el Progreso.*

The Brazilians, by coincidence, happened to have a program already drafted, and they sent it to Washington. They called it *Operacão Pan America.* The theme of it was that the ills of Latin America derive from its being underdeveloped; each underdeveloped Neighbor should have access to unlimited credit.

Stirred by Nixon's misfortunes, the Republicans bought this lusitanian horse opera in a flurry of evangelical fervor, notwithstanding the fact that they had rejected the same scenario six years earlier. No longer did the Republicans deprecate soft loans: they established the Development Loan Fund for the announced purpose of making loans so soft that the repayment provisions were printed on Kleenex. No longer were the Republicans left cold at the thought of a hemispheric bank with a single depositor; they voted for an Inter-American Bank with twenty checkbooks in the hands of the twenty Good Neighbors. No longer did the Republicans oppose a Marshall Plan for Latin America; they asked themselves why they had not thought sooner of all these patriotic ways to create happiness and well-being.

Viva Operacão Pan America, declared the Republicans.

Hurray for Underdevelopment, shouted the Neighbors.

The upshot was not lacking in irony. Just as their Republican parents in the Hoover administration renounced armed intervention in Latin America, thus opening the way for Franklin Roosevelt and the Good Neighbor Policy, so the Republicans of 1960 assembled for the benefit of their Democratic successors practically all of the ingredients that today form that rich pudding distributed under a Democratic label.

When the Democrats took over, they quickly suppressed the Portuguese sub-title and dreamed up *Alianza para el Progreso* instead. They earmarked one billion dollars of U. S.

Treasury funds. They announced they were open for business. Nor did the Democrats neglect to make the customary bow to the Guilt Complex. "We have not always grasped the significance," said President Kennedy in a speech in 1961 launching *Alianza,* "of the hemisphere's common mission. . . . We have not always understood the magnitude of your problem, nor accepted our share of responsibility for the welfare of the hemisphere."

The U.S. quota for *Alianza* was upped to *three* billion dollars.

Interpreting these portents as the whistle on the most opulent gravy train since the one piloted by the Coordinator of Inter-American Affairs in World War II, the Neighbors were shortly incensed by remarks on the part of White House professors about "necessary social reforms" and "archaic tax and land-law structures." First the remedial action by Latin America, averred the professors, and then the *Alianza* handouts.

The Neighbors characterized this as intervention, and they said so in shrill, rasping voices. They intimated that if Uncle Sam expected to get his eagle back with *any* feathers left, Uncle had better stop promoting social revolution and stick to minting gold coins for Rising Expectations.

Thus admonished, Washington retreated. Although the gravy train then puffed out of the station with hemisphere flags on the U. S. Treasury baggage car, it has not been a happy expedition. There have been open switches and innumerable hotboxes. The travelers, frustrated trying to rifle the baggage car, have complained of carsickness. What should have been a delightful run, with impressive scenery and expenses paid by the railroad, generated instead cinders in everyone's eyes, and recrimination.

For a simple and comprehensible reason. The rules for American subsidy having been progressively relaxed since the first prudent stipulations were shouted down in Uruguay in

185

1961, what the Neighbors are really talking about are American-controlled safeguards of *any* description.

"Just give us the money, and we'll figure out a way to use it," is what the *Alianza* partners are trying to tell us.

Three decades of shaking golden feathers out of the hair shirt of the eagle support the expectation that if the Neighbors complain loudly enough and behave abusively enough, Uncle Sam will capitulate. The odds, therefore, are that the shivering bird is in for another plucking.

Unless, of course, Congress should intervene.

Where, then, do we stand, after a generation of handouts, apologies, and ingratitude? The eagle has lost a great many feathers, and the United States has little to show for them. After years of generosity and good intentions, the only motion picture that interests the Good Neighbors is Mutiny on the Bounty — their mutiny against Uncle Sam's bounty.

Of friends in the hemisphere who would stand up for the United States and be counted, we have practically none. The Neighbors, with scarce exception, are stumbling around in a morass of self-pity and self-righteousness, enjoying the luxury of helping Uncle Sam blame himself, but taking few steps on their own behalf. Brazil has been a prime example. Argentina is another.

In an altercation involving the United States on the one hand and a Latin American country on the other, almost everybody is automatically against the United States, regardless of the issue or its merits.

It is also clear that no matter what the treaties say, effective sanctions will never be voted by the Latin American members against a wayward *latino* brother. Conceivably, in a specific instance, a majority of republics might favor some sort of disciplinary measure; they might agree, for instance, to beat Santo Domingo over the head with a toothpick. But no numerical majority that does not include Mexico, Argentina and Brazil (or at the least, two of them) is worth anything, and by no stretch of the imagination would two of these three key countries line up on the side of efficacious action. Rio Treaty or no Rio Treaty. Castro or no Castro. No matter what the provocation.

It is thus naïve — and a waste of time — to think about collective sanctions.

What in all these circumstances should the United States do as a responsible member of the New World family? We have been patient and forgiving for so long that the muscles which turn the other cheek are frayed almost beyond recovery. Our ready assumption of guilt has been a bonanza for the Communists, who have profited by manipulating into hatred for the United States the effects of our self-inflicted remorse-for-everything.

The prescription is inherent in the analysis of hemispheric relations. The first and most important requirement is the reestablishment of *respect* as the basis for inter-American relations. There is no better formula than the Good Neighbor Policy as originally expressed in 1933:

"The policy of the neighbor who resolutely respects himself and, because he does so, respects the rights of others . . . who respects his obligations and respects the sanctity of his agreements, in and with a world of neighbors."

That covers practically everything. Emphasize that the Good Neighbor Policy is a two-way street, and statesmen would search far indeed for a better foundation for hemispheric association.

As a first step toward regaining American self-respect, the Guilt Complex should be exorcised. We must purge ourselves of the idea that the problems besetting Latin America are the fault of the United States, or that their solution is the primary responsibility of anyone except the nations concerned. Let us recognize, albeit sadly, that some of the Neighbors may never rise far above poverty; their resources, human and material, are too meager.

We do the Bolivians no favor by chattering about Utopia, or by humbling ourselves for our failure to produce it. We do the Panamanian people no service by echoing the childish diatribes of their prehensile politicians.

Viewed realistically, little of *Alianza para el Progreso* makes much sense. *Alianza* would dedicate the United States to the "principle of collective responsibility for the welfare of the peoples of the Americas."* That means the welfare state for everybody, from the Aleuts of Alaska to the Alacalufas of Tierra del Fuego, plus those rapidly multiplying millions in between. From Nome to Ushuaia, eleven thousand miles of welfare state, and all at the expense of Uncle Sam.

Alianza ignores the fact that the bureaucracies of most undeveloped countries — disorganized, inexperienced, and frequently corrupt — are incapable of assimilating foreign aid or putting it to profitable use. It ignores the further fact that without birth control, no amount of American assistance can raise the Latin American standard of living.

Suppression of the Guilt Complex should likewise take care of the hallucination, popular in Latin America, that American business abroad is something to apologize for. The record of American business is proud. Without it, countless Latin Americans would still be reading with whale-oil lamps, and many of the rest would either be walking to market or riding their burros.

There is no objection to a modest and selective aid program. Unless, however, the proposed beneficiary gives honest treatment to United States citizens, the American government should decline to assist. Fair treatment should be the number one requisite for American aid. Expropriators of American property should no longer be invited to make visits to Washington. (One of the most shameful spectacles is the sight of Uncle Sam negotiating with a neighbor an agreement so that

* John F. Kennedy, White House, March 13, 1961.

when the neighbor swindles an American investor, the swindling government permits the American government to bail out the victim — at the expense, naturally, of the American taxpayers; this is known as the Investment Guarantee Program.)

Along with burial of the Guilt Complex and interment of the notion that the underdog is always right, the American government should stop worrying so much about its image in foreign countries. On this issue, the *latinos* are more sophisticated that we are; they are bewildered by what seems to them to be an irrational Anglo-Saxon desire for popularity. The *respect* of the Neighbors is what the United States should seek, not their votes in an international forum, nor their signatures on even the most eloquent of inter-American resolutions.

When its vital interests are involved, the United States may someday again have to go it alone. Then the *respect* of the hemisphere will be a far more valuable asset than *liking* or *friendship*. Nor will unilateral action render the United States so unpopular as some internationalists suppose, especially if the United States acts with determination and despatch, and above all without apology.

Reestablish respect — reciprocal respect — and many of our preoccupations in the New World will evaporate.

The hemisphere could then be invited to take note that henceforth a hair shirt ill becomes the American eagle.

Part 2

Having spent half my career in Latin America, including two Washington assignments on hemisphere problems, I am often asked what our policy toward the Good Neighbors ought to be. Some of the answers are implicit in the foregoing paragraphs, which indicate that my enthusiasm for turning the other cheek can often be kept under control. So can my eagerness for Good Works as an overture to playing "Happy Days Are Here Again" on the U. S. Treasury barrel organ.

In 1961, when I was ambassador to Greece, I was invited by an amiable Leading Statesman to accompany him as his adviser on a trip around South America — one of those cyclonic expeditions visiting eleven capitals in sixteen days, at the end of which few survivors can remember the name of the country-before-last that they slept in. One of my recommendations was:

Don't Waste Money on Northeast Brazil.

The *polígono do seco* is a afflicted area, scorched and marginal, and occasionally flooded. Northeast Brazil contrasts with millions of acres of virgin territory, awaiting development. If someone gave Brazil an unlimited credit, no strings attached, scarcely a *cruzeiro* would be allotted to the Northeast. Leastways, not by a Brazilian government.

Whereat Washington decided to rescue Northeast Brazil, at the expense, of course, of the American taxpayer. Uncounted dollars later, the venture has succeeded only in opening another endless vista of bureaucratic spending. A further example of Uncle Sam's rushing in, checkbook in hand, to save somebody from something.

Much of this compulsion to fill his neighbor's Easter basket with gold parsley originates in that old American craving for popularity. Joined to it is the erroneous belief that in Latin America the United States not only ought to but *can* be popular. That proposition is nonsense, as any reflective student of foreign affairs should know. Weak nations mistrust strong nations, and twenty weak nations greatly mistrust a single great power.

That is a fact of life, not necessarily immutable, but certainly enduring throughout the twentieth century. Recognition of it should replace those repetitious schemes to disguise Uncle Sam as a wholesome American girl with a thirty-eight-inch bust and then have her elected Miss Alliance for Progress.

If the United States spent as much time trying to be respected as it wastes looking for approval, progress in hemispheric relations might follow. The energy saved could be devoted to constructive behavior.

Among themselves, the *latinos* are often quarrelsome and parochial. One of the worst of the Spanish-American legacies is geographic fragmentation. Proposals looking toward regional agreements, understandings among contiguous countries (as among the Central American republics), customs unions, commodity agreements, and even amalgamation of countries, should engage American sympathy and interest. While a fusion of existing political units may at the moment seem far-fetched, as a long-term objective it possesses considerable merit. How much stronger the expanded political units would be than some of the ones now scrabbling about on the *llanos, pampas,* and *selvas.*

Canada should be encouraged to play a role in hemispheric affairs. The interests in Latin America of our northern neighbor are already substantial, but in terms of responsibility commensurate with ability, Canada has been coasting along, in effect enjoying the benefits of membership but paying no dues and few of the expenses. It would be naïve to expect Canada to vote always with the United States, and counter-productive if that occurred, but adding the Canadian voice to hemispheric councils would strengthen the association in every particular. Canada should become a part of the inter-American system.

If Brazil should ever reach its potential, that might take some of the "curse of strength" off the United States. Brazil has the elements of a great power: area, resources, elbow-room, a sophisticated upper class, a capacity for political invention. But Brazil lacks a sense of direction, and above all

191

discipline. Should the military establishment disintegrate, Brazil's promise of greatness could easily remain unfulfilled. It could even evaporate altogether, leaving a frightening gap in hemispheric leadership and geography.

And then there is Cuba. Theirs is a time of trouble. And yet the worst thing for Cuba might have been a successful Bay of Pigs operation in 1961. The time was not ripe for it. The post-Castro regime would have been a puppet administration, established and maintained by the United States. As soon as the American prop was removed, it would have collapsed or been overthrown. At worst the United States might have been committed to indefinite occupation and re-occupation of an ungrateful island. At best, the United States might have exchanged a Castro pesthouse for a post-Castro asylum.

There are other factors to consider:

Castro as a menace to the United States, as in 1962, when missiles were aimed at our cities. Then the Russians backed down. The recollection of their humiliation plus the knowledge that the American government is still prepared to act if national security is affected, should be sufficient to deter the Russians from comparable adventures in Cuba. Castro without Khrushchev is not a menace but a nuisance.

Second, Castro as a carrier of rabies into the hemisphere. That danger is diminishing. The spectacle of Cuba in the grip of commissars and *barbudos* has not reassured the other American republics. *Fidelismo* as an export product is shoddy. It finds a declining market.

That does not mean that the United States can whistle up a set of inter-American sanctions against Cuba. But by skillful diplomacy, enough Latin American vigilance and collaboration ought to be possible to keep Castro neutralized and and relatively innocuous outside the Caribbean. Inside the Caribbean, Castro is a headache — at times a throbbing headache — but not a menace to the survival of the neighborhood.

There remain the Cuban people. Castro is their responsibility. It is not the United States which will rescue Cuba from Castro. That must be done by Cubans — the people who bred Marti, and the heroes of the long struggle against Spain. This also may be a dark and bloody business, but it is still a Cuban responsibility.

The fact that the Cubans themselves must solve the problem does not mean that the United States cannot assist. Instead of announcing hypocritically from time to time that the United States does not encourage or condone commando raids and other anti-Castro preliminaries, officially the American government should try the novel experiment of keeping quiet. Whether the American embargo is still effective, or more trouble that it is worth, I leave to others to argue. But there are different ways, both overt and clandestine, in which the United States can help anti-Castro Cubans. I pray they are not being overlooked. And above all I pray that a Cuban leader of stature may again arise, and mobilize his people behind him.

XII.

A Magnolia Tree for Brasília

WHEN, in 1958, Secretary of State John Foster Dulles accepted an invitation from Brazil to make an official visit to that country, he agreed that Brasília — the new capital city then a-building on the plateau of Goiás, six hundred miles from Rio — ought to be included in his itinerary. Brasília was included, and that was how Secretary Dulles became involved in the magnolia project, which, before the tree was finally planted, had enlisted the participation of the President of Brazil and most of his cabinet, plus sundry legislators, electricians, reporters, photographers, and jeep drivers. Not to forget one American ambassador, who was responsible for getting the magnolia tree from Washington to Brasília in the first place, and two harassed Secret Service aides, who were responsible for getting one intact Secretary of State back to Washington from Brasília.

The episode illustrates that while you may be able to discipline some of the Brazilian people all of the time (but not many, to be sure), and perhaps all of the Brazilian people for some of the time (but, to be sure, not for long), it is impossible to discipline many of the Brazilians for much of the time. Their natural condition is one of uninhibited exuberance, and they are likely to erupt in unexpected directions — as when, in a recent political campaign, the citizens nominated a rhinoceros from the São Paulo zoo as a candidate for Congress. That, they declared, should teach their *paulista* politicians a lesson.

The American embassy in Rio endorsed the Secretary's trip to Brasília for two reasons. Going to Brasília would immensely gratify Mr. Dulles' host, the President of Brazil, who had declared on more than one occasion that whatever claim he might have on posterity would result from his having sponsored the new capital, which had been in the Brazilian Constitution for over fifty years, with no previous chief executive having lifted a finger to build it.

And secondly, the trip to Brasília should simplify — so we naïvely imagined — the problem of security for our visiting statesman. For this was only a few weeks after the students at San Marcos University in neighboring Peru had mounted a hostile demonstration against the Vice President of the United States. This was followed a few days later by a rioting mob threatening the life of Mr. Nixon on the road to Caracas. Washington suddenly became so security minded that it began mistaking the ticking of its own nervous arteries for the sound of an enemy Geiger counter.

Thus the first business for our embassy in Brazil was fixing the schedule of Secretary Dulles' visit, without which no local security arrangements could be initiated. We met for that purpose in the air-conditioned ambassadorial office overlooking the incomparable harbor of Rio de Janeiro.

The number of public activities in which a foreign dignitary can usefully engage during a two-day official visit are few. For example, to address the legislature is helpful only if the visitor has some pronouncement to make. Secretary Dulles had business to transact with the government of Brazil, but not in the legislative marketplace. So we crossed off the Brazilian Congress.

Receiving an honorary degree used to be appropriate for a visiting statesman, but nowadays you never could tell about Latin American students. Likely as not the lifting of the ceremonial hood would be the signal for a barrage of tomatoes. So we crossed off the local university.

195

Laying a wreath beside the statue of a national hero is a sound if unimaginative gesture. However, inaugurating something is better than wreath-laying because whatever you inaugurate will surely last longer than tired tropical flowers at the base of a monument. Unfortunately the embassy had in reserve no pavilion or exhibit to unveil, and there was insufficient time between Secretary Dulles' acceptance of the Brazilian invitation and the date of his visit to invent one. So we regretfully crossed off those possibilities.

What we needed was something calling for an outdoor appearance by the Secretary of State. Something with a not too complicated security ratio. Something with a built-in public relations content, which meant the presence of the press and photographers, which automatically meant the presence of Brazilian spectators and officials.

It was then that tree-planting entered our calculations. "Mr. Ambassador," said one of my embassy colleagues, "why not have the Secretary plant a tree? An American tree, that is. We could probably get one flown down from the States."

"You mean, plant an American tree, here in Rio?" I asked. I was visualizing the lush Jardim Botanico, under the peak of Corcovado, and the tall royal palms planted a century ago by the Emperor Dom Pedro. Those palms were an impressive memorial. To have Secretary Dulles plant a tree that would grow into something as stalwart as that should certainly be more profitable than leaning a wreath against the martyred Tiradentes.

Another colleague elaborated the idea. "Wouldn't Brasília be better than Rio, Mr. Ambassador? Rio has plenty of trees, but Brasília has nothing but scrub. President Kubitschek's lawn, in front of Alvorada Palace, hasn't even a bush growing on it."

That was a fact. The Palace of Dawn, as the President named his official residence, had recently been inaugurated at a celebration complete with captive diplomats flown from

Rio and a local bishop, who froze on the microphone. Beside the reflecting pool there was a surrealistic statue that nobody could explain, called Order and Progress; and there was a Niemeyer chapel that looked like an Eskimo Pie wearing an Easter bonnet. But from the bronze doors and the plate-glass main entrance of the Palace of Dawn, there was a noble view of nothing in particular.

A tree was just what that empty prospect needed. Furthermore, tree-planting was appropriate to the burgeoning aspect of the infant capital; it would be right in the great-oaks-from-little-acorns-grow tradition. It would give additional point to the Secretary's visit. It would involve — so we optimistically believed — no difficult security problem. And finally, unless we were greatly mistaken, President Kubitschek would love it.

So tree-planting was added to the schedule.

But then the question arose — what kind of tree should Secretary Dulles plant? Summoned to give technical advice, the Agricultural Attaché embarked on an exposition of the chemistry of the soil of Brasília in its relation to the climate of "a rainfall-deficient area nearly four thousand feet above sea level." We were reminded that whereas the United States is several thousand miles *north* of the equator, Brasília is one thousand miles *south* of the equator. Soon the bloom was in danger of being rubbed off our entire arboreal proposition. I suggested to the Attaché that he ask the Department of Agriculture in Washington what kind of tree would grow well in Brasília.

This inquiry evoked a reply of even more devastating thoroughness. All manner of factors were listed, taken into account, and considered by the savants of the Department of Agriculture. After rejecting several varieties for one deficiency or another, the tree that Agriculture was finally prepared to endorse for Brasília was *Magnolia grandiflora,* the American magnolia tree, which was described as "a handsome ornamental evergreen, bearing large white flowers; it is native

197

to southeastern coastal United States, but should be cultivable in other warm temperate areas."

Agriculture added — helpfully — that a suitable specimen of *Magnolia grandiflora,* four feet high, was available; still more helpfully, that it could be packed for shipment on the same Air Force airplane that would bring the Secretary of State to Rio de Janeiro. Presumably the embassy could arrange to have the tree forwarded to Brasília for planting. Further information by air mail.

Slightly shaken by the complications that develop when the experts take over, I consoled myself with the thought that my Portuguese-speaking friends could at least pronounce magnolia without uprooting their tonsils. If the Department of Agriculture had sponsored a horsechestnut, or a shagbark hickory, there might have been no solution short of transplanting the new capital, instead of transplanting the sapling. I was further mollified when the promised additional information arrived, including color photographs of a magnolia tree in flower. Beautiful.

The Air Attaché was sent for, and I arranged for him to fly the Agricultural Attaché *and* the magnolia tree to Brasília in the embassy C-47, as soon as the tree reached Rio with the Secretary of State. That would give the Agricultural Attaché time to dig a hole in the presidential lawn and to accomplish whatever else might be needful in advance of the tree-planting ceremony two days later.

"That's quite a tree, for a fact," observed the Air Attaché, admiring the photographs. "Dom Juscelino will sure go all out for that one."

Dom Juscelino was the President of Brazil, with whom — clearances from Secretary Dulles' office for the proposed schedule having been obtained — I was shortly thereafter closeted. That affable Chief Executive expressed himself as enchanted with the suggested arrangements, including the planting of the magnolia in Brasília. In fact, the President was

198

so pleased that the Secretary had agreed to accompany him to the new capital, that he would probably have settled for our digging up his lawn and installing a bowling alley, provided reporters and photographers were present to record that the American Secretary of State had been a principal participant. The President was equally cooperative about Rio security arrangements. "Anything you wish, *Senhor Embaixador,*" he said. "I'll tell Colonel Danilo . . ." Kubitschek was determined that no matter what had happened to Vice President Nixon, nothing would be permitted to mar the visit of the Secretary of State.

"Thank you. That's fine for Rio," I said. "But how about security in Brasília, Mr. President?" I remembered that the only thing we had discussed about the new capital was planting the magnolia tree.

President Kubitschek made me a wide and confident gesture. It took in the entire Planaltina plateau and all of the new Federal District, plus contiguous areas of the State of Goiás. It guaranteed the hospitality of all the inhabitants.

"*Embaixador,*" concluded the President severely, "*deixa Brasília comigo.*" Leave Brasília to me.

That was all I could get out of the President about plans for Brasília, except that the Secretary and Mrs. Dulles would be looked after personally by the President and by dona Sara Kubitschek, the wife of the President. "*Deixa Brasília comigo,*" were the President's final words on the subject.

They were good enough words, in a local context, but they were poor nourishment for an ambassador to have to serve, by cable, to a critical and suspicious Washington security establishment, still burping with political indigestion over the Nixon Spanish American exposure. I eventually pacified the bureaucrats by throwing them an expensive Potomac past participle: I cabled that plans for Brasília — the last six hours of the fifty-hour visit — could be *finalized* after the Secretary of State and his security aides reached Rio de Janeiro.

199

For that fearless understatement by the American ambassador to Brazil, no medals or decorations have as yet been forthcoming . . .

Thus the afternoon of the fourth of August, 1958, arrived, and at three o'clock Secretary Dulles' airplane touched down at the international airport at Galeão, deep in Guanabara Bay. Emerging into the warm winter sunshine, Mr. Dulles looked as fresh as if he had just enjoyed ten hours of sleep at his north-woods retreat, instead of five in an airplane, with little to regale him but three Assistant Secretaries of State, a pile of whodunits, and the Lebanon crisis.

The Secretary's security detail, in light raincoats and snap-brim hats, swung down from the forward exit of the Constellation while I was presenting Mr. Dulles to the Foreign Minister. And as the Secretary stepped out to inspect the honor guard of Brazilian soldiers, I was pleased to observe that my Agricultural Attaché and my Air Attaché were taking charge of a wooden crate being unloaded from the luggage compartment. "Keep from Extremes of Heat and Cold" was stenciled on the side of the case.

An enterprising Brazilian correspondent, observing the object of my attention, scented a possible story. "Does your Secretary of State travel with the atomic bomb?" he demanded.

The Secretary's arrival took place on the military side of the field, a mile from the passenger terminal. The security arrangements were exemplary. As he swept through the airport gates, the blue flag of his office flying from the left fender of the long black Embassy Cadillac, there were troops in abundance, and they all saluted. We were an impressive cavalcade. In following automobiles there were the three Assistant Secretaries of State, brought along for contingencies. There was the Brazil Desk Officer, the author of a briefing book two inches thick that as usual nobody on the trip had time to read; it would nevertheless prove useful after the visit as a compendium for the Embassy to study. There was the Secretary's communications officer, who would presently be operating a code room through which would flow more telegraphic messages than used to pass through the entire State Department in Washington a scant few years earlier. And there was Mr. Dulles' incomparable personal assistant, who with experience gained in palace, Quonset hut, pagoda, and Pullman would within five minutes of unpacking her toothbrush have established in the embassy residence the office of the Secretary of State of the United States — open and ready for business.

Our procession had an escort of sixteen special policemen, each mounted on a motorcycle and each wearing a cap with a bright red top that inflated, balloon-like, as our forward speed increased — which it immediately did. Each motorcycle was equipped with an oversized siren. Multiplied by sixteen conscientious policemen, sound waves generated by the escort shook the funnels of ships approaching the harbor. These were the armed escort of the Presidency, and the red-capped riders swept up and down the line of our official cars. They dashed ahead to immobilize traffic on avenues intersecting our route to the city. They foraged deep into alleys and *praças*. Automobiles overtaken braked cheerfully to a curbside halt, where they blew their horns, further swelling the decibels smiting the city. Pedestrians, scattering from the right of way like windblown confetti, beamed on us from the comparative safety of doorways.

Our cavalcade was also a security triumph. Contrary to Washington apprehension, there was no anti-Dulles demonstration. On the long ride from the airport to the residence we passed one banner, hung from the balcony of a Communist students' union, which read, "Mr. Dulles, Go Home." That was the nearest anyone came to compromising the hospitality of South America's most sophisticated city. When they recognized Secretary Dulles, the *cariocas* responded with applause. Moreover, they heartily approved of the noise: organized pandemonium is the lifeblood of the city.

Like many professional travelers, Secretary Dulles had a philosophical approach to his personal safety. He left arrangements to the specialists, and then put the matter from his mind. Nevertheless, he winced as one of the escorting motorcycle redcaps — gesturing with both hands to a colleague — shot by the Cadillac with an eyelash of clearance.

Making conversation, I remarked there would be a bottle of Old Overholt on the Secretary's table, once we reached the embassy residence.

"*If* we reach the embassy residence," growled Mr. Dulles, wincing again as we shot, unscathed, through a series of teeming intersections. "What's it like in Brasília?" he suddenly asked me.

"No traffic problem," I assured him. "Brasília is a frontier town. When President Kubitschek started it two years ago, the nearest settlement was fifty miles away. Now Brasília has twenty thousand workmen. Town looks like a Grade B Western, except there are jeeps instead of horses. Everything is knee-deep in red dust . . ."

Secretary Dulles was running a finger down the official program given him by the Foreign Minister at the airport. "What about this tree-planting in Brasília?"

I told him about the magnolia ceremony on the lawn in front of the President's Palace.

"Hmm," said Mr. Dulles. "I'll have to say something, I suppose. Let me have a note on it when we get there."

The Secretary of State spent two crowded days in Rio de Janeiro. It is no part of this chronicle to dwell on the business that brought him to Brazil, except to observe that since Mr. Dulles was prepared to accept President Kubitschek's proposition that underdevelopment in Latin America (which Dom Juscelino called *sob-desenvolvimento*) was deplorable and ought to receive greater attention in Washington, and since President Kubitschek was prepared to agree that international Communism was a menace in Latin America and ought to re-

202

ceive greater attention in Brazil, progress toward an acceptable joint statement to be issued by the two governments was amiable and rapid.

Thus Secretary Dulles was able to chew a contented pencil, and President Kubitschek was able to say *Viva sob-desenvolvimento*. Both statesmen were happy, and the visit prospered. Nothing, during those forty-eight hours in Rio, marred the picture of Brazilian welcome. Agenda, protocol, and security arrangements were so smoothly blended by our Brazilian hosts that I overheard the Secretary's senior Secret Service aide telling Colonel Danilo — who had trained the special motorcycle escort — that in all his travels with the Secretary of State, he had never participated in better-planned arrangements.

Remembering reports of how many thousand miles a month Foster Dulles was accustomed to traveling, Colonel Danilo beamed — and so did I, for, having had something to do with those same preparations, I was aware of the temptation to improvisation the Brazilian officials had resisted and of the possible cost of this unaccustomed self-discipline to people whose talents lay in other directions. The perfection of Rio arrangements might be too good to last as far as Brasília. Satisfaction, that was to say, might be premature.

That proved a prophetic misgiving. The first intimation that all might not be well on the organizational front in Brasília occurred while we were waiting, the senior security aide and I, beside President Kubitschek's Viscount, for the takeoff from Rio. The aide had just learned that the invaluable Colonel Danilo was not accompanying us to the new capital.

"All I can find out," he complained, "is that before the tree-planting ceremony, the President is taking Secretary and Mrs. Dulles sightseeing in Brasília. But nobody can tell me about automobiles, or police arrangements, or anything . . ."

On the flight to Brasília, I tackled the President's Chief of Ceremonial, usually a geyser of information. Aluízio confirmed the sightseeing, but said that was all he knew about it; possibly

203

the President's Military Aide might know what was projected. But it turned out that the Military Aide had flown to Brasília ahead of us, and I went back to Aluízio, who was abstractedly drumming his fingers on his elegant London bowler — a hat brought along, I suspected, to establish himself as an urban official. His current preoccupation was, however, the President's "family supper" (as it appeared on the official program), which meal the Dulleses had assumed meant a private affair with the Kubitschek family. Questioned, Aluízio conceded that members of the Brazilian Cabinet might turn up, and perhaps some Senators and Representatives. There had been extra planes, he reminded me, beside the runway when we took off from Santos Dumont airport in Rio. *His* problem was the number of guests, and seating the presidential table.

I passed on the amended "family supper" news to the Dulleses, warning the Secretary that another speech might be in order. He also confirmed the President's sightseeing proposal. He hoped they could do without the Brasília equivalent of the Rio motorcycle escort.

It was from the President himself that I eventually learned what he had prepared for Secretary and Mrs. Dulles in Brasília, but by then it was too late to do the senior Secret Service aide any good.

"Don't look now," I whispered to Mrs. Dulles as we approached the new city, "but I think a helicopter is waiting."

While we circled in the Viscount over the site of the future capital, President Kubitschek proceeded in a torrent of Portuguese French to lay out the plan of Brasília for his Washington visitors. Silhouetted against the horizon, under oyster and white cumulus clouds, were the steel skeletons of buildings, and connecting them a skein of unpaved avenues. Congress looked like a knitting needle, impaled beside an upsidedown teacup. The dam of the artificial lake was finished, and the depression, twenty-five miles long, was beginning to fill with water. The Palace of Dawn was a row of gleaming white triangles, upended in the late afternoon sunlight.

And all about, as far as the eye could compass, there stretched the reddish Goiás landscape, with gray-green bushes, and endless scrub, and pillars of brick-red dust wherever work was in progress. Yet a decade hence, Brasília might well be a city of half a million people.

Against the noises of his descending airplane, President Kubitschek switched from French to pantomime. He raised his arm, with a finger pointing aloft. With the hand and finger he made circles in the air. *"Piqueno passeio,"* he shouted enthusiastically to the Dulleses. "A little trip." More circles with his finger. *"Helicóptero . . ."*

And helicopter it was, there on the airstrip at Brasília, with the rotorblades already turning. No sooner had we handed in the Viscount — large amiable crowd and no police protection — than the President sailed away with his guests in the helicopter. I had a glimpse of the slightly bewildered faces of the Secretary of State and his wife through the H-19 window, and of the anguished expression of the abandoned security aide, just before everything disappeared in choking clouds of brick-red Brasília dust. Sightseeing by helicopter. *Un piqueno passeio . . .*

It turned out that no one at the Brasília airport — in fact, no one in all Brasília — knew exactly where the President's helicopter was going, how long it would be there, or where the President proposed to land at the end of his little *passeio.* That, I surmised, might be precisely the President's idea of how best to arrange things. If nobody knew what the plans were, how could anybody interfere with those plans? And if there were no plans, then so much the better! A man shackled to a program was no match for a man gifted with improvisation.

Like the voters of São Paulo who became bored with the

electoral campaign and nominated the rhinoceros, the President of Brazil became impatient with the rigidity of security precautions. His solution was to nominate a helicopter. And away he flew in it.

These meditations, plausible to an admiring foreigner in Brazil, seemed unlikely to comfort Secretary Dulles' senior security aide, who now approached me through the thinning haze of the helicopter's departure. He was the unhappy man, for it is a serious thing for a warden to be deprived of his keys, or an ambassador to mislay his diplomatic passport, or a security man to become separated from his principal.

With eyes smarting from the dust, we followed the flight of the presidential chopper, visible above the treeless Goiás horizon. While we watched, the machine began to descend, the spot — about a mile away — marked presently by a dense pillar of dust as the downdraft bit into the parched Brasília earth and then bounced up again, augmented by topsoil.

"Your guess," I told the aide, "is as good as mine. Way it looks from here, that might be the site of the new Foreign Ministry, or maybe the new American embassy property. They'll probably wind up — if the rotorblades stay on — either back here at the airport or, more likely, at the President's Palace. If you want, I can get you a jeep and you can try to catch them."

The Secret Service man looked dismally around. Behind us, on the airport runway, additional airplanes from Rio were landing: a DC-4 with the newspaper correspondents and photographers; the Secretary's Constellation with the three Assistant Secretaries of State and the rest of the Dulles party; planes with Brazilian Cabinet members, legislators, and politicians. Everyone would soon be heading through the dust for the Presidential Palace, the magnolia tree, and the "family supper."

With the assistance of Aluízio, I got the Secret Service man a jeep. Aluízio explained to the driver what was up. The machine took off in a spurt of red, spinning around a corner like a water spider on a millpond. Then the Chief of Ceremonial and I commandeered a similar vehicle and we set out for Palácio da Alvorada, one jump ahead of the arriving contingent from Rio de Janeiro.

The helicopter reappeared, before the security aide could possibly have reached it. We had further views of it, Aluízio and I, as we drove along. The chopper came down now and then, each time in a great pillar of dust, and I pictured my wretched colleague, roaring frantically up and down the new Federal District, but always outmaneuvered because nobody knew where his quarry was going.

By the time the Chief of Ceremonial and I reached Palácio da Alvorada, Aluízio's London bowler looked like a red-painted Bolivian derby, and the handkerchief I tied around my neck resembled a bandanna.

True to his trust, the Agricultural Attaché was waiting on the lawn in front of the President's Palace. The magnolia tree was there, and the hole for the planting was there. Garden hoses connected the Palácio with the edge of the hole, against the moment when the dry Brasília earth would first touch the roots of the sapling. There were two ceremonial shovels, painted white; one with green and gold ribbons was for the President of Brazil, the other with red, white, and blue for Mr. Dulles.

The three Assistant Secretaries of State, possibly disgruntled at not having come in the President's Viscount, bore down upon me with a draft departure statement; they wanted immediate time out to discuss it. And where, they inquired, is the men's room? The junior security aide, who had come with the Assistant Secretaries after taking care of tips, luggage, and the tag ends of Rio departure, was dashing about, looking for the senior security aide; failing to find him, he appealed urgently to the American Ambassador.

"Security arrangements," he wailed. "Mr. Ambassador,

there aren't any arrangements. Nobody here is in charge of anything . . ." He appeared to be coming unzipped.

I told the Assistant Secretaries to relax; I'd see them about the communiqué right after the magnolia ceremony. I told the junior security aide to be thankful he wasn't bucketing around the State of Goiás in a jeep, trying to catch a helicopter with a butterfly net. Sighting my Air Attaché, who alone in all the confusion seemed to be observing developments with detachment, I detailed the Colonel to chaperone the Assistant Secretaries and to pacify the Secret Service man. The Attaché was in uniform. He had three rows of ribbons and he spoke tolerable Portuguese. I hoped he had a deft hand with overwrought visitors.

For the moment, that was all I could do in the name of security. The Secretary of State, the magnolia tree, diplomacy, and Brazilian-American relations: they would damn well have to take their chances together, there in the garden before the Palace of Dawn.

Nevertheless, the rotorblades were still on President Kubitschek's helicopter; we could hear it chopping away in the distance, apparently getting closer. If the pilot had not already dropped his passengers into the non-existent lake, or deposited them in the nave of the unbuilt cathedral, or abandoned them in the mythical bar of the still unconstructed Brasília Yacht Club, then the chances were that the swirling paddles would stay on long enough to deposit the President and his guests on top of the spectators beside the Palácio da Alvorada.

There might be worse maxims, I thought as I surveyed the seething turmoil around me, than "God is a Brazilian," whereby sixty million people sought daily refuge behind the skirts of the improbable. It might even be that the citizens now stomping about among the electric cables and live wires and garden hoses in unregimented enjoyment would scatter sufficiently so the helicopter pilot could find an open space to come down on.

208

Sure enough, as the short twilight of the tropics deepened across the plain of Brasília and the cumulus clouds turned from crimson to purple, President Kubitschek's sightseeing machine settled softly and safely beside the flagpole, with no casualties except a ruined flowerbed. Clearly, God was still a Brazilian.

As soldiers set about forming a lane from the helicopter to the magnolia, the jeep of the senior Secret Service aide at long last caught up with the program. Its occupant, almost unrecognizable under his coating of dust, was rescued by the Air Force Colonel in time to fall in with his colleague behind the Secretary of State, as protocol and security demanded.

Looking alert and by no means daunted by the afternoon's adventures, Secretary Dulles accompanied his host across the lawn. The lights came on, and the crowd edged forward. Bowing to the President of the Republic, I handed him the white shovel with the green and gold ribbons. A moment later I gave Secretary Dulles the shovel with the red, white, and blue ribbons. Each dutifully transferred a few shovelfuls of earth from the pile beside the hole to the roots of the magnolia.

Cameras whirred. Flashlight bulbs were a popping accompaniment. A murmur of delight arose from the crowd as the two Secret Service men came under the illumination — the one with the neat blue suit, and the other coated a quarter of an inch thick with the rich red powder of Brasília.

"O Orfeu Vermelho," I heard someone exclaim. "The Red Orpheus. Now all we lack is a Pink Eurydice . . ."

With the photographers shouting "outra vez" and "one more," the ceremony was dutifully repeated, with increased illumination. The blinding lights stayed on as the President and the Secretary of State shook hands with each other across the little magnolia. Additional enthusiasts, members of the Cabinet and of the Brazilian Congress, competed for possession of the shovels. The hole filled so rapidly that it needed all the agility of the Agricultural Attaché to get the burlap off the roots, and to get himself out of the diminishing hole before there was no hole left to get out of.

When the President of Brazil called for order, fifty persons helpfully took up the refrain, each shouting for silence with every bit of his lungpower. The noise and the heat of the television lights were terrific. As the commotion gradually diminished, Secretary Dulles stepped forward. There was applause. Briefly he scanned the paper I had given him, blinking under the brilliance. Microphones were held up before him.

"Mr. President, Ladies and Gentlemen," the Secretary of State began. The Secret Service men, one on either side, edged closer to Mr. Dulles' elbows. This was the moment, I thought with a flash of nostalgia for all those wonderful security arrangements in Rio de Janeiro, when a hostile attempt might have the largest chance of succeeding.

"This is a happy occasion," said Mr. Dulles. "The planting of a tree shows faith in the future — faith in the future of Brazilian-American collaboration. And now as we commit this beautiful North American magnolia to the warm hospitality of the red Brazilian soil . . ."

At which instant — six thirteen P.M. on the evening of August 6, 1958, darkness having spread like a canopy across the sky over central Brazil — the overloaded electric circuits of the new Federal District collapsed, and every fuse and transformer in Brasília blew out simultaneously.

It was two hours before service was restored, and longer than that before the tangle of wires, pipes, cables, hoses, cameras, floodlights, and microphones were sorted out in the headlights of the assembled jeeps. By that time the presidential lawn — except for the still erect little magnolia — looked like a polo field at the end of a dozen desperately fought chukkers.

It was later still when the President's "family supper" — a formidable *feijoada* — was served to sixty-seven persons assembled in the State Dining Room of the new Alvorada Palace, each guest sorted out and seated in order of precedence by

210

the indefatigable Aluízio. The Secretary of State of the United States, refreshed by a candle-lit rest and fortified by a shot of Old Overholt from the flask of his diligent representative in Brazil, spoke graciously of the hospitality he and Mrs. Dulles had received at the hands of the Brazilian government and people.

And then, fifty-six hours from the time when the wheels of the Air Force Constellation touched Rio de Janeiro with the Secretary of State, his aircraft departed from Brasília for Washington. The last aboard was the senior Secret Service man. He started to say something to the American Ambassador about Brazilian security arrangements. It would, no doubt, have been a memorable and pithy observation. But just then the first engine caught, and whatever it was, was lost in the clatter.

211

XIII.

The Care and Feeding of Dictators

As a young man in the State Department a good many years ago, I was briefly in charge of our relations with Romania, and the experience taught me several useful things: for one, not to underestimate the readiness of American spectators to interest themselves in somebody else's behavior; for another, that the temptation to substitute a moral judgment for the national interest is rarely conducive to the successful transaction of a government's overseas business; and for a third, that the care and feeding of dictators is a difficult operation.

Carol was ruler of Romania in those far-off days, and in Bucharest his coronation was about to take place. On the advice of the State Department, President Hoover appointed the American minister to Romania to serve as special ambassador during the ceremony.

American participation in Carol's coronation was a routine undertaking. Little importance attaches to such representation, whereas failure to participate would be adversely remarked. Furthermore, by selecting the resident American minister in Bucharest, instead of sending someone on special mission from the United States, the American government was playing its participation in King Carol's coronation about as far down the ceremonial scale as it could go, short of deliberately giving offense to Romania.

For Carol, it must be conceded, was hardly a model monarch, even by the relaxed Danubian standards prevailing a generation ago.

The desk officer of Romania went on leave and his responsibilities were parcelled out among his colleagues in the Western European Division. That was how I found myself in June of 1930 with the affairs of Romania on my desk. I was given that country in addition to my regular duties, on the assumption that, with the coronation arranged, nothing untoward was likely to happen. That proved correct as far as Romania was concerned, but it overlooked the American people, an astonishingly large number of whom took a surprisingly poor view of the appointment of a special ambassador to honor King Carol. No sooner was this announced than the startled State Department was deluged with letters and telegrams.

Secretary of State Stimson was belabored for having anything to do with Carol, who was variously labeled adulterer, usurper, and dictator. Carol had taken off with a mahogany-haired siren, abandoning his wife and his royal career for sinful frolic in Paris. Carol and Magda had returned, unrepentant, to Bucharest where, his son having mounted the throne, Carol unceremoniously threw the boy out and seized the scepter for himself. And now, while Carol prepared to have himself crowned King of Romania, Madame Lupescu was measuring the royal dormitory for curtains.

None of which, these volunteer statesmen declared, should be condoned by right-thinking people. The letter-writers directed the Secretary of State to manifest their disapproval by denouncing King Carol and boycotting the coronation proceedings.

These communications soon found their way to the acting desk officer for Romania, where they were joined by an avalanche of comparable messages addressed to President Hoover, forwarded by the White House with the notation: "Transmitted for appropriate consideration and acknowledgment by the Secretary of State."

Few of the letter-writers appeared to have any personal stake in Romania. Nevertheless, several hundred American cit-

213

izens, observing the appointment of an official to attend a ceremony in a distant Balkan dictatorship, were stimulated to
make known their dissent, and even to demand that something
be done about it. As the interim Mr. Romania in the State
Department, it was my responsibility to prepare replies.

The replies said that Romania was a power friendly to the
United States, and that it was customary for a country maintaining relations with such a power to participate in its major
celebrations, including coronations. No significance, the writers were assured, attached to American representation at the
crowning of Carol. Least of all did it signify personal approval
by the President of the United States or the Secretary of State
of the Matters Mentioned in Your Letter.

The amiable Bill Castle signed the letters as Assistant Secretary of State for European Affairs, but he vetoed my proposal to insert in each envelope a limerick then current on the
third floor of the old State War Navy Building:

> Declared the red-headed Magda Lupescu
> As she came to Romania's rescue
> "It's a wonderful thing
> To be under a king.
> Can democracy beat it — I ask you? "

Thus the coronation of King Carol the Second. It might
have pacified the critics if the State Department had been able
to predict that seventeen years later an exiled Carol would
marry Madame Lupescu. Foreign offices are seldom, however,
that much more clairvoyant than their crystal-gazing constituents.

The propensity for getting excited about somebody else's
business and then reading moral judgments into the conduct
of foreign affairs is an American phenomenon, for dissection at
another opportunity. It is not a propensity that eases the burdens of the Secretary of State as he seeks to deal with a dictatorship or a regime regarded as disreputable by an articulate

214

segment of the American people. The indignation over King Carol, a relatively innocuous reprobate, led me to speculate about how our government goes about handling those prickly situations that involve a really vicious or unprincipled dictatorship. How does the American government respond to those problems?

Since dictatorships of all shapes and sizes have flourished throughout recorded history, and rarely in greater profusion than during the last thirty years, there was no lack of raw material for study.

At the outset, the alternative courses of action are limited to one or the other. Either the American government has relations with another government, or it does not. And if it is decided to maintain relations, notwithstanding the evil character of the regime, there are, generally speaking, only three choices facing the American ambassador.

First, an envoy can disparage the dictator in private and skirt the edges of criticism in public, hoping that disapproval may weaken the usurper and encourage his enemies, thus promoting his overthrow. This procedure appeals to many well-intentioned amateurs in foreign affairs. No new administration in Washington is immune to their revelations. Despotism is evil, they declare, so therefore let us all help extirpate despotism. Ambassadors included.

There are several drawbacks, however. A police state is always well supplied with informers. The conversations of an ambassador criticizing a chief of state do not long remain confidential. They do not enhance the envoy's subsequent effectiveness in dealing with the despot or his government. If relations were not strained when the Ambassador arrived, they shortly become so.

And as for public criticism, if an ambassador wants to shorten his days in the country of his accreditation, a belittling speech or even a careless public comment can be by all odds the quickest shortcut to the nearest frontier crossing. Dictatorships are sensitive to anything the dictator interprets — or misinterprets — as an unfriendly reference to the existing Utopia.

The case of George Kennan when he was ambassador to Russia over a decade ago is pertinent. Kennan was in Berlin when, in response to a question by a newspaper correspondent, he made an observation concerning the lack of freedom under Communism. That gave Moscow the peg on which to hang a *persona non grata* demand, and Kennan did not return to the Soviet Union. Similarly, shortly after World War II, the articulate Adolf Berle, a former Assistant Secretary of State who was ambassador to Brazil, departed from Rio de Janeiro on the heels of a speech commenting on various aspects of the dictatorial regime of President Getulio Vargas.

Nor are dictatorships alone in their resentment of what they construe to be unwarranted activity by a foreign representative. President Cleveland over seventy years ago requested the recall of the British envoy in Washington for suggesting to a naturalized citizen that he vote for a Republican candidate. That was deemed interference in the domestic affairs of the American people.

There are more recent examples. In 1962 the American Ambassador to Peru was withdrawn when it became clear that the military junta which seized power after an inconclusive election, was not going to crawl into a Rimac cave and eat spider webs just because the American envoy considered their coup d'état immoral. By his show of disapproval, the Ambassador forfeited his usefulness.

And in 1963 a dictator in Haiti, who is a comic figure only to those out of reach of his jungle claw, declared *persona non grata* a competent American ambassador because he represented a government that had indicated it viewed Papa Duvalier with something less than admiration.

Another reason why criticism of a dictator by a foreign representative is rarely efficacious is that it can easily play into the ruler's hands by giving him the opportunity to raise the cry of intervention. The dictator promptly casts himself in the role of defender of the fatherland. Controlling the press and radio, he conveys so unedifying a portrait of the bullying Colossus of the Potomac that local patriotism is aroused. The oppressed multitude closes ranks. The dictator is strengthened.

Standing up to American pressure is thus a favorite posture among dictators. Even when no pressure has been applied the same maneuver can serve, this time as Operation Red Herring. An irresponsible President of Brazil was not above attempting such a gambit against the American ambassador in 1961; to its discredit, the State Department let the Brazilian politician get away with it.

Even when American diplomatic activity succeeds in unseating an unsavory ruler, the results can be disappointing. In 1933 Sumner Welles went to Cuba with a mandate to get rid of President Machado. When the dictator fled the country, Welles engineered his replacement by a tidy, housebroken liberal, with an immaculate program. The only fly in the ointment of this diplomatic achievement was that with the fall of the hated Machado, pent-up tropical passions exploded, and Cespedes — the hand-picked substitute for the dictator — lacked the necessary toughness to govern. Cespedes lasted only a few days, but for weeks thereafter the Pearl of the Antilles, torn by revolution, resembled a madhouse.

Order was finally restored by an ambitious young man of mixed antecedents, who had been an Army sergeant under Machado. Fulgencio Batista, with some shrewd professional assistance from Welles' successor, finally managed to get the lid back on the Pandora's Box that early New Deal diplomacy so recklessly opened.

All in all, the maneuvers of an ambassador seeking to bring about a change in local government are rarely triumphant. When they succeed, the results are not as foreseen, and Uncle Sam is likely to be left holding the bag. And when those activities fail, the representative concerned is frequently an *ex-*

American ambassador, in circumstances that add little to the prestige of the United States.

Many of those who speak glibly about the New Diplomacy and the alleged desirability of having the accredited representative of the United States play a more positive role are really asking that the American envoy take out a license as a busybody-with-all-the-answers. Their fellow dreamers, who would have the American representative not only disparage dictators but also operate as an accelerator of social evolution in what Washington describes as Underdeveloped Countries, would also do well to examine the record.

Overzealousness was identified with failure in diplomacy long before M. Talleyrand gave voice to his famous advice about it.

Alternatively, an envoy, hoping to discover a dictator's better nature and then to manipulate it in the direction of more decent behavior, may seek to become intimate with the chief of state to whom he is accredited. This aspiration often gratifies the dictator, and personal relations soon become cozy. The ambassador and the dictator are photographed dedicating public works projects and judging poultry exhibits. At the Jockey Club they share the Presidential Box, overlooking the races. The dictator's yacht is mobilized, with a discreet intimation that entertainment need not be confined to fishing for marlin.

Before long the ambassador and the dictator are practically on a first-name basis. The ambassador is flattered by being asked all manner of questions about how the local government should operate. He modestly reports this to Washington. He concludes that, notwithstanding some past mistakes and repressions, the chief of state is really a capital fellow, patriotic at heart, and with well-conceived plans for liberalizing his regime at the first opportunity. It takes a while, the ambassador observes, to prepare the natives for the tasks of administration. Meanwhile his subordinates are discouraged from developing contacts with opposition elements. The picture is rosy.

Numerous American representatives have subscribed to this Butter-Up-the-Dictator school, which owes something of its popularity to the fact that the person whom the leader delighteth to honor has a much more pleasant time of it in a dictatorship than if he undertakes to criticize the way things are going or to hold himself aloof from them. Certain envoys accredited to Juan and Evita Perón during the decade of their depredations in Argentina come to mind in this connection. There are others who enjoyed the lush aspects of Havana living in the 1950's. It is possible that the wartime relationship with our Soviet ally, regarded today as a disillusioning experience, may have conditioned the American people toward believing that there might be some good in even the ugliest political system. More than a few Americans went along with Uncle Joe when he declared benignly that the Chinese Reds might not be Communists at all, but Simple Agrarian Reformers.

A fault with the Butter-Up-the-Dictator treatment is that it rarely succeeds in influencing the chief of state in any significant direction. Ruling through fear and accustomed to living in the atmosphere that fear engenders, the dictator has little inclination to experiment with tactics his instinct tells him may be dangerous to survival. Or he may have no better nature to be appealed to by the ambassador. In either case, chances are that the indigenous strong man, playing before his home audience and familiar with local conditions, will succeed in using the ambassador, rather than that the latter will temper the character of the dictator. And the liberal reform program is always around the next kilometer post, to be adopted after the people have had further experience.

The spectacle of the American diplomatic representative, arms around the neck of a despot, disheartens the friends of liberty, who ought to be the friends of the United States. Decent people are disgusted, and the prestige of the United States is not enhanced. Moreover, when at long last the tyrant is overthrown, people remember the photographs of him and the ambassador having good times together. The ambassador is almost as discredited as the cast-out oppressor. The victorious revolution may even shout for the scalp of the ousted dictator's diplomatic crony. The envoy beats an ignominious retreat, citing Impelling Personal Reasons for returning to private business. A new United States envoy must hastily be appointed.

The back-seat drivers and volunteer statesmen, often strangely quiet while the dictator and the ambassador are caressing one another, suddenly burst into an indignant chorus. They urge that the new American representative be instructed to demand the holding of immediate elections . . .

There remains a third ambassadorial approach to the problem of dealing with dictatorships. It is rarely publicized at the time, for its success often depends on inconspicuousness and lack of glamour, rather than on public gestures susceptible of daily newspaper coverage. It lies midway between the critical and the butter-him-up schools, and its successful execution requires more professional competence than either.

A description of this third approach comes, curiously enough, from one of its less ascendant practitioners. To the genuine democracies, said Vice President Nixon at the end of an unprofitable safari around South America, I would give a warm and brotherly *abrazo,* whereas dictatorial governments should receive no more than a correct and formal handshake. Oversimplified, but it gives the idea. It implies that the ambassador should not lend himself to the vainglory or self-advertising of the dictator, or become identified personally with the dictator or his projects. Public speeches lauding the regime should be avoided. While standing apart from these things, the envoy should not hesitate to act on behalf of American interests.

Mr. Nixon would probably not claim to be the inventor of the policy of disassociating one's diplomacy from a dictator. In a small way in a small country, I myself pursued such a policy two decades ago in the Dominican Republic. Those efforts

220

were endorsed by the Secretary of State, and they succeeded as long as Washington backed them.

The dictator was Rafael Leonidas Trujillo, self-proclaimed *Benefactor de la Patria*. He ran the Dominican Republic as his private *hacienda*. The tragedy of Santo Domingo was that President Trujillo's qualities as leader and executive were overshadowed by almost indescribable personal excesses and by a vanity the satisfaction of which required adulation on a fantastic scale.

Trujillo's was as vicious a regime as has afflicted the New World since Columbus discovered it.

The character of the Trujillo dictatorship was, of course, known to the State Department. As a young man the Under Secretary of State had written a definitive history of the Dominican Republic. The same official had also, not long before my appointment as Ambassador, done his best to force Trujillo out of office for the massacre of several thousand Haitian peasants along the western frontier. With the other American republics rising against him, the *Benefactor* beat the charges by bribing the President of Haiti to concede, in effect, that there were two sides to the machete.

And Cordell Hull, no friend of tyrants, must have known that while the American government was paying its Ambassador ten thousand dollars a year to carry out official policies in Santo Domingo, Trujillo was paying a prominent American politician one hundred thousand dollars to frustrate those policies in Washington. In a battle of pocketbooks, the representative of the richest country in the world is often outgunned.

Having nevertheless been instructed before I left Washington to resist efforts to utilize the American Ambassador for the further aggrandizement of President Trujillo, the means to accomplish this were wisely left undefined. The first moves, possibly taking the *Benefactor* by surprise, were gratifyingly successful.

During the war, the United States undertook to feed the entire Caribbean area. The Dominican Republic is one of the few islands producing a surplus of foodstuffs, and a contract was entered into whereby President Trujillo agreed to sell to the American government, for distribution to the food-deficient areas, all the beans and meat and corn not required by the Dominican people. The contract stipulated that the prices paid by the United States would be published in the Dominican Republic; Washington wanted to make sure the Dominican farmers knew what President Trujillo was receiving. Trujillo, of course, did *not* want the prices to become public. The contract had been signed several months before my arrival, but no publication of prices had taken place.

When the omission was called to the attention of the Dominican Foreign Minister, he professed astonishment. "An oversight that will be corrected immediately, *Señor Embajador*. Think nothing of it."

I waited for two weeks and then took the contract to President Trujillo. He, too, professed astonishment. "Think nothing of it, *Señor Embajador*. An oversight that will be remedied without delay."

And when again nothing happened, except that by now the food crops were being harvested, and sold by the farmers for a fraction of the American prices, the embassy bought space in the Dominican newspapers and published the schedule. Whereupon the take of the farmers was increased.

While these events were occurring, President Trujillo decided to organize a Victory-in-Europe parade, to advertise the satisfaction of the Dominican people with the Allied landings in France. It was my first experience with a Spontaneous Popular Demonstration as generated in a dictatorship, and it must be admitted that when the *Benefactor* snapped his fingers, and his police went from house to house with the Word, Trujillo really put the population of his ancient capital on the streets, flags in hand and arrayed in order of marching.

The parade lasted three hours, under a broiling midsummer sun. Even the women of Santo Domingo marched, with banners that took note of the *Benefactor's* mother, referred to as *La Primera Madre de la Republica.* President Trujillo himself wore one of his gaudiest uniforms, corresponding to his five-star rank of Generalissimo of the Dominican forces. Foreign ambassadors, whom the President grouped around him while innumerable photographs were taken, wore by request striped trousers, cutaway coats, and high hats.

Horse blankets would have been as appropriate for the ardent Caribbean summer, and three hours was a long time, even for diplomatic non-marchers.

It was definitely a score for the dictator of Santo Domingo, who managed to convey to foreign countries reached by his heavily subsidized publicity agents the false impressions of popular support for his regime and of international respect for his obtrusively bedecked person. In fact, so satisfying to the *Benefactor* was this display of solidarity that he shortly cranked up another parade, this time in honor of the Dominican contribution to the patriotic war effort — a contribution which in fact consisted of the aforesaid food contract, plus a commitment to grow as much sugar as possible, at attractive wartime prices.

More sartorial splendor for the *Benefactor,* and more sartorial roughage for the diplomats. Contemplating these portents and the advantage that might accrue to the dictator from another meretricious display of diplomats-in-his-pocket, I sent word to the Chief of Protocol that the American ambassador would be pleased to attend the projected celebration in a white suit and a Panama hat or, should that not be considered suitable, to be represented at the parade by an attaché in uniform.

Since President Trujillo needed the personal presence of the American envoy to add verisimilitude to the flexing of his patriotic muscles, the white suit was tolerated — and it created a sensation. In the atmosphere of pervasive terror that a truly

223

evil despotism can create, the serfs are so conditioned to leaping at the sound of the bell that when someone does not leap, the effect is far out of proportion to the circumstances — and the wonder of it runs like a fire before the wind.

President Trujillo was not amused — neither by the publication of food prices in his newspapers, which affected his pocketbook, nor by my sartorial declaration of independence, which affected his conceit. His serfs took note. The diplomats were delighted.

It was the brandy incident, trivial in itself, that I found the most satisfying of my personal tilts with President Trujillo. My predecessor had written me that the *Benefactor,* a two-fisted drinker, was addicted to only one kind of beverage. He would not, to be sure, reject a sip of ceremonial champagne when the national toast was proclaimed at the end of a dinner, but the liquor the dictator really liked to drink — in the place of cocktails before a meal, as a highball with soda and ice instead of wine during the meal, and undiluted when dinner was over — was a vituperative Spanish brandy called *Carlos Primero,* distilled by the firm of Pedro Domecq at Jerez de la Frontera and, incidentally, not easy to come by. It just so happened, wrote my predecessor, that at the time of my appointment he had on hand half a case of that rare beverage so admired by the chief of state, which he would be happy to leave for the new ambassador.

Remembering wartime transportation difficulties, I was appropriately grateful — until I received a chit from my predecessor, after I myself had reached Ciudad Trujillo. The outgoing ambassador billed me $210 for six bottles of *Carlos Primero*. Two hundred and ten dollars represented in 1944 one week's salary as American representative in the Dominican Republic. My predecessor also informed me that President Trujillo, who may have heard of the Borgias, expected wherever he went to have a new bottle of *Carlos Primero* opened in his presence.

The embassy representation allowance, then as now inadequate to the demands of official entertaining, was not geared to that sort of drinking. Neither was the American ambassador, who could not see adding thirty-five dollars for one bottle of brandy to his personal tab every time the President of the Republic accepted Embassy hospitality. The first time around, the *Benefactor* accordingly had his unopened bottle, when he attended the customary dinner given by the newly arrived ambassador: *Carlos Primero* was resplendent in crinkly cellophone and a ribbon, with seal, around the neck of the bottle.

But when the dictator appeared at the Embassy for the Fourth of July reception a few weeks later, I signaled the Dominican houseboy. "Roberto," I said, "bring me the President's bottle."

And when Roberto, almost palsied with apprehension, placed the obviously violated *Carlos Primero* on the garden table beside us, I hefted the bottle for Trujillo and the other guests, concentrating on the proceedings, to see. The bottle was still half full, just as the President left it the night of the dinner.

"*Vuestra Excelencia,*" I told him politely, "your own bottle. I have been saving it for you."

For these and other reasons, the Benefactor of Santo Domingo had no love for the American ambassador. However, he could hardly expel a foreign envoy over a brandy bottle: the power exercised by a dictator, although appearing absolute, is inherently fragile. Trujillo would have had to run the risk of making himself ridiculous, which no despot is eager to do. To have the incident be public knowledge was a double frustration. The Benefactor was fuming . . .

In the context of harsh Dominican dictatorship, those gestures were not absurd. They were independent and unintimidated; they earned the dictator's respect, if not his liking. They also maintained self-respect, which no American representative should surrender.

225

The Trujillo dictatorship lasted thirty blood-soaked years. Then one day the medicine he had prescribed with such cynical ferocity for so many of his fellow countrymen was administered to President Trujillo himself, the protagonist of ruling by murder. In 1961 the *Benefactor* was assassinated.

In the words of Hilaire Belloc: "I wept — for I had longed to see him hanged."

The question is sometimes asked, paraphrasing the amateurs in foreign affairs who complained a generation ago about a minor civility to King Carol, what purpose is served by having diplomatic relations with governments we disapprove of, or that declare hostility toward the principles on which our own country is founded. Soviet Russia. Spain, before the rehabilitation of the Caudillo. Papa Duvalier's Haiti. Red China. Castro's Cuba. The Hungary that in 1956 crucified freedom. Nazi Germany.

In considering these pernicious regimes, the notion should be discarded that the morals of a government (assuming it has any) control the desirability of recognizing it or transacting business with it. The only intelligent criterion is the interest of the United States, which may sometimes be advanced by dealing with an unprincipled government, or sometimes retarded. Though the incidence may vary from time to time, or country by country, the interest of the United States should remain constant — the primary, the only criterion. It may be deplorable that all governments are not freely chosen and incorruptible, but until that millennium arrives, there will continue to be disreputable regimes which it may be prudent as well as expedient not to ignore and sometimes to deal with.

Therefore the search for a doctrine to serve as a guide for recognizing regimes or entering into relations with them is generally futile. If found, such a doctrine could easily become the refuge of unimaginative politicians and textbook statesmen. The Estrada Doctrine, which would have relations exist automatically, is too rigid for general applicability.

It follows that the *attitude* of the American government to-

226

ward having diplomatic relations — as distinct from the *tactics* to be employed when such relations have already been established — ought to be as flexible as possible. It should likewise be realistic, tough, and pragmatic. It should not be cluttered up with wishful thinking, nor moist from having been dunked in an ethical culture.

It is only after a decision is made to maintain relations with a dictatorship that the question, What Kind of Relations, arises. Here tactics have to be considered. Here the element of choice enters. Here what are you going to do next becomes an immediate practical problem.

Not all dictatorships are equal, much less are they all equally evil. For example, the history of some of the American republics gives little encouragement to believe in their ultimate ability to use the instruments of democratic government. In the present conjunction of their affairs, a so-called benevolent dictatorship in a Paraguay or a Nicaragua may provide a practical solution, although a Perón in Argentina proved an unmitigated disaster, and the people of Santo Domingo will long wear the scars inflicted during the era of Trujillo.

The future of the Asian and African succession states remains obscure, but not much thus far is discernible to encourage the belief that a paramount chief is less (or more) efficient in the administration of justice than his son with a veneer of foreign education and ambitions to rig an election.

Governments do not often perish because other governments disapprove of them. Embracing a moral judgment can be stimulating, but it can also lead to painful bruises and contusions, from which the State Department has not always been saved in the clinches. Although the analogy of the treatment of individuals — if you sup with the Devil you need a long spoon — may have only limited validity in foreign affairs, the lesson derived from experience is that a safe way to treat bad dictatorships is at arm's length, so that the self-respect of the American government and people is unimpaired.

There can be little excuse for countenancing intimacies with a regime such as the one ended by the extermination of the Benefactor of Santo Domingo. An American decoration should no longer be awarded to an oppressor because he shouts anti-Communist slogans. No American official should cultivate a supple spine before a tyrant, nor should he become the sycophant of a despot.

For the rest, the care and feeding of dictators should not be left to nature lovers, however well intentioned, but to professional animal trainers.

XIV.

The Korean Armistice — A Decade Later

THIS chapter was completed a few weeks before the death of General Douglas MacArthur in the spring of 1964. There has been no significant addition since his death to the information available on the decision to end the war by stalemate instead of victory. That was a judgment the dismal consequences of which grow more apparent every day. I see no reason, therefore, to modify the text which follows.

Whenever I see Vietnam or Laos on the front page, I am reminded of my first interview with President Rhee of Korea, when he told me that peace without victory in the Korean War would be an illusion, and that if the Communists were not forcibly ejected from his country, Korea might remain permanently divided.

"And what is more," warned the old gentleman, "if we don't defeat the Communists in Korea, it may all have to be fought over again, somewhere else in Asia."

That conversation took place when I presented my credentials in the battle-scarred capital of Seoul, in November of 1952. The armistice negotiations at Panmunjom had been stalled for over a year in acrimonious debate over the prisoners of war, and meantime the shooting continued, with mounting casualties. For President Rhee, the occasion of my arrival served as a rehearsal for his impending meeting with the President-elect of the United States, who had promised a few weeks earlier, just before the end of his political campaign, that if elected he would hurry out to Korea and do something about the war. Eisenhower's first task, he announced, would be to "review and reexamine every course of action with one goal in view: to bring the Korean War to an early and honorable end."

One result of this promise was that President Truman told me to curtail my leave and to make no unessential stop between the Potomac and my new post. "Because if you do," said the President, "General Eisenhower will get to Korea before the new American ambassador. I've offered him the Independence to fly out in, but whether he uses it or not, you had better get going."

By leaning-in on a Great Circle course, with a day snowbound on an Aleutian island and another spent listening to General Mark Wayne Clark in Tokyo, I managed to reach Korea before the visit of the President-elect. When Eisenhower arrived, he toured the front, and the cheers of the startled GI's echoed in the thin December air. It is not recorded whether the applause was for the successful Republican candidate, or for the man who had promised to extricate them from the Korean trenches.

At dinner at Eighth Army Headquarters, only Americans were present. The mickey-mouse boots of the patrolling MP's crunched on the deep-frosted ground outside, and the two-inch steaks had been flown all the way from Australia. Young Major Eisenhower mixed the drinks in General Van Fleet's hitherto dry mess, and the whiskers of Charles Wilson, unmowed since he left the United States, were a formidable addition to the decorations.

Around the table that night eight American officers — seven in uniform and an eighth who was the guest of honor — accounted for thirty-five stars. But for all of that there was little discussion of the stalled military operations, possibly because the views of some of the generals and admirals were closer to those of President Rhee than they were to those of the veteran soldier who was about to become President of the United States.

Next morning at Kyun Mu Dai, against the shoulder of North Mountain, General Eisenhower paid a courtesy call on Syngman Rhee, who had spent sixty of his eighty years struggling for the independence of Korea. Rhee rubbed the tips of his stiffened fingers together and urged his guest to throw the Chinese Communists out of his country. Any other ending, he reiterated, would settle nothing. With his fine new ROK army, trained and equipped by the Americans, the Korean President, unlike his United Nations allies, was full of martial spirit. If he could have persuaded Vice Admiral Clark to take USS *Missouri,* then flagship of the Seventh Fleet, on a mission to bombard Dairen or Antung, President Rhee would gladly have gone along as supercargo.

But warlike words were not what the President-elect of the United States wanted to hear in the autumn of 1952, nor the American people either. And as for the fifteen allies, most of them wanted no further part in the fighting.

The armistice itself came eight months later, and it is doubtful whether it was substantially influenced, or even accelerated, by the pre-inauguration Eisenhower visit to Korea, albeit the campaign speech promising to go there may have attracted some additional votes for the Republican candidate.

President Rhee opposed the armistice throughout, and at one time Washington believed he all but wrecked the negotiations. That was when Rhee liberated the twenty-five thousand North Korean anti-Communist prisoners of war, thereby defying the United Nations Command. His action almost caused hysterics in Washington, where it was widely believed that the Communists might seize the excuse to cancel the truce talks.

General Clark and the American ambassador were accordingly instructed to remonstrate, in terms reflecting bitter Potomac anguish, but the venerable Korean statesman had us over an A-frame, and he knew it, for as soon as the Korean POW's had accepted Rhee's invitation to leave the stockades, there was absolutely no way to round them up. Within minutes the

231

happy prisoners melted into the rest of the population of South Korea, and no one, least of all United Nations Command, could possibly get them together again. In many quarters there was sympathy for Rhee's action, which some observers believed was overdue, but it would have been worth the ambassadorial toga to say so at that time to the State Department.

Up at Panmunjom, vilification filled the air as the Communists screamed their heads off, but it was largely an act, for they had no intention of terminating the truce negotiations. Instead, they charged collusion between President Rhee and the American government in springing the prisoners, an accusation which so annoyed Washington that presently an Assistant Secretary of State was dispatched to Seoul to supplement the monitory fingers shaken at the unrepentant old President by Generals Wayne Clark and Maxwell Taylor, plus the American ambassador.

The best the Assistant Secretary could accomplish was to extract from Rhee a qualified promise not to violate the impending armistice, if and when it should be signed, but the Korean President continued to decline to have anything to do with the negotiation of the truce, and he continued to proclaim that a cease-fire without victory would be the equivalent of a United Nations defeat, and that it would store up trouble for the future.

A defense pact brought personally to President Rhee by Secretary of State Dulles within a week of the signing of the armistice mollified Rhee somewhat, but it failed to change his attitude toward implementing the truce. He refused to allow the five thousand Indian troops, dispatched to superintend the prisoners-of-war exchange, to set foot on Republic of Korea territory — a decision which multiplied the logistic problem of United Nations Command. The Indians had to be transferred from their troopships to an America carrier anchored off the Korean coast, whence they were flown by helicopter to the demilitarized zone now separating North from South Korea — all five thousand of them, with all of their equipment. It was the largest helicopter lift attempted up to that time, and for days the choppers shuttled back and forth between the flat-top and the peninsula, ferrying warriors in turbans. Had Rhee not objected, the Indians could easily have made the journey from the port of Inchon, by rail across Republic of Korea territory to the demilitarized zone, at a fraction of the effort that the United States expended in moving them by air.

At the same time, President Rhee made it so hot for the Czechs and Poles on the Neutral Nations Supervisory Commission that those members practically had to be smuggled from place to place in South Korea by the Fifth Air Force. Rhee argued that, unlike their opposite numbers the Swedes and Swiss, who were genuinely neutral, the Czechs and Poles were not neutral at all, but the same sort of Communists his soldiers had just been fighting, and would still be fighting if his allies had shown any gumption.

Nor was the President of Korea alone in his attitude toward the armistice. Although for the most part the American generals maintained at the time a disciplined stillness, many of them, in contrast to the GI's in the trenches, were nearly as unenthusiastic about the truce as Rhee was. Whereas Rhee's reason was political, based on his estimate of the future of Korea, to the generals the war had been a sterile and unrewarding experience. Aware of the preponderant resources of the United States over those of Communist China, the generals wanted either a clear-cut military decision, or at least the satisfaction of pushing the Communists sufficiently far beyond the 38th Parallel so that Washington's boast about "repelling aggression" would have some measure of validity.

Nevertheless, the fighting stopped on July 27, 1953, and the armistice, which the dictionary defines as "a temporary cessation of hostilities," has now endured for over a decade.

Conceived on the Communist side in vituperation and on the side of the Americans in frustration, the cease-fire did not

233

lead to a peace treaty, nor to any solution of the Korean problem, and as President Rhee predicted, the Communists have succeeded in keeping the Korean people divided.

From the point of view of the United States, the Korean War was "the most unpopular war we ever fought . . ." * There is no question but that the armistice responded overwhelmingly to the wishes — in 1953 — of the American people. Presidents Truman and Eisenhower and both political parties supported the truce, not to forget the American soldiers who had been doing the fighting.

Our United Nations allies were as eager for a truce as the American people. Several of them had never been interested in military victory, but only in pushing the North Koreans back to the 38th Parallel. That done, those allies favored calling it a day. And from the moment the Chinese Communists intervened, the Europeans experienced an almost psychopathic fear lest the Korean struggle expand into a third World War.

It remains to consider in the light of the ten years that have elapsed since the Korean armistice was signed, whether that truce was *good,* as it seemed at that time to most Americans and to the majority of our allies, or *bad,* as the armistice seemed to veteran President Rhee — the only chief executive whose territory was directly concerned.

The armistice stopped the carnage, and that is still the most important thing that can be said about it. American casualties had exceeded 137,000, including thirty-three thousand dead. Of the way the war was fought, the soldiers themselves have already written; no civilian can add to their valor. Korean military losses were immensely greater than those of the United States, plus one million non-combatants killed and approximately four million more made homeless or destitute. For thirty-seven months the peninsula had literally been drenched in blood.

* *The Eisenhower Years,* by Richard H. Rovere.

In the decade that ensued, the people of South Korea have had an opportunity to resume the process of national recuperation that began with the withdrawal of the defeated Japanese in 1945, after forty years of domination of the country. The territory of South Korea, rehabilitated since the truce by the United States at a cost of several billions of dollars, has not only been restored as the traditional food-producing area of the peninsula, but to a considerable extent it has been industrialized as well, to compensate the Republic of Korea for the loss of the manufacturing facilities of the north, which remain in Communist hands.

Substantial political experience has accrued to the Republic of Korea in the past ten years, even though the notion is still far from proved that the people are desirous of adapting themselves to a Western-type democracy, or that they ought to be subject to continuing pressure to make them conform to an alien pattern. Until almost the turn of the century Korea was a hermit kingdom, and the idea of popular government dates from the end of the Japanese occupation, less than twenty years ago. It should be remembered, too, that for half of the country Japanese occupation was exchanged for Communist control, with the 38th Parallel cutting the nation in two.

Before 1950, few Koreans except old President Rhee had experience in governing or in making a bureaucratic administrative machine operate. But by the end of the war, there was a whole new class of tough, able, and patriotic young Korean generals, their competence tested and their ambitions aroused. It was inevitable that with the departure of Dr. Rhee, the generals should fill the political vacuum. What has been remarkable is the order the generals have maintained and the efficiency with which they have gone about civilian political business.

Another result of the armistice — or perhaps more accurately of the Korean war itself — was the precedent it created in the direction of international effort and multinational un-

235

dertaking, under the aegis of United Nations. That is an aspect broader than Korea alone. Granted that the Korean War as a United Nations enterprise was made possible by the boycott of the Security Council by the Soviet member in June 1950, nevertheless the forging of over a dozen different national military units into a United Nations Command was a formidable achievement. It reflected credit upon all the governments concerned, and especially on the United States, which bore the brunt of the operation.

Although the separate national contingents may have been small beside the United States and Republic of Korea divisions, they were made up of professional soldiers and experienced fighting men. The Filipinos and the Turks and the Thais fought as stoutly as the British or French or Canadians. The Greeks joined the struggle, even though their own Communist war had scarcely ended. The Ethiopians lost not a single soldier to a prison camp.

Thus the blue and white emblem of the United Nations in Korea became a symbol of man's long struggle toward international cooperation. Few witnessed unmoved a United Nations honor guard, with sixteen sergeants in sixteen different national uniforms, each carrying his country's flag in review by a commander holding authority from a world organization. Without the Korean experience, it would have been far more difficult to organize United Nations security forces in Suez in 1956, in the Congo in 1960, and on Cyprus in 1964. The current NATO project for a multinational force likewise owes much to the success of United Nations military collaboration in Korea.

Notwithstanding these achievements, which are substantial, the debit side of the armistice ledger is heavily weighted.

By accepting a military stalemate in 1953, the Allies practically guaranteed that there would be no predictable settlement of the Korean problem, which the United States itself had created by an ill-starred military decision in 1945, that

236

north of the 38th Parallel the surrender of the Japanese forces would be to the Russians, and south of it to the United States. Although Soviet Russia had done no fighting in Asia, the Potsdam Agreement made them partners in the Far East victory. Arrived in North Korea, the Russians did just as they were doing in Europe: they dug in.

A Communist regime was quickly established in North Korea, and belated American efforts to work out an arrangement for free elections and the unification of the country were blocked by the Soviet government. With that background, there never was any reason to anticipate that the Korean armistice would produce a different outcome on unification; the failure of the Geneva Conference, held in 1954 pursuant to the armistice, should have surprised no one.

The Korean people were thus condemned by the cease-fire to indefinite separation, with half the country still in bondage. The only way that could have been avoided would have been by military victory over the Chinese Communists, as demanded by President Rhee. In 1953 the United States and its United Nations allies were unwilling to pay the price of such a victory.

It is interesting to speculate on the point at which the will to win the Korean war was replaced by American eagerness to accept a stalemate. In the first ten weeks, the North Korean Communists overran almost the entire peninsula. Everything except the tiny "Pusan perimeter" was shortly in Communist hands. The first United Nations-United States objective was to preserve the small remaining piece of Korean territory while counterstrength could be mobilized and brought to bear. To stem the onslaught, to contain the North Korean advance, and then to push the enemy out of South Korea — back to the 38th Parallel — that was what was meant, initially, by "repel the Communist aggression."

General MacArthur's surprise landing at Inchon on September 16, 1950 — less than three months after the Communist attack — turned the tables on the North Koreans. The landing was a brilliant operation. Outflanked, the North Koreans collapsed. They fled northward, over the Parallel. The war was transformed almost overnight into a mopping-up operation.

At that point, Communist aggression had in fact been repelled. Seoul was liberated, and President Rhee was back again in his capital. In the United States, everyone relaxed. It remained only to watch MacArthur chase the vanquished North Korean Communists out of the country.

This military picture was reversed again with equal suddenness, after MacArthur's miscalculation of Chinese intentions. In October, 1950, during his only personal conference with President Truman, MacArthur reportedly assured the President that the Chinese would not enter the conflict. Late in the following month, on the very eve of Chinese intervention, General MacArthur was still predicting the end of the war by Christmas. Almost in sight of the Yalu River, his lines over-extended and his forces divided, MacArthur's troops were suddenly attacked by one million hard-bitten Chinese, and nearly overwhelmed by them.

There followed the heroic but ignominious escape of the mauled UN forces, back again to positions south of the 38th Parallel. Those who could not escape died, or were captured, and of the prisoners taken by the Communists many were not to survive their captivity. Seoul fell a second time, and the Korean government fled to Pusan.

At some moment between those dark days that ended 1950, and Russian U.N. Ambassador Malik's New York speech proposing a cease-fire six months later, American ambition to win the Korean War disintegrated.

Contributing to the inability of American leadership to make Korea intelligible to the American people was a babble of inconsistencies emanating from high quarters. In January of 1950, six months before the Communists tried to seize the country, the Secretary of State of the United States publicly declared that Korea was outside the perimeter of American defense. But within hours of the dawn when the Communist attack on Korea began, the United States not only committed its forces to go to the rescue of the South Korean Army, but the American government began mounting a United Nations campaign and mobilizing world public opinion.

In view of the official disclaimer of interest in Korea, all this must have bewildered the Communists as much as it probably enraged them. It likewise bewildered a considerable segment of the American people, who wondered whether that kind of talk might not have encouraged the Communists to believe they could gobble up South Korea with impunity.

The United Nations undertaking was shortly described in the United States as a crusade, but the crusading spirit lasted only so long as the North Koreans alone were involved. When the Chinese Communists crossed the Yalu and ambushed MacArthur's forces, the alliance came apart. When MacArthur appealed to Washington for war against the Chinese, including the bombing of Communist industrial targets and troop concentrations in Manchuria, our principal United Nations partners took fright.

The Prime Minister of Great Britain declared that "total victory means unlimited war" — meaning that any victory risked expanding the war — and he pointed a trembling finger across the horizon toward Siberia, where the Soviet Air Force crouched, watching events and presumably glowering. France joined the British Commonwealth in urging an impotent conclusion.

General MacArthur was a proconsul unafraid, who in addition was charmed by the sound of his own voice: he spoke and he wrote, and his controversy with President Truman over how the war should be fought simmered and smoked through the winter of 1951. It burst into flame with the General's dismissal.

MacArthur's phrase "there is no substitute for victory" appealed strongly to President Rhee, and privately to many American generals, but by then the American people had grown allergic to slogans. They were unhappy over the casualties, disillusioned with the crusade, and bewildered by all the altercations — including American congressional turmoil and the din generated by everyone shouting at once in the General Assembly.

The Soviet truce offensive was shrewdly timed.

By mid-1951, General Ridgeway, as successor to MacArthur, had made a start toward rolling the Communists north once again, but the Malik speech came at a moment when the American desire to win had been superseded by a desire to emerge from the Korean quagmire as quickly as possible.

When President Truman directed Ridgeway to arrange for peace talks, responsive to the Soviet suggestion, his decision was widely supported. Few then envisaged the two years of haggling and bloodshed before the truce would finally take effect, for, as far as the American people were concerned, in 1951 the Korean War was over.

It is conceivable that, with a cork in some of the purveyors of public discord and perhaps with different leadership, the American spirit might have been sustained or even revived following the Yalu disaster, the defection of the allies, and the MacArthur dismissal. Conceivable, but not probable, for after President Truman's courageous decision to go to the rescue of South Korea, our policy was poured into an international mold. Instead of maintaining flexibility and keeping our elbowroom, we committed ourselves to the United Nations Crusade.

Having capitalized on the Russian boycott of the Security Council to obtain veto-free directives on which the existence of the United Nations Command depended, the United States found itself chained to the U.N. concept of conducting the war, even though our allies, whose votes in the forum of the United Nations had been crucial there, furnished on the battlefield only three per cent of the effort. The United States made so much of the mere presence of our United Nations allies that when those allies wilted before what they thought was the menace of World War III, the United States was stymied. The American government had nowhere to go except into unilateral adventure — in partnership, to be sure, with stout-hearted Syngman Rhee — or else toward the cease-fire-without-victory that seemed the only other alternative.

It was a classic example of the wisdom of the injunction, Never allow a weak ally (in this case several of them) to make the decisions for you.

Ten years after the event it is easy to say that the United States ought to have chosen differently. But few sounds of the coming Peking-Moscow discord were audible a decade ago, and the prospect that Russia might join China if the United States bombed Manchuria could not be dismissed. To our European U.N. allies, themselves so recently under fire, the specter of World War III was a palpable menace.

At all events, the decision not to bomb beyond the Yalu gave the Communists safe haven there, thus to an important degree neutralizing American air and naval superiority and ensuring delivery of the Communist supplies and munitions wherewith they continued to fight, through all the tedious and stultifying months the truce talks were in session. Next to the decision to intervene on the side of the Republic of Korea in June, 1950, not to bomb Manchuria was the key decision of the war.

Only by the most optimistic stretch of the imagination could the armistice of 1953 be regarded as "repelling Communist aggression." What had really happened was that the Chinese Communists had reconquered half the country, and held it. The demilitarized zone separating the two Koreas begins on the west below the 38th Parallel, and angles across the peninsula to a point a few miles north of the Parallel on the Sea of Japan. It follows the battle-line that existed when the truce

241

was being drafted, but for practical purposes it is the status quo before the Communist attack of June 25, 1950. The hocus-pocus emitted by those who sought to convey the notion that the Communists had reeled out of the Korean ring with a bloody nose was scarcely convincing to anyone, even without old President Rhee shouting dissent from the sidelines.

By whatever name it is called, the armistice gave enormous prestige to the Chinese Communists, and prestige does not attach to failure. Not only had the Communists driven out of North Korea the Americans and their allies (including the British and French, whose troops had dealt so summarily with Chinese forces during all the nineteenth century), but the Chinese had then contained their adversaries along the 38th Parallel for over two years.

It would be difficult to overestimate the importance of this achievement. And added to the military renown that flowed from the establishment of the Chinese soldier as a fighting man was the fact that for two long years of negotiation, first at Kaesong and then at Panmunjom, the Communists had publicly pilloried, abused, and vilified their opponents, who sat there and took it. By behaving publicly, at the truce table, in the most deliberately offensive fashion, and by getting away with it, the Chinese added further to their stature, especially among other Asiatics, and in uncommitted areas as well.

The Chinese Communists were able to do this because they correctly comprehended that the eagerness of their enemies to reach an armistice agreement was greater than their own. While the Communists likewise sought a truce, they were in no great hurry about it. They were prepared to defer reaching an agreement and meanwhile to go on fighting. That gave the Communists a negotiating advantage that they exploited every hour of every day.

The same vicious and abusive truculence that was in evidence during the truce talks characterizes to this day the meetings of the joint commission that oversees the armistice. Every time the Communists shoot a United Nations soldier, they declare he was caught *in flagrante delicto;* they offer to spit in the eye of the complaining American general to prove it. And when the Communists shoot down an unarmed helicopter, they either deny it or refuse to discuss what they have done with the pilot.

Another result of the Korean armistice was the acceleration of the defeat of the French in Indochina, and the emergence of Laos, Vietnam, and Cambodia. If anyone can think of three more throbbing headaches than those three limp and dismal succession states, let him proclaim his discovery and become the first argonaut to light a bonfire on the floor of the ocean. As soon as the shooting stopped in Korea, the Chinese Communists were able to turn their attention to Southeast Asia, and Dien Bien Phu was next. The same Geneva Conference that uselessly debated Korea in 1954 also ratified the partition of Indochina, along the 17th Parallel.

France was doubtless destined eventually to relinquish her Asiatic colony, but the Korean truce hastened the process. The eviction proceedings looked to the Orient, and to the rest of the world as well, like La Belle France getting the Old Heave Ho from Ho Chi-minh, with an assist from the victorious truce champions of Panmunjom, the Chinese Communists.

Lastly, the Korean armistice paved the way for neutralism, a Pandora's box still polluting the international atmosphere. Neutralism may well be one of the most unfortunate of all the results brought about by allied acceptance of the stalemate in Korea. A whole covey of nations was perched on the fence, awaiting the outcome in Korea. When it became apparent that the United States and its allies were not going to win, those countries within a prudent radius of Mao Tse Tung and his merry men got off the fence and climbed aboard the neutralist garbage wagon, that depository of dead hopes and decayed ambitions. Three out of four of them have remained there to this day, neutral *against* the United States. Other states in other hemispheres have been content to be neutral neutrals, while still others have preferred to bore their contemporaries with philosophical neutralism. And most of them, as underdeveloped as their leaders are overarticulate, have coupled their neutrality with demands for American largesse, for which they believe it would be un-neutral to give anything to the United States in return.

Although the moving finger has not yet finished writing the history of twentieth-century Korea, more of the script is legible today than at Panmunjom when the armistice negotiations were in progress. Enough now can be deciphered so that it seems doubtful whether the Korean truce of 1953 is likely to be listed as an act of statesmanship on the part of the American government.

President Truman has received full marks for going to the rescue of Communist-attacked Korea in June of 1950, but what of his change of heart less than six months later, when General MacArthur wanted to counter the equally unprovoked onslaught of the Chinese by blasting their lairs in Manchuria? What deterred the President then was his fainthearted allies, to whom Truman was mortgaged by his United Nations diplomacy; but the same fortitude which saw the United States intervene in Korea in the first place might also have carried the war to a more successful conclusion than the truce that settled nothing.

No one thus far can compute the value of forcing Communism to disgorge the first piece of looted territory. For altogether too long, Communist adventures have resulted in Communist gains, with each stolen acre added to those already enslaved. The effect on the affairs of the world of turning this tide remains to be experienced, but it could be prodigious. In Korea, an opportunity to do so was frittered away at the cease-fire conference table.

Korea may have been "the wrong war, at the wrong time, in the wrong place," as some in the United States ten years ago were proclaiming. In Korea, nevertheless, the United States had a stalwart ally, whose citizens hate Communism and have steadfastly opposed it. Compared to those in Southeast Asia who seem incapable of fighting for their own salvation, the Koreans were assets of incalculable value, but at the cease-fire table those assets were squandered.

And in the ultimate assessment, the Korean armistice brought not peace but neutralism: a refuge for the cautious and a haven for the faint-hearted.

XV.

No Charge for the Extra Buttons

THE next three chapters are stories of Greece. They contribute nothing to archaeology, but they may perhaps illustrate some of the matters that face a twentieth-century diplomat when he is not signing a treaty, or trying to persuade his government not to get involved in the Cyprus question, or taking a Congressman to visit the Acropolis.

How to present credentials to a king, and how to prepare a birthday cake for that same monarch are, moreover, tributes to my friend the Grand Marshal of Greece. Having from time to time said certain things about some of those who afflict the conduct of foreign affairs, it is a pleasure to record my admiration for the professionals of protocol who, like Dimitri Levidis, arc rarely thanked and too often taken for granted.

Because no table has been invented that will permit all guests to sit at the same distance from the host and hostess, and no doorway is wide enough so that everyone can pass through it at once, protocol exists. It is the science of determining who does what and who goes where, in what order. Without protocol, most international occasions would be riots, and the intercourse of nations would soon be paralyzed.

Protocol is often of labyrinthine complexity, and the distinctions even among officials of the same nationality are frequently tenuous and subtle. Each hazard is multiplied when foreigners are present. Furthermore, protocol deals with exacerbated and hence often unreasonable human beings — officials exhausted by lengthy public display; irritated by sun-in-eyes, interminable oratory, popping flashlight bulbs, inaccessibility of facilities, or overdue victuals; people feeling that if they are not accorded the precedence they deserve (or imagine they deserve), they may be denounced when photographs of the ceremony reach distant homelands.

Precedence, an inseparable component of protocol, can be an apple of discord second only to a ticking bomb in destruc tive potential. In the name of precedence, otherwise honorable and trustworthy citizens have been known to plot, scheme, bribe, steal, and swindle, all in order to switch place cards at an official table or to get through a doorway ahead of a rival. Monitoring these problems of pride and frustration does not enhance the popularity of the protocol officer, who is vulnerable because he stands apart from substantive operations, and also because he wears fancy regalia.

Protocol is likewise the organizing of such official events as presidential visits abroad, and ceremonies incident to the acceptance by a chief of state of the credentials of a newly arrived ambassador — the latter one of mankind's oldest confrontations, going back to the initial tribal chieftain who sent an emissary to assure a second tribal chieftain of the first chieftain's creditable intentions.

Notwithstanding a current Washington effort to reduce the credentials ceremony to the equivalent of one Rotarian meeting another Rotarian at a Wednesday luncheon, the reception of a foreign envoy has traditionally been a formal occasion. An ambassador is still the personal representative of his chief of state, as well as the official representative of the sending government.

I nevertheless welcomed the opportunity to be presented to the King of the Hellenes, wearing the white mess jacket authorized by the Grand Marshal of the Court. The garment detracted nothing from the ceremony in King Paul's summer palace on the Island of Corfu, and the mess jacket was less uncomfortable on a Greek summer day than either the white-tie-and-tails or the morning coat and striped trousers which the Grand Marshal could have decreed for my reception.

It was my first encounter with Dimitri Levidis, and I was grateful to him.

This same hero of my credentials ceremony played a key role in the visit shortly thereafter of the President of the United States to Greece, as described in Chapter XVI. For half a century Colonel Levidis had served the Royal Family with unsurpassed devotion. Experience had bred into the Grand Marshal a knowledge of procedure and ceremonial and of the practical details of arranging people at events. This gift of five decades of experience Dimitri Levidis placed at the disposition of the American ambassador, as soon as the American Presidential visit to Greece was announced. Levidis was of incalculable assistance to the Embassy not only during the Presidential visit itself, but also during the weeks of preparation and the elaboration of those ruthless details, inattention to which can wreck a mission.

I had hoped that Dimitri might be able to read this tribute. These pages that praise his name and talents might have given him pleasure. They would have been a modest payment on account, in the coin of admiration and friendship.

Dimitri Levidis died in February of 1964, in the fifty-second year of his service to Greece, and two weeks before the death of his sovereign, King Paul.

My words are offered, therefore, in a broader context, as an obeisance to the Grand Marshal of Greece, and also to the international guild of ceremonial officers, who toil so diligently and are thanked so seldom. From Washington to Tokyo, from Helsinki to Canberra, may their craft be honored.

Then in my sadness I remembered various royal travels outside Greece. I recalled that when King Paul left Athens on a trip, he was customarily preceded by the Grand Marshal of the Court, who went ahead to make arrangements and to look after the reception and comfort of his monarch abroad.

Whenever the King arrived, he found a welcome and everything set in order by his Grand Marshal. And it occurred to me that when King Paul made his final voyage, and reached his final destination, there he would have found Dimitri Levidis, loyally waiting.

Dimitri would have liked that. It was a comforting thought.

It is a notion widely held by those having little to do with diplomacy that diplomats love to dress up like elephants at a rajah's wedding.

Legend further holds that American diplomats resent the restrictions put upon them by an unsympathetic Congress which, notwithstanding occasional lively debate, refuses to authorize gold braid for the American Foreign Service.

Both notion and legend are false. Professional diplomats measure their success, nine times out of ten, by their inconspicuousness. They wear their striped pants on demand of foreign ceremonial officials. Privately, most of them have as little use for a diplomatic uniform as a ski jumper for the Green Umbrella of the Bey of Tangier.

Only twice in nearly four decades in the Foreign Service did I make an honest dollar out of my overstarched pinafore. The first was in Peru and the second, a generation later, was when the Grand Marshal of Greece allowed me to present my credentials to King Paul in a white mess jacket. The moral of which is that whereas official servants participate in public spectacles as one of the accepted hazards of their profession, those hazards are multiplied by the irrationality of the rompers in which their acts of contrition are often committed.

To begin with the honest Peruvian dollar: Lima, in midsummer. New Year's Day in Peru is like the Fourth of July in Washington. I was Third Secretary in an embassy presided over by the late Alexander P. Moore, of Pittsburgh. Uncle Alec, as hard-boiled and colorful as an Easter egg, had been ambassador to Spain, where he delighted King Alfonso by calling

249

him Boss and Queen Victoria by presenting her with a set of aluminum kitchen utensils made by his friend Andy Mellon. President Coolidge thereupon sent Uncle Alec to Lima to work on the Tacna Arica problem after a toothache had worked on General Pershing so acutely that the general threw in the towel of diplomacy and left it to be picked up and laundered by the Foreign Service.

The diplomatic corps in Peru was invited to congregate in Pizarro's Palace, once occupied by Spanish Viceroys but now by the President of the Republic, to congratulate him on having chalked up another year in office. At twelve degrees south of the equator the white tie, boiled shirt, and black vest decreed by Peruvian protocol made as little sense as a bikini at the North Pole. All the diplomats except those whose countries had diplomatic uniforms — who were in a worse fix than the un-uniformed diplomats because uniforms are heavier and hotter in addition to smelling of mothballs — wore white tie and tails, as prescribed by the Peruvian Foreign Office. We looked, as we trooped in one after the other, like penguins attending a wake.

Feliz año nuevo, Señor Presidente, we dutifully declared as we filed past President Leguia. The Papal Nuncio made an unmemorable speech, to which the President of Peru was moved to reply. Magnesium powder exploded in our faces as photographs were taken for the benefit of *La Prensa* and *El Comercio* the following morning. Then Ambassador Moore departed in his maroon and silver Rolls Royce to meet his friend Irvin Cobb, who was arriving that morning by Grace ship from New York — all this being before the days of commuting by airplane.

Emerging from the Presidential Palace, I set out on foot down the broiling Giron Union, perspiration soaking my garters. I was heading for the Hotel Bolívar where in the shaded bar — this was also before the days of air conditioning — a *pisco* sour was in order. As I crossed the lobby I was inter-

250

cepted by Irvin Cobb himself, complete with inked-in eyebrows, an uncorseted figure, and a heavy winter overcoat.

"Hey, waiter," shouted the author. "Check this coat for me, please. I need a coat here the way Lucifer needs a pass to hell. And tell me, son, how do I get from this hotbox to the American embassy?" Radio addicts of a generation ago will remember the intonation. "You speak English?" Cobb demanded.

"Me spik ingleesh good," I told Cobb, accepting a garment that might have been made by Omar the Tentmaker. Part of the weight turned out to be a bottle of Old Overholt, two-thirds empty, for this was New Year's morning.

"Cuide el abrigo y no se meta con la botella," I told the hatcheck scorpion. "Take care of the coat and keep your hands off the liquor." Returning to Cobb with the check, I said Ambassador Moore lived just down the street from Plaza San Martín. "Out the door and turn right. Past the Club Nacional. You'll see the embassy shield over the entrance. Thanks, Mr. Cobb. The Ambassador is expecting you."

And I spent Irvin Cobb's dollar on the first *pisco* sour of 1929, with my white collar wilting around my neck and my boiled shirt soggy against my chest. New Year's morning, with the fragrance of brandy and lime and with icy beads sliding down the glass to make a bright ring on the mahogany, is a good time for meditation and vows. I meditated on the silly clothes imposed on foreign diplomats by the Chief of Peruvian protocol. And I vowed, if I stayed in the diplomatic service as long as I hoped, to try to do something about them. Additional *pisco* sours fortified my resolution. They also extinguished Irvin Cobb's dollar.

A vow is a vow, but fulfillment lay around a good many corners. After Lima, a transfer to the State Department gave me a chance to help smuggle six pairs of muskoxen from Greenland to Alaska on behalf of the Department of the Interior, and to draft some spirited correspondence for Secretary

Stimson in reply to a Scandinavian protest about our alleged theft of "mush oxes" from a restricted glacier, but President Hoover's Washington of a generation ago afforded few opportunities for a junior officer to strike blows for sartorial freedom. I also dealt with India, where a little man wearing a sensible tropical toga was twisting the British Lion's tail; and so convincingly did I handle American affairs with Liberia that I was presently sent there — still without having had a chance to tell Secretary Stimson about the virtues of seersucker suits as official regalia. That was a pity, for Stimson patronized Henry J. Goodman's haberdashery on Pennsylvania Avenue — the only store in the District of Columbia where you could buy a mackinaw in August. Stimson, I felt as I sailed away to Monrovia with a sun helmet in one hand and my high hat in the other, would have endorsed my project for rational raiment for diplomats.

There followed years shinnying up the Foreign Service totem pole in the direction, I hoped, of achievement. All of it was rewarding and most of it was fun. But some of it, identified with inappropriate bibs in unlikely climates, went a long way to prove that the smaller the country the more prone are its officials to stage gaudy public formations, which they embellish with diplomats, like maraschino cherries nesting in the foam of an eggnog.

My top hat developed a bent brim and a permanent list to starboard. Long after mildew had turned it as green as the north side of a New England pine tree, I retained that hat, from mixed motives of penury and contempt: each hairshirt has its hermit.

Occasionally I rebelled, as in the early days of World War II, when I found myself chargé d'affaires in Cuba. Fulgencio Batista, then constitutional president of the Pearl of the Antilles, was unveiling the bust of a soldier of the Spanish American War, whose contribution might have been forgotten had it not been for a turn-of-the-century philosopher named Elbert

252

Hubbard, who cast Lieutenant Rowan in the hero's role in a fable called "A Message to Garcia." Cuban survivors hired a sculptor to immortalize the lieutenant, and President Batista agreed to be present. He chose our Independence Day for this display of Cuban-American solidarity; Fidel Castro, ten years old at the time, was not consulted.

Chancing on one of Batista's aides in the Floridita Bar and recognizing that the Havana noon of the unveiling ceremony would be capable of giving sunstroke to a Galápagos iguana, I bought the aide a daiquiri and, while Constantino performed his incomparable magic, I observed that bathing suits and sunhelmets would be better than the morning coats and *pantalones de fantasia* that the Cuban State Department was demanding. The aide bought me a daiquiri, and I reiterated the suggestion. I ordered a third round, and the aide decided it was his idea in the first place.

This conversation got back to the President of Cuba. He sent me word that he was holding political office even if I wasn't, but that he would settle for white sharkskin suits — which is what I gratefully wore, and I carried a natty Panama hat, acquired in Guayaquil in 1929, when I was stranded there with malaria.

The Message to Garcia ceremony was a drawn match, at that, for the principal speaker was Major Miranda, Under Secretary of State of Cuba, who claimed to have been General Garcia's adjutant; he paid me back for cancelling his taffeta pajamas by declaiming for an extra half hour, with the Strait of Florida a molten mirror searing my eyeballs. It was weeks before I could pass the Cuban memorial to the good Lieutenant Rowan, there on the Havana Malecon, without making an uncivil gesture.

More years passed, and more embassies. I was moved from Latin America to China and back again to the Good Neighborhood. From there to Europe and back to the Orient, like a disc on a checkerboard in the hands of someone playing against

253

time. The Foreign Relations Committee of the United States Senate, I am gratified to observe, has raised its eyebrows about the phenomenon of diplomats-in-motion, demanding that we be left in one place at least long enough to learn how to order breakfast in Hindustani, Amharic, or Guarani. I applaud that proposal.

Eventually I was assigned to Greece, my first experience with a monarchy. What the *Almanac de Gotha* might portend in the way of ceremonial vestments replaced my speculations about weightier questions of policy. From Rio de Janeiro, as we assembled our battered possessions for shipment to the Mediterranean, I communicated my misgivings to the deputy chief of my forthcoming mission in Athens.

His Acropolis answer caught up with me in Washington, where I was pondering the effect of trying to learn Greek on a three-year diet of Portuguese. I already knew what Portuguese had done to my Spanish.

"The Court goes to Corfu," Sam wrote, "before you reach Athens. The Grand Marshal says protocol is relaxed in the summer. You can present your credentials in a white mess jacket. After that, King Paul invites you to luncheon. If you can't find a mess jacket in Washington or New York, you can have one tailored here. In that case, please cable your measurements . . ."

This was an encouraging message. Long years after my Peruvian exposure, the diplomatic haberdashery business seemed at last to be looking up. Not for nothing had the Greeks invented our western civilization. I was all for the Greeks — especially the Grand Marshal.

"Mess jacket OK," I wired Sam in Athens. "Will bring. Please thank the Grand Marshal."

Whereupon my diligent deputy chief, who up to that time had never owned a mess jacket himself, went to the royal tailor, stopping en route to thank the Grand Marshal.

All this occurred while I was still in Washington, being

254

briefed, as the phrase has it, on the problems of Greek-American relations. Between briefings I thought benign thoughts about the Grand Marshal; someday I would propose a monument to that enlightened public servant; perched on his pedestal, jauntily, he would be wearing a Key West sport shirt, vintage of Harry Truman. And in New York, just before sailing, I would buy myself a white mess jacket chez the Messrs. Brooks Brothers on Madison Avenue. It would be an elegant garment, in the tradition of that urbane emporium. Then, like Lord Byron, I would be off with the wind to Parnassus.

Brave thoughts, and I savored them as I sought to unravel Greek politics in the Foggy Bottom cubicle assigned to the Ambassador-designate to Athens. Greek politics cannot be unraveled, but while I was finding that out, there came a further message from Sam, wherein he gave details of the credentials ceremony. Efficiently he enclosed the scenario prepared for my predecessor, when Jimmy Riddleberger presented *his* letters of credence. Sam even enclosed a diagram of the Corfu Palace Throne Room. The entrance was shown, and the raised dais, X marked where I would stand, with the members of my staff shown as little squares behind me; K for King Paul, C for Crown Prince Constantine, and FM for the Foreign Minister on His Majesty's left. And, sure enough, GM for the Grand Marshal, who would precede me into the Throne Room, announce me to His Majesty, and then stand to one side while I presented my credentials to the monarch. Sam added that the royal tailor was now well along with the construction of his mess jacket; he hoped I would have no trouble finding one to bring with me.

"That coat," my deputy observed, "is going to cost me a pretty penny."

I accomplished my Washington consultation and, replete with information about Macedonian tobacco and the Cyprus question (if still hazy about Greek politics), I proceeded to

New York. I called on the Orthodox Archbishop of North and South America, who served Turkish coffee, hard candy, and Greek cognac in rapid succession and in that order. Later, in company with Greek Americans I was taken to a Manhattan restaurant where I had shiny dark olives and a dozen different kinds of hors d'oeuvres, each fortified with Peloponnesian garlic and washed down with *ouzo* and *retsina,* only to discover that a huge luncheon was to follow. Later still, slightly comatose but otherwise intact, and full of well-founded impressions of the quality of Hellenic hospitality, I reached Madison Avenue.

Establishing my identity at Brooks Brothers, I ascertained to my dismay that they no longer stocked mess jackets. They hadn't, said the salesman, sniffing the heady aroma emanating from his client, for over a decade. He implied I had mistaken my era.

"Now if the Ambassador is going through London . . ."

I said, curtly, that I was going to Greece. Furthermore, I reflected bleakly that there would now be no time between my Attic arrival and the presentation of my credentials on Corfu to engage the services of Sam's regal tailor. Clearly the situation was of crisis proportions. Wistfully I eyed a pile of Bermuda shorts on an adjacent counter: now *there* was a garment that made sense out of midsummer letters of credence.

A floorwalker got in the act, sniffing. To him I explained the acuteness of my need. Sailing tomorrow. Flying to Athens. Credentials the Tuesday thereafter. My need was compelling.

The floorwalker made sympathetic noises, although perhaps he was only gasping for breath. He went away and presently returned with an assistant manager. The latter said, also sniffing, that if I insisted I had to have a mess jacket, there was the Brooks Costume Company, over on the West Side.

"The Brooks Costume Company has no connection with Brooks Brothers," the assistant manager warned me. "We cannot guarantee their products." His attitude reminded me

256

of a Foreign Office official who once discussed with me the extension of recognition to a distant, underdeveloped, and slightly disreputable country. I thanked the assistant manager, who withdrew with alacrity, and while the floorwalker obligingly hunted for the address, I laid in some Bermuda shorts, just in case I might someday be in luck. I charged the shorts and then took a taxi across town. It was an air-conditioned taxi, but as we crossed Fifth Avenue, the driver rolled down his window.

"Hop out, buddy, this is it," said the driver over his shoulder as I gazed in popeyed immobility into the showcase of the Brooks Costume Company, where an anthropologist seemed to have joined forces with a taxidermist from the Smithsonian Institution. Only here the subjects were neither Siberian tigers nor former White House First Ladies; they were stuffed midtown New York City doormen, wearing the fanciest clothes I had seen since I was Ambassador to the Dominican Republic.

The Stork Club was represented, and Twenty One, and El Morocco. The Copacabana bouncer was about to try three falls out of five with the St. Regis Hotel headwaiter. Purple uniforms edged with crimson, and pale blue uniforms edged with orange. Red uniforms with bright green facings, with enough gold braid to have outfitted in the days of the Holy Roman Empire half the Courts of Europe, plus the Knights of Malta. If Rafael Leonidas Trujillo, then Benefactor of Santo Domingo, had no talent scout assigned to casing the Brooks Costume Company, he was missing the richest source of inspiration in the New World.

Somewhat shaken I paid off the taxi and entered the store, where all was activity and bustle. Swarthy little men, not unacquainted with the kind of food I'd been eating, were speaking a variety of languages and waving thin purses. These were the novices, the acolytes petitioning for restaurant employment, the candidates for kitchen and pantry. The big shots were all outside in the showcase. Eventually I got the eye of

257

a salesman. He was unimpressed by, or at any rate impervious to, the fine Byzantine aroma of my Hellenic-American luncheon.

"White mess jacket?" he repeated, eyes pinching the bridge of a nose as sharp as an icepick. "You come to the right jernt, mister."

He gestured upward with his thumb. Over our heads there were hundreds of white mess jackets, hanging from a rod which, supported from the ceiling, stretched all the way across the store. They began at one end with tiny mess jackets, fit for an organ grinder's monkey. Hence monkey jackets, I suddenly remembered. The coats gradually increased in size as the line progressed toward the opposite wall; there they looked like sails for a four-masted schooner. Sizing me up with a squint that matched his icepick nose, the salesman took a boathook from behind the counter and fetched down a sample from the middle of the line. Too small, he decided, moving ten feet in the direction of the barkentine models.

That coat fitted, if you weren't counting details. The V at the back just reached my belt; it stuck out jauntily from the ambassadorial hips. The sleeves reached to my knuckles on one side, to my fingertips on the other.

"Shorten sleeves while you wait," offered the salesman. "Eight dollars and a half. Two for sixteen bucks. Wear one while the missus washes the other. Buttons ain't sewed on — see? Button goes through this hole, with a ring on the inside." He demonstrated, removing a button. "Detachable buttons — see? Give the missus a break, with the washing. Some jernts," he explained, "calls for fancy buttons. We got fancy buttons, too. Buck extra the set."

I examined the fancy buttons, regretfully declining a tagua nut model, with a cameo mermaid who would have done well in the brassiere business. The standard buttons were mother-of-pearl, each nearly as large as a quarter. They seemed adequate for diplomacy, if not for a West Side chophouse. Agreeing that it was a good idea to give the missus a break, I counted out sixteen dollars for the bright-eyed salesman, who magnanimously said he hoped I'd get the job.

"We got a more elegant rig," he gestured with reverence toward the showcase full of stuffed doormen, "whenever you get promoted." He accepted a cigar. "Thanks, mister." He bit off the end with teeth as sharp as an Allagash beaver's. "*Thanks, mister.*"

In a thoughtful mood I left the Brooks Costume Company, the two mess jackets under my arm. I had a flashback to Irvin Cobb and the Hotel Bolívar in Lima. From waiter to waiter in thirty-five years — that seemed to sum up my life in diplomacy.

The King of Greece was an affable monarch. My introduction to him was painless and pleasant. Bowing at the door as prescribed by my new friend, the Grand Marshal of the Court, I advanced to the spot marked X on Sam's chart, where I said:

"Your Majesty, I have the honor to present the letter of the President of the United States of America which accredits me as ambassador to Greece, together with the letter of recall of my distinguished predecessor and good friend, Ambassador Riddleberger."

King Paul said: "I am happy to recognize you as ambassador of the United States of America."

The King stepped off his dais and we shook hands. He accepted my two envelopes with their white wafer seals containing the letters of credence and recall, but he did not open them. Chiefs of state rarely do, and I wondered how many of those archaic messages, beautifully engraved by hand, each beginning "Great and Good Friend. Having made choice of J. Sediment Peachpit, a distinguished citizen of my country, to reside near Your Majesty in the capacity of . . ." are regularly filed, seals intact, in dusty foreign archives.

Since his accession to the throne of the Hellenes in 1947,

King Paul had probably received two or three hundred letters of credence from arriving ambassadors. He handed my envelopes, seals intact, to his Minister of Foreign Affairs. The King remarked that he hoped Jimmy Riddleberger was well, and that he looked forward to seeing me an hour later at luncheon.

"Informal," King Paul said, glancing at his chestful of orders and then at my mess jacket with its mother-of-pearl buttons. That completed the ceremony. I was now recognized by the Chief of State as American ambassador to Greece.

Back at my Corfu hotel, before changing into a silk suit and a club tie for my first meal with the Royal Family, I gave the customary reception for the officials of the Court who had arranged the credentials ceremony. The champagne was French, and the caviar came from Teheran. The hors d'oeuvres had a minimum of Peloponnesian garlic. My mess jacket was commented upon politely by the Grand Marshal. He hoped his ruling on credentials costume had caused the Ambassador no trouble nor inconvenience.

"And where, may I ask," said the Grand Marshal of the Court, "did you find your mess jacket, Mr. Ambassador?"

"Brooks," I told him.

"Ah. Brooks, in New York," said that cosmopolitan courtier.

But it was the mess jacket of Sam, my deputy, which attracted attention. The officials of the Court were ecstatic. And with reason. Whereas the ambassador's stuck out in the back like a pointer pup's nose. Sam's was a form-fitting garment. Mine seemed to be made of white drill, possibly sailcloth, fine for kitchen or pantry, or for giving the missus a break with the washing. Sam's was as soft as moleskin. His sleeves sloped gently from his shoulders; the arms of my mess jacket resembled semaphores.

All my new Greek friends, immaculate in their summer uniforms emblazoned with decorations and ribbons and with dress swords and gold sword-hilts, complimented Sam on his mess jacket, but I thought he accepted their enthusiasm with reserve. Sam's sunny disposition is proverbial, but today I sensed that something was wrong in the sartorial bleachers. Today, on the terrace looking across aquamarine water toward Epirus, Sam's sun was in eclipse. Our praise of his mess jacket seemed to give him small pleasure.

As we flew back to Athens that afternoon, after my luncheon with King Paul and Queen Frederika, I probed for Sam's trouble. "Your mess jacket," I declared, "is the envy of the gods on Olympus. You can make a mint of money at parties. Charge a small fee just to let the other guests stroke it. You have the most elegantly tailored job since Mark Anthony gave Cleopatra a mink-lined kimono, with gold bells on the extra tippet."

"I bought mine," I went on, "at Brooks — the Brooks Costume Company, which is *not* on Madison Avenue. My mess jacket cost eight dollars and fifty cents, with a cut-price spare, just in case Marshal Tito someday decides to make an official visit to Athens. No charge for the extra buttons."

Sam choked. Under the wings of the embassy C-47, Homer's wine-dark sea covered the Saronic Gulf as we let down toward Piraeus, and Sam's face matched the reflection. "Eight dollars and fifty cents!" The words came out of his throat in a gargle. "The royal tailor took me for exactly ten times that much. He charged me eighty-five dollars for my mess jacket. And the buttons — the buttons were ten dollars extra . . ."

Sam sulked for the rest of the flight back to Ellinikon Airport. But the newly accredited American ambassador to Greece spent those moments arranging, in his nimble mind, the details of the monument proposed for his new friend, the Grand Marshal of the Court. I discarded the idea that Colonel Levidis should be wearing a sport shirt. Not even a sport shirt inspired by former President Truman. No. The Grand Marshal of Greece would be sculptured in pentellic marble, and by the most distinguished descendant of Praxiteles now discoverable

261

in Athens, wearing a mess jacket — a mess jacket designed by the Brooks Costume Company. (And no charge for the extra buttons . . .)

What's more, in due course I was able to wear my spare mess jacket in Athens. Not for Tito, but for the official visit to Greece of the President of the United Arabic Republic. But that is another story — with a small surcharge for the buttons.

XVI.

A Birthday Cake for the King

CHRONIA POLLA means Happy Birthday in Greek, so when King Paul reached the Athens airport five minutes before President Eisenhower's plane was due to arrive: "*Chronia Polla,*" I said, meaning "Happy Birthday to you, Your Majesty." For on that December 14 the King of Greece was fifty-eight years old.

His Majesty, with an accurate notion that the rest of my Greek might have had difficulty getting me a shoeshine in Piraeus, was possibly surprised. He grinned and said, "Thank you very much, Mr. Ambassador." And together we waited for the President's plane, which had left New Delhi at four o'clock that morning, to let down through the overcast that covered Attica.

Chronia Polla, I mentally repeated, reviewing events that led to that greeting. And if I didn't clear the King's birthday cake with the President, I would be in my wife's doghouse. Not to forget the disappointment of George-the-Cook, who baked the cake for President Eisenhower to give to the King of Greece on his fifty-eighth birthday.

My wife, who has the inspired ideas in the family, was the one who discovered that the day the President of the United States would reach Athens was also the birthday of the King of Greece. "We'll have a birthday cake," said my wife. "George-the-Cook can bake King Paul a cake, and the President can give it to him at the Palace the night he arrives."

George-the-Cook was summoned, and when George is enthusiastic, dry bulbs put out green shoots and jasmine blooms ahead of its season. George was enthusiastic. "Uppum uppum," he said. "Hot damn" — meaning he would bake the best cake since the one Penelope made for Ulysses. George learned his English on Crete, cooking wartime goodies for British guerrillas.

The cake conversation occurred two weeks before the Presidential visit, when I was busy with less profitable calculations. "Sure, sure," I murmured to my wife. "Happy Birthday. *Chronia Polla*. I bet the King would love it."

By then my wife and George-the-Cook were in executive session. "Sure, sure," I repeated. "And eighty-four correspondents will need forty-two hotel rooms. There will have to be a press room, and special wire services. Typewriters. Cigarettes, Bourbon whiskey . . ."

"I said," repeated my wife, "that the icing better be blue and white, the Greek national colors. Maybe George could make a silver crown to sit on top of it. How many people have the King and Queen invited for dinner that night at the Palace?"

"It's a family dinner," I answered. "And forty-two rooms will need forty-two phones. Did anybody say whether Jim Hagerty is staying at the hotel with the correspondents? Bob Murphy, by the way, is staying with us. Oh, at the King's dinner, you mean. The Royal Family — that's five. Three Eisenhowers and Bob Murphy — that's nine. You and me. The Prime Minister and the Foreign Minister. Some Court people. Wives. Twenty, maybe. But about the correspondents . . ." And I went back to my computations, which did not include the cake. I was to regret that they did not include the cake.

A visit by the President of the United States is a complex operation. The President as an individual is no problem. His personal wants are few, and he is usually undemanding. He can only be in one place at a time, and those places are identified beforehand; they are not only identified, they are scouted, inspected, and, when the moment comes, carefully guarded. But our Constitution makes no provision for an Acting President while the Chief of State is out of the country. Where the President goes, goes also the Presidency, and with it the White House. And with the White House goes security, and communications, and the Secretariat.

Security means the Secret Service, charged by law with protecting the President sixty seconds each minute, twenty-four hours each day. A detachment from that dedicated corps was to work with their Greek opposite numbers for ten days before the President's visit.

Communications means that at any moment a given word can reach the President by phone from Washington. A White House switchboard was installed in the Chancery, tapping strategic Athenian locations, including Ambassador Murphy's bedroom in the Embassy residence, and the sideboard in our dining room where the President would breakfast. During the visit one of the correspondents was to wander into a White House suite in the hotel, seeking ice cubes and soda. There were three telephones which the correspondent sampled in hopeful succession — object, room service. The first phone answered: "American embassy, Paris. What number do you want?" The second said: "Embassy Athens, Marine Guard speaking." And the third one replied: "This is the White House, Washington." Slightly shaken, the correspondent slid down the bannister five flights to the ground and flushed a bellboy out of the lobby. Communications also means cables, to and from everywhere, and in impressive volume.

Secretariat means the accompanying individuals from the White House staff, regulating the executive machinery twenty hours per person per day, on a diet of benzedrine and nembutal; they handle the documents, jet-planed in sealed pouches from the Potomac, to be signed by the President in Rome, Ankara, Karachi, Kabul, New Delhi, and now Athens.

I meditated upon this panorama of endeavor as I stood beside the King in the damp Attic dusk, waiting for the President to reach Ellinikon Airport. King Paul was tall and handsome in his uniform with medals, decorations, and a dress sword. I wore a business suit because that was what the President would be wearing; in fact the business suit had been cleared for me in advance by Jim Hagerty with the Master of Ceremonies, who took a dim view of it. There was the youthful Crown Prince, in a junior version of the parental uniform. The Prime Minister, starched and elegant, was holding a black Habig homburg. And there was the Grand Marshal of the Court, in striped trousers and a cutaway — the only man among us who had the good sense to carry an umbrella, which he nevertheless had to keep furled because the King didn't carry an umbrella.

And all about us, making three sides of a large square, were the Honor Guard and the band — the latter twiddling practice bars from "The Star-Spangled Banner" — the Greek Cabinet and civilian authorities augmented by the senior officers of the American embassy waiting to be presented, and the press aforesaid, eighty-four of them, just arrived from Iran ahead of the President, with fourteen thousand miles of living out of suitcases behind them and nearly ten thousand more miles to go. The correspondents were already cranking their cameras, testing their floodlights against the oncoming gray twilight, aiming their television equipment. An hour after the President's arrival, a press plane would streak west, with film for tomorrow's American TV audience.

Chronia Polla, I thought, as the President's airplane touched down. Here is the climax of four weeks of collective endeavor, which began — for Embassy Athens — with a Washington telegram marked "Eyes Only for the Ambassador" outlining the proposed trip and concluding with the crisp directive: "Inform Department priority telegram whether visit convenient government to which you accredited." Here also, I thought, is

266

where — I hope — I clear one birthday cake with the President of the United States.

For, alas, I had forgotten about the cake, after that first conversation, until my wife reminded me of it three days before the President reached Athens, by which time the expedition was already in New Delhi.

"George-the-Cook," said my wife that morning, "is baking the most beautiful cake. Blue and white for the national colors. And he's making a silver crown to sit on top of it. He wants to know how to spell Happy Birthday. Or do you think *Chronia Polla* would be more appropriate?"

"What cake?" I asked, over my breakfast tangerines.

"I told you," said my wife with restraint, "that December 14 is the King's birthday. You remember. Cake. C-a-k-e. For the President of the United States to give to the King of Greece. Right after dessert. Birthday cake. For the King. Catch on?"

"I'm sorry," I said, "but you can't spring a birthday cake on the President. It would have to be cleared with the White House in advance. Everything has to be cleared with the White House in advance. The President might think it was a corny idea. Maybe they don't give birthday cakes in Greece."

"They do give birthday cakes in Greece," said my wife. "George-the-Cook says so."

Summoned, George testified with conviction. The gist of it, omitting gestures, was that a birthday cake is an essential ingredient of the culture of Greece. "Lovelly kek," George declared. "Uppum uppum. Hot damn." Which signified he was confident his ambassador would never sell him or his cake down the river. George went on to explain that he was a friend of the royal chef, whom he had appraised of impending developments, enlisting the support of that patriotic fellow citizen. Finally, George would like to accompany us to the Palace on the birthday night, to deliver the cake to the King's chef in person. "Lovelly kek," George repeated, beaming upon us.

267

"And so," said my wife, "you will please clear the King's birthday cake with the White House."

At the time that unprofitable exchange took place in the American Embassy in Athens, the President was standing beside Prime Minister Nehru, opening an agricultural fair in New Delhi. I entertained misgivings about inserting a telegram about a birthday cake among the urgent embassy messages forwarded from Athens to the President of the United States in India. Plans for the forthcoming NATO meeting in Paris: "NIACT for Amb Murphy from the Secretary. Prime Minister MacMillan says . . ." "From Emb Paris, personal for the President from Amb Houghton. When I saw Pres de Gaulle this afternoon, he . . ." Plans for Tunis. Plans for Madrid. Plans for Morocco . . . Somehow a birthday cake, even a royal birthday cake, did not seem to fit into that flow of correspondence. Relaxation is fun, but statesmanship seldom has time to enjoy it; relaxation misinterpreted as frivolity might backfire and melt the blue and white icing. A cake telegram, I decided, might also get lost in the shuffle. There must be an alternative procedure.

There was. The embassy received a telegram directing Sam, my deputy chief of mission, to meet the Presidential plane in Teheran, the last stop before Athens. There Sam would go aboard and during the three-hour flight between Iran and Greece, brief the White House staff on final Athens arrangements. Since the cake was a part of Athens arrangements, nothing more appropriate than that Sam should also clear the cake. Or so it had seemed at the time.

Trouble was, now, at the Athens airport, with the President arriving, I couldn't get hold of Sam. The bright orange face and black radar nose of the Presidential Boeing was taxiing toward royal hospitality, and Sam was presumably aboard, but inaccessible because of the rigidity of arrival protocol, to which I myself had contributed. We had rehearsed the arrival as recently as the day before, complete with a borrowed

268

Air Force plane, a substitute President, a live Master of Ceremonies, the full Honor Guard, the band, and a fleet of genuine Palace automobiles.

The front entrance, forward of the sweptback wings, would successively frame the Presidential visitor, his son and daughter-in-law, Ambassador Murphy as the ranking State Department representative, and the President's interpreter — temporarily out of a job because Greek wasn't one of his seven languages; besides which, the King of Greece spoke English as well as we do. A Secret Service contingent, unobtrusive and competent, was already mobilized around us. But everybody else, including upper echelons of the White House staff, the President's valet and Sam, would disembark from the rear door, one hundred feet away and on the far side of the plane from His Majesty and the official welcoming committee.

With the King of Greece at my elbow and the President of the United States descending the stairs, with floodlights focused and television cameras grinding away for posterity, there was no way for the American ambassador to scuttle under the belly of the plane and yell: "Yoo-hoo, Sam! Has the King's birthday cake been cleared with the White House?" and then scuttle back again to his square on the protocol checkerboard.

The President arrived, smiling his friendly smile and looking — heaven knows why — rested as well as affable. Greetings were exchanged. The King and the President were friends from wartime days when one was heir apparent to a Nazi-occupied throne and the other a general. Ambassador Murphy, urbane and genial, was led away by the Prime Minister. The President's interpreter, whom I had last seen on another continent, saluted me in Portuguese, which *was* one of his seven languages. The King accompanied the President to review the Honor Guard, to present his Cabinet — after which I presented my embassy staff — and then to the radio platform

269

where the President acknowledged the greetings extended by His Majesty in the name of the people of Greece.

Before I knew it, and also before the cake was cleared, we were in our designated automobiles and off in procession toward Athens, eight miles away.

First rode the Grand Marshal of the Court, all alone with his furled umbrella, in deference to which the rain had stopped. Next went the King and the President, riding together. The Crown Prince went third, with the junior Eisenhowers for company. Ambassador Murphy and the Prime Minister rode away together. Then the Foreign Minister and the American ambassador. The Minister made me a gracious little speech about the visit, and about how well the President looked. I nodded, and thanked him, and brooded about the cake, which I saw no profit in mentioning to the Foreign Minister. Birthday cakes for the King were clearly in Palace, not Foreign Office, jurisdiction.

There had been no sign of Sam, who I hoped was riding in the parade a few cars behind me. I reflected that both Sam and my wife were scheduled to be at the Palace for a reception just preceding the King's dinner. That was cutting the cake pretty thin, but that was the way it was.

The ride to Athens took nearly an hour, with traffic stopped on the opposite side of the Piraeus-Athens highway so that a busload of correspondents, perched with their cameras on a platform built on top of a truck, could keep abreast of the President and the King, who had a trick Rolls Royce for state occasions, with a detachable Plexiglass roof, now removed so the occupants could stand up. They stood up, and the President raised both arms in salute.

There was an American flag on the right fender and a Greek flag on the left. I recalled that the royal Rolls Royce and its companion the American embassy Cadillac had been removed from circulation two days before, to have special mounts installed on the fenders, with grooves to take the

270

thread of the Presidential flag staffs. Directly behind the royal automobile, in an unnumbered vehicle marked X on the arrival schedule, rode two Evzones, the one on the right holding the Royal Standard and the one on the left holding the blue Presidential flag, resplendent with fifty white stars — in case Alaska and Hawaii were looking.

And all along the Athenian way as many of the inhabitants as the sidewalks could hold pressed against the police lines, waving Greek and American flags and cheering. Having witnessed official welcomes in other lands, where the dictator advertises a "spontaneous demonstration" and then turns the crowds on and off like sprinklers in a garden, it was heartwarming to witness a genuine spectacle, based on good will and affection.

By Hadrian's Arch the outriding motorcycles gave way to a troop of cavalry, with lances and pennons brave to see. Thus we came to the Tomb of the Greek Unknown Soldier, where we paused for wreath-laying while the two national anthems echoed across Constitution Square between Parliament and the ancient Acropolis, which had looked down on twenty-five centuries of parades and processions, and finally to the Royal Palace. By then there was only an hour between me — and my uncleared cake — and the King's birthday dinner.

In the Palace reception room where she waited with the Court ladies, my wife caught sight of Ambassador Murphy and me at the same instant. To me she said: "Put out your cigar. You can't smoke cigars in the Palace until after dinner." To Ambassador Murphy she said: "Bob, darling. How wonderful . . ." And to us both my wife said: "Has the birthday cake been cleared with the White House?"

"Ho! The birthday cake!" said Ambassador Murphy genially. He removed lipstick with his pocket hankerchief. "Sam told me about the cake on the plane. Sam couldn't see the President because he went to sleep as soon as we left Teheran. But I asked the President just before we landed in Athens. He

271

thinks the cake is a fine idea. He is for it, but there's one condition. The President says you better clear the cake with the Queen."

"Thank you, Bob dear," said my wife. "Perhaps," she added gently, "I should have done it myself in the first place."

Then the Royal Family, with the President and his son and daughter-in-law, entered the reception room where everybody was presented to the President. Sam arrived just in time to meet, in Athens, his Principal Traveling Companion from Teheran. And twenty minutes later Bob and my wife and I were on our way to the embassy residence to change our clothes and come back to the Palace for dinner.

"The Queen said OK?" I asked, pushing a button that ran up the glass partition separating us from Tassos, the chauffeur.

"The Queen," said my wife, "didn't ask a single question. She couldn't have been nicer . . ."

"Have you heard," asked Bob in the midst of a considerable silence, "that Tyler Thompson is going to Iceland?"

The cake was a fine success. It rode back with us from the embassy residence to the Palace, George-the-Cook on the front seat, wearing his white chef's hat, balancing the cake on his lap. It was, as George declared, a lovely kek. And when the King cut the first slice the Crown Prince struck up "Happy Birthday to You," with the guests joining in lustily, until we reached the punch line "Happy birthday, dear . . . ," when everybody trailed off, not knowing whether to say "King Paul," or "Your Majesty," or what. But it was an elegant birthday cake, and an inspired idea.

It had two sequels:

The next morning the President came to the embassy for breakfast, whereof the dishes from orange juice to medium steak were duly reported by the international press. Soon there was a great scurrying up and down our back stairs with semi-final and final-final pages of the President's address to the Greek Parliament, to be delivered at ten o'clock that morning. Each page was typed on stiff white paper, 10½ by 8 inches, with three holes on the lefthand side to fit into a black leather holder; and the footprints of the typewriter, brought from the Presidential airplane, were the largest I had ever seen. Meanwhile, members of the Secret Service ate scrambled eggs and drank coffee in the kitchen, and George-the-Cook, wearing his white hat, was the happiest Greek in all Greece. Until the President left the embassy for Parliament, when George became happier still.

We departed in some pomp, the Prime Minister accompanying us. Just outside the door was George, now enjoying the benevolent regard of the Secret Service, who were replete with his scrambled eggs and coffee. I presented George-the-Cook to the President of the United States of America, who beamed on George while George beamed on the President.

"That," said the President, "was a wonderful birthday cake. Thank you very much for baking it."

As we drove away, George waved his white chef's hat. "Uppum uppum," he shouted. "Hot damn!" Meaning that he would be glad to go to the United States and vote the straight Republican ticket, indefinitely.

Later that day, when the Marine helicopter with the departing President aboard had zoomed off the stadium plaza and coasted past the Acropolis, heading for USS *Des Moines* waiting in Phaleron Bay to take the President to Tunis — later than that, when the visit of the President of the United States to Greece was a warm memory — I inquired of my wife how come she got so quick an assent when she asked Queen Frederika if the President could give the King a birthday cake at the Palace dinner.

"Seemed to me," I observed, "almost as though the Queen expected your question."

"So she did," said my wife. "She knew about it three days ago. George-the-Cook told the Palace chef, and the chef told the Queen. George and the chef cleared the cake with the

Queen. All you had to do, dear, was clear the cake with the President . . ."

I was mixing myself a double-sized, six-to-one martini; the kind of martini an ambassador thinks he rates at the end of a Presidential visit. I raised my glass to my wife. *"Chronia Polla,"* I said. "Uppum uppum. Hot damn." Meaning that when better birthday cakes are baked, George-the-Cook would not only bake them but clear them!

XVII.

Nick-of-The-Gotham Builds a Church

I HAVE included this tale of Nick-of-The-Gotham-Hotel because I think it is a pleasant story of a good little man, who deserves well of Greece and of his adopted America. The cordiality with which Nick's story was received when it first appeared has tempted me to seek for it a wider audience; I hope I am not mistaken.

There are over two million Greek-Americans in the United States, and among the things they do well is remember the land that gave them birth. They are loyal American citizens, with room in their hearts for the mountains and islands and care-worn little villages of Greece, where change has been slow to come across the centuries. Nick got the idea of going to America, five thousand miles from his native Peloponnesus, from a gypsy fortune teller. But his dream was strictly his own: it shows that if you do one thing at a time, with your heart as well as your head, people after a while begin to take notice. In Nick's case, the governments of Greece and the United States took notice, including the American embassy in Athens.

As Nick tells it, he was a small boy when he consulted the fortune teller, half a century ago. His life had been spent uneventfully on a rock-strewn slope overlooking some of the oldest olive trees in Greece. He had never been as far north as Sparta, forty miles away, but he had seen the blue Aegean because his father shipped olives from the ancient port of Monemvasia, in the shadow of a crumbling Venetian fortress.

275

"You will soon go," said the fortune teller, "on a long voyage, to a new land."

"As far as Athens?" asked Nickos. His father had once been to the capital. In the village *taverna* he often talked of the wonders of the Acropolis and the ways of the politicians.

"I said a *long* voyage," said the gypsy. "And while you are in that new land, you will meet famous people. Kings and Queens. Millionaires and ambassadors . . ."

Nick had a vague idea what a Queen was because her picture was in the town hall, beside that of bald King Constantine. He had never heard of millionaires or ambassadors, and in 1910 millionaires and ambassadors had certainly never heard of Pakia, where the farmers wore pom-poms on their shoes and their wives rode their burros two miles to get water. Nickos gravely withdrew his small hand from the gypsy's. He wished he had spent his ten-*lepta* coin for caramels at the shop of Yannis, which smelled delectably of coffee and *retsina*, of *ouzo* and goatsmilk cheese.

The fortune teller went away but was still remembered when Nickos' father received a letter. "It is from a village called *Nea Yorki*," said his father. "Your Uncle Gregorio says they do not grow olive trees there but that many people are rich in America. He sends money for your ticket. How would you like to go to *Nea Yorki,* Nickos?"

"Is it far?" asked the boy, wriggling his toes as he remembered the fortune teller. "Is it as far away as Athens?"

"Much farther. America is across the ocean."

"Does America have a king and queen, Father?"

"No, *pedimu*. America has a President, chosen from time to time by the people."

"And after I have been to America, and seen the President, can I come back — back to Pakia?" asked Nickos, the germ of his dream stirring within him.

His father smiled. "That's as may be," he said. "Perhaps if

276

you work hard and save money. I may not be here, but your brother and sisters will be glad to see you."

Nickos' eyes were shining and the dream fluttered in his heart. "Some day I shall come back," he promised. "Back to Pakia."

That year the olive harvest was not good. Nevertheless by eating less at home and spending less time in the village *taverna,* Nickos' father managed to outfit his son for the United States, including the first pair of shoes Nickos had ever owned, with a wonderful built-in squeak that lasted as long as the shoes did. Nickos kissed his three sisters goodbye and embraced his father and brother. He cried a little and was seasick part of the voyage, but his dream now sustained him. Some day he would return to his village. Some day he would do something for Pakia.

After Ellis Island, Nickos discovered that *Nea Yorki* wasn't a village and that Uncle Gregorio was right — no olive trees grow on Manhattan. Soon *Nea Yorki* became New York, and Nickos became Nick, and he had a job in a midtown hotel, working in the pantry and seeing all manner of amazing dishes the likes of which a boy from a remote hillside in the Peloponnesus could never have imagined. More than four decades later he was still working there.

Nick was a quick boy with serious eyes, light hair that is not uncommon in Lakonia, and a small body full of cricket-like energy. After what seemed to him a long time in the pantry and kitchen, during which his deftness and eagerness were noted, along with his warm smile and his efforts to learn English, he was promoted to bus boy, which included the privilege of serving bread and butter and filling glasses with ice water. And he suddenly knew the splendid world of the dining room and the glitter of patrons in evening dress, of weddings in private suites, and of a strange phenomenon called Prohibition.

Later, with English conquered, Nick began to achieve

277

status for himself. He took orders with precision; he was always cheerfully polite; he recognized guests and guests recognized him. Mrs. Chapin, who wanted her toast browned on only one side and a dab of ketchup on her breakfast poached egg, got her poached egg with a dab of ketchup and her toast browned on only one side. Colonel Fisher (Cavalry, retired) knew that when he ordered an Old Fashioned "without all that damn fruit salad" he would receive from Nick a bourbon on the rocks, with no bitters and a double slug of bourbon to replace the sliced pineapple, the wedge of orange, and the maraschino cherry, which in other midtown latitudes prostituted Mark Twain's favorite beverage.

Guests took to giving Nick telephone messages which were delivered accurately, and with discretion. In those days the University Club, behind The Gotham on Fifty-Fourth Street, had no ladies' dining room, and Nick became a life-saver for stranded wives. Entering the club one evening through the basement, bent on retrieving a husband, Nick saw President Hoover in the lobby. A Secret Service man barred the way, but Nick saw the member he was looking for and the member saw him. "He's okay," said the member. And then he took Nick by the arm and presented him to the President of the United States of America. "Mr. President," he said, "this is my young friend, Nick-of-The-Gotham."

By 1939, when he became headwaiter of The Gotham, Nick had served Queen Marie and Princess Ileana of Romania, and the Queen of the Belgians. He had seen a young man called the Prince of Wales, and the same man five years later as the Duke of Windsor. He had waited on three Secretaries of State, beginning with Charles Evans Hughes, who made a memorable buzz through his whiskers with minestrone, and Cordell Hull, who did not. He had served ambassadors, and more millionaires than he could remember, including an aseptic old gentleman from Tarrytown, New York, who gave Nick-the-bus-boy a shiny new dime which he accompanied, under the eye of another patron called Ivy Lee, with a ten per cent tip for the waiter.

The boy from the Peloponnesus with the warm, welcoming smile was now a contented American, doing competently a job he respected. He did not marry and the hotel and its guests remained the center of his life — an American life. Nick was pleased when so many of the guests congratulated him on being promoted to headwaiter. Now they all called him Nick-of-The-Gotham. So did taxi drivers on Fifty-Fifth Street. And the Irish policeman, spotting a nattily dressed little man on his way home after midnight, used to say: "Hi, Nick. How's tricks at The Gotham?"

It was pleasant to be an American. And Nick's dream of doing something for Pakia was kept alive every time he sent money to his three sisters, whose letters were harder and harder to read as the Greek of his boyhood became overlaid with the idiom of Manhattan.

The war that began in Greece in 1940 made little initial impact on Nick. Europe was a long way from Fifth Avenue, and Greece was separated from the rest of Europe by the mountainous Balkans. True, Greece and Mussolini were fighting, but that was in Epirus, where Nick had never been, and the Greeks seemed to be doing all right without him. The hotel barber was Italian but a barber is not to be classed with a headwaiter, and after *Oxi* Day Nick put the barber in his place with a rude Levantine gesture that startled the patrons.

And then, without warning, in the spring of 1941 Greece was attacked by Germany, with overwhelming force and equipment. Two weeks later the Nazis were in Athens; they were invading the Peloponnesus. The King and Queen flew to Crete, to make a stand there with the British. In the New York papers Nick read that Crete would be assaulted by paratroopers, who were massing on the plain south of Sparta. That was the plain of Malaoi, the nearest flat land to the island of Crete.

279

The village of Pakia overlooks that plain, and the first casualties were the olive trees, chopped down by Nazi soldiers to make a takeoff strip for the Luftwaffe paratroopers. The next casualty was Pakia, whose sons hid behind rocks to snipe at the invaders. Soon there were few sons left in Pakia, and Nick had no brother.

The war flowed away but an occupying army remained, while Greece starved. Nick's father died without ever knowing that his son was the headwaiter of a Fifth Avenue hotel. It was three years before Nick had word from his sisters. Nor did the Nazi capitulation in 1945 end the struggle: the Communist war continued to ravage the country for four more years. One by one the satellites were betrayed and thrust behind the Iron Curtain, but Greece went on fighting for freedom.

Young Queen Frederika, who during the occupation had been a refugee princess in Africa and England, came to the United States to plead for assistance against the Communists. There Nicholas Demakos, American citizen, met the woman who would have been his sovereign if he had remained in Pakia. The Mayor of New York gave the Queen an official reception and Nick, who had learned how tickets are obtained in New York, had a ticket.

"I'm Nicholas Demakos," said Nick-of-The-Gotham. "I'm an American citizen, but I come from Pakia, in Lakonia. Forty years ago a fortune teller told me I'd meet you."

The Queen smiled. "A fortune teller? But I wasn't born then. I know Pakia. Do you want to return there?"

Nick, who was accustomed to many people in the dining room of his hotel, felt all at once that he and his queen were alone, talking by themselves, cool in the shade of an olive tree with the plain of Malaoi around them. His native language came back to him. *"Ime amerikanos,"* he declared. "I'm an American. But I want to do something for Pakia. My father and my brother died there during the war. Our village church was destroyed. Perhaps, if I could help to rebuild the Church of Saint Demetrius, in Pakia . . ."

Queen Frederika, too, may have felt for a moment the illusion that they were alone in the shade of an ancient olive tree. "Do that," she said gently. "That would be a fine thing to do. Good luck, Nickos of Pakia."

Nick kissed the Queen's hand, in the same way as a little boy he used to kiss the hand of the village priest.

To the Mayor of New York the young Queen said, "Nickos of Pakia. I liked that little man. Who is he?"

"That was Nick-of-The-Gotham, Your Majesty. Been a waiter there longer than anyone can remember. Everybody knows Nick. Was that Greek you were talking?"

Nick thought a long time about his meeting with Queen Frederika. He had never before tried to raise money and he wasn't sure how to go about it. Sending money to his sisters, yes, for their dowries and at christening time for his nephews and nieces. But that was his personal affair, not involving other people. Finally he had an idea: he would start his church fund with a contribution from himself, and then he would talk to the guests of the hotel about it.

The first the American embassy in Athens heard of Nick's project was a letter that reached me from a retired American diplomat, now a New York commuter.

"In my wanderings about town," he wrote, "I now and then lunch at The Gotham. The maître d'hôtel, who is the size of a chipmunk and twice as active, finds out everything about everybody. The other day he asked me if by chance I knew the American ambassador to Greece. When I incautiously admitted that his daughter is my godchild, I almost missed a later afternoon appointment. Seems that Nick-of-The-Gotham has been working for years to raise money for the reconstruction of the church in the little town where his family originated. Now the church is almost finished and Nick wants you to attend the dedication ceremony. He says he is writing the State Department to ask that you be invited. I haven't the faintest notion where Pakia is, but I don't suppose anything in Greece is very far from Athens."

I didn't know where Pakia was either, but by then I had a good deal of experience with the devotion of American citizens from Greece to the families and towns of their birth. While I was still studying a map, looking for Nick's village, there arrived an official communication from Washington, enclosing a copy of his letter to the Secretary of State. Nick's letter read:

Honorable Sir,

My name is Nicholas Demakos, known here as Nick-of-The-Gotham. I am the maître d'hôtel and have worked here the past forty years. I have had the pleasure of taking care of some of the best families of America, including your predecessor's parents, who lived at The Gotham.

A few years ago I started a campaign for my home town, Pakia, Lakonia, Greece, to help rebuild the church that was destroyed during the war. Up to last fall I collected $25,000. Persons who contributed are having their names engraved on a plaque. I have almost 250 names on the list, including presidents of big corporations, judges, etc., some of the best names in America helping to rebuild this small church in Greece. People of all faiths and religions — Protestants, Catholics, Jews, and Orthodox.

This summer I contemplate to go to Greece to be present at the church dedication and it is my wish I have with me the American Ambassador to Greece, to represent all the Americans on this honor roll which will have written at the top "This Church was built with the help of American friends of Greece." I want to impress the Greek people that American people are always willing to help poor countries of the world. Please ask our Ambassador to represent all the American contributors who helped rebuild Saint Demetrius Church in Pakia.

Respectfully yours,
Nicholas Demakos (Nick-of-The-Gotham)

282

A transmitting slip from the State Department read: "Forwarded to Embassy Athens for appropriate action." Which meant that Nick and his church were up to me.

By the time Nick himself reached Athens, in the middle of a busy week and only a few days before his ceremony, I had ascertained that Pakia was a long way from being a suburb of Athens. It would take eight or nine hours by automobile to get there. South of Sparta the map showed a thin line, which if my experience in Greece meant anything indicated "secondary road, probably passable in dry weather." It might turn out to be a cart track or a goat trail. In no circumstances would the official embassy limousine thrive on an expedition to Pakia, nor would the aging American ambassador. I could, I concluded, send a member of the embassy staff to represent me. I was tempted, as Nick was announced, to do so.

Nick-of-The-Gotham wore a bright bow tie and a sport jacket, the elegance of which made me think that maybe I was in the wrong business. And on his lapel he proudly wore the Gold Cross of the Order of Phoenix, awarded to him in the name of the King by the Minister of Foreign Affairs. He had, said Nick, come straight from the ceremony to see his ambassador. And then he proceeded to tell me about the church of Saint Demetrius, which was to be dedicated by the Archbishop of Sparta on the following Sunday.

Nick's eloquence was impressive. He wanted no part of an embassy representative. He wanted the American ambassador. And so, he indicated, did the Nomarch of Lakonia, the mayors of Malaoi and Pakia, the Archbishop and his parishioners, not to forget the American citizens whose names were on the plaque. Nick was as persuasive as he was earnest. If he had chosen life insurance instead of the hotel business, he might, I reflected, have reached Greece in his private yacht. I summoned my Air Attaché, who produced additional maps. The nearest landing field was not at Pakia, for at the end of the war the survivors immediately replanted the Luftwaffe

283

takeoff strip with new olive trees — which Nick confirmed, adding that he wouldn't like to ask the citizens of Pakia to cut the trees down again. The nearest landing field was on the far prong of the Peloponnesus, miles away from Pakia and connected with it by "secondary roads." Clearly the embassy C-47 was out.

I recalled that my Naval Attaché had an amphibian. The Captain was sent for, and he brought another set of maps. The nearest port to Pakia appeared to be Monemvasia, on the far side of the plain of olives, but the Captain had never been there. He volunteered to fly down to see if a landing could be made. He guessed it might be a half-hour flight from Athens, *if* he could find sheltered water. I passed this word to Nick, who was waiting in the embassy reception room admiring the photographs of my predecessors and the flags of the countries I had served in. "Sure," said Nick cheerfully. "Monemvasia. There's a fine bay there. My father used to ship olives from Monemvasia."

I told Nick I'd be in touch, and that I hoped to be in Pakia with him for the ceremony. He beamed, he gave me the smile that generations of his dining room patrons remember. "Sure, sure, Mr. Ambassador. I knew you would help me." He skipped out, nimble as a chipmunk.

But when the Captain reported to me, he was a frustrated pilot. He had landed in Monemvasia without incident. "Hell of a big rock there. Like the Morro at Arica, with the ruins of a Venetian castle on top, instead of guano. Good bay behind the rock. No problem. But on the way back I had engine trouble. Conked the starboard governor. Nearest replacement is in Naval Stores at Port Lyautey, in Morocco . . ."

By that time I was sold on Nick and his project. "Hasn't the Greek Navy a seaplane?"

"First thing I thought of, too," said the Captain. "None

284

available. And the nearest carrier with a plane I could use is with the Sixth Fleet at Naples."

"It looks," I observed bleakly, "as though the Brazilian jeep I brought with me from Rio de Janeiro to Greece is going to have a fine workout in the Peloponnesus. How would you like to come along, as co-pilot?" But the resourceful United States Navy had a better idea. "If you don't mind an early start," said the Captain, "and a bumpy ride if there's a sea running, the Navy can still get you to Monemvasia. We got a crashboat, sir, at Piraeus."

I asked How Early, and What was a Crashboat.

"Around four o'clock in the morning, Mr. Ambassador. It's a four–five hour run from Piraeus. Boat's for air-sea rescue practice. Burns avgas. No smoking. Twenty-five knots, but it bumps, it really bumps, on rough water."

And that was how I made the trip to help Nick dedicate his church in Pakia. Nick himself went the day before. He met me at the pier of Monemvasia, which was decorated with Greek and American flags. The Governor was there, and the Nomarch and the Mayor and the representative from Sparta in the Greek Parliament. There were newspaper correspondents, and photographers. And on his white jacket, Nick wore the Gold Cross of the Order of Phoenix.

There was oratory at the pier and more thereafter. The hot summer sun of Greece poured from a cloudless sky. We reached the church, across the plain of olives from Monemvasia, at ten-thirty Sunday morning. The Archbishop was waiting. And all the population of Pakia, one thousand and thirty-four men, women, and children, were in the church and the square outside it. There was an honor guard of Greek soldiers, and on our arrival the village band, brave in new uniforms, played the Greek national anthem and "The Star-Spangled Banner."

After the mass Nick unveiled the plaque recording that

285

Saint Demetrius Church was rebuilt "with the help of American friends of Greece" — just as Nick had dreamed it.

There was a village feast in the schoolhouse following the dedication, and Nick made a speech, first in English and then in Greek, telling about the fortune teller and how he went to America, and how years later he met Queen Frederika, who encouraged him to undertake his campaign to restore the village of Pakia. He presented to me his sisters Stamata and Katerina, plus at least a dozen of his nephews and nieces, the boys in Evzone suits and the girls wearing the village dresses of Lakonia. As I worked away at a mountain of roast lamb and rice, washing them down with Pakia *retsina,* the Mayor told me of Nick's third sister, whose passage Nick had paid to Canada so she could marry a Pakia boy in Alberta. Nor had his benefactions ended with his family: the band, said the Mayor, with their new instruments and uniforms; also running water for the school, from a spring on the side of the mountain . . .

For this was Nickos Demakos Day, to honor Nick of Pakia. And the American ambassador was proud to be present.

It was late when I returned to Piraeus. The Aegean breeze freshened in the afternoon and, as my Naval Attaché had predicted, the crashboat bumped on rough water, one hundred nautical miles of which separated Monemvasia from the port of Athens. I fortified myself with gin and tonic, brought aboard with dry ice in a flight bag, while the correspondent of the *New York Times* wrote an account of the day for his paper. It had been a long day, but I had witnessed the rebirth of an ancient village.

Nick called at the embassy the next week, exhausted by feasting and family reunions, but as exuberant as ever. I asked about his plans for the future. "Forty years in one job is a long time," I told him. "Won't you soon be retiring? Pakia seems to be in pretty good shape. The school with its water supply — good water it is, I mixed it with Pakia

286

retsina. That monument you built to the Pakia soldier. And now the Church of Saint Demetrius. You've had a good life, Nick. Greece and the United States are grateful to you."

It was Nick-of-The-Gotham who answered for Nickos of Pakia. "It's a long way," he said, "from Pakia to Sparta — that's the nearest hospital. A lot of sick people can't wait that long to be treated. We need a thirty-bed hospital for the villages around the plain of olives. The Greek government says that if I can raise half the cost — that's only a *fifteen*-bed hospital, Mr. Ambassador — they will find money for the rest. I'm an American. This is my vacation. I'll be back at the hotel, on the job, in the autumn."

Which I report by way of advance notice of Nick's next campaign. Acknowledgements will be signed: Nick-of-The-Gotham.

XVIII.

The Shrunken Toga

TIME was when an American ambassador was a pretty important fellow. The doorman at the Metropolitan Club knew his name. His credit was good at The Willard, and strolling back to the old State War Navy Building through the unguarded White House grounds, Chief Usher Ike Hoover (no kin of the future President) not only recognized the ambassador but usually remembered the name of the country he served in. The ambassador's diplomatic passport was signed personally by the Secretary of State, and when the ambassador displayed it, officials at home and abroad took notice.

Prestigious days. And prestige is an essential ingredient in the ability to conduct successful diplomacy. Conversely, anything that reduces the esteem in which an envoy is held renders his task — and that of his government — more difficult.

There were only thirteen American ambassadors in the world when I entered the Foreign Service in 1925. Each ambassador was serving in a country that possessed power as well as sovereignty — a country, that is, of importance to the United States. For a vice consul in those days to aspire to become an ambassador was to reach for a handful of stardust; vice consuls were not discouraged from aspiring, but kindly counselors of embassy saw to it that they recognized the odds were against them.

Today, we have over one hundred ambassadors, plus two dozen spares, freewheeling through international organizations. Today the State War Navy Building, its diplomatic tenants evicted, is full of overflow professors from the White House cellar, and whiz kids with tuning forks pressed to the bosom of an electronic computer. Today, the Chief Usher of the White House is called Ceremonial-Officer-Chief-of-Protocol; he keeps an ambassadorial title on the side, just in case he needs diplomatic immunity from an irate Washington hostess.

Today, much of the stardust is dandruff.

Every person who has served as ambassador in the years since World War II has at some time received his private intimation of the decline of ambassadorial influence, and of the diminished size of the ambassadorial toga. My intimation came in Korea, the first spring after the armistice in the Communist war, when I encountered three youthful GI's. Their ages, added together, possibly approximated my own.

It was during a Sunday morning walk, within the great wall that encloses North Mountain. The three soldiers paused, and we conversed. I told them something about the old Koryo barricade, and of the invasion route of Genghis Khan, followed for centuries before him by the wild tribes pushing east from the Gobi desert and south from Manchuria — tribes, I remarked, not unlike the Communist hordes that attacked General MacArthur. And I warned the three soldiers to stay on the marked paths, for unexploded mines were still scattered about the forest, reminders of the bitter fighting for Seoul in 1950 and 1951.

Presently one of the GI's inquired what I did in Korea. Civilians were then scarce in the land, and seldom encountered by soldiers.

I replied, not without urbanity, that I was an ambassador. "*Your* ambassador," I explained, for the faces of my three young friends were as blank as shreds of birchbark.

There was a pause while the warriors sought to digest this information. Clearly they had never in their lives heard of an ambassador, far less met one. Suspicion struggled with po-

289

liteness. Finally one of the GI's said, giving me the benefit of the doubt:

"Jeepers, mister," he said, "you sure speak English good!"

Well, looking back on it, I hope I do. Worse things have been said about diplomats. But if I had expected the soldiers to come to attention in the presence of the representative of their Presidential Commander-in-Chief, I was wasting my time on illusions. Ambassadors might outrank generals on the pages of a diplomatic list, but obviously not in the barracks surrounding Eighth Army Headquarters in the capital of Korea.

Shortly after that incident, I was sent to Peru, where my diplomatic stock rose slightly in the presence of Viceregal tradition; to Brazil, where a wildly irresponsible government was too busy digging a grave for the economy of the country to pay much attention to foreign representation; and to Greece, which has been suspicious of all ambassadors, especially its own, since the days of Pericles.

As I moved from capital to capital, in charge of the operations of the American government in each country, I remembered my encounter in Korea with the three young soldiers, whose estimate seemed to emphasize the declining importance attached to the office of ambassador. How has this come about? I asked myself. Why is it that nowadays a traveling ambassador, exhibiting his diplomatic passport, is lucky to be allowed to buy a package of cigarettes at the Blue Danube Snack Bar? Let alone cash a check there. Why, I wondered, is the ambassadorial toga so shrunken . . .

The reasons are not far to seek, nor difficult to identify: At the Congress of Vienna, the statesmen who foregathered to feast on the bones of Napoleon undertook in addition to sort out the diplomats. Four grades of representatives were recognized. Chargé d'affaires was the lowest, followed by minister resident, then minister, and finally ambassador, since 1818 the highest diplomatic representative sent by one government to another.

290

The difference between a minister (whose full title is Envoy Extraordinary and Minister Plenipotentiary) and an ambassador (in formal parlance, Ambassador Extraordinary and Plenipotentiary) is this: A minister, representing his government officially and accredited to a foreign head of state, nevertheless does not represent the "person and dignity" of the chief of his own state. The ambassador on the other hand represents his sovereign — or president — both personally and officially. It is the *personal* representative capacity that spells the distinction.

Contrary to popular belief the first United States representative of ambassadorial rank was not Benjamin Franklin, but an envoy appointed over one hundred years later by President Cleveland, in 1893. Until that time the Republic had managed with commissioners, diplomatic agents, chargés d'affaires, and ministers. For many years the rank of ambassador was regarded in the United States as too exalted for a democratic nation. Commenting on the pre-ambassador situation, a recent publication of the State Department observes that American envoys of the last century "frequently chafed" at being outranked in foreign courts by the agents of smaller and less important countries who bore the impressive title of ambassador; American representatives complained that this detracted from the dignity and prestige of the United States.

Beguiling prose, in view of what was in store for American representatives.

The first American ambassador went, appropriately enough, to London, and by the turn of the century the list had been extended to Paris, Berlin, Rome, and Saint Petersburg — but not yet to Constantinople, the capital of the Ottoman Empire. The reason for the change in American representation in Turkey, which took place shortly thereafter, demonstrates more graphically than international law the difference between a minister and an ambassador. It was because of the Armenians.

The Armenians, a minority group in the Ottoman Empire,

were objects of missionary zeal on the part of many philanthropic Americans. Sultan Abdul Hamid, an unregenerate character, was massacring Armenians. The missionaries, loudly lamenting, converged on Washington, and the State Department hastily instructed the American minister on the Bosporus to demand an audience with Abdul Hamid. The minister was to remonstrate with the Sultan for his unchristian behavior — an ironic touch — and to seek a stay of execution on behalf of the Sultan's surviving Armenian subjects.

The American minister dutifully went about his humanitarian task, but old Abdul Hamid saw him coming, and the Sublime Porte did not open. What was more, the Sultan was within his rights in refusing to grant the requested audience to the United States representative because, as a minister instead of an ambassador, he did not represent the "person and dignity" of the President of the United States. The Sultan's Grand Vizier said he was sorry, but that was the way it was, and the uniformed *kavasses* on guard beside the Sublime Porte rendered the honors relevant to an Envoy Extraordinary and Minister Plenipotentiary, but not to an ambassador.

The upshot was the raising of the American legation in Constantinople to an embassy. That having been accomplished, the American ambassador was able to demand an interview with Abdul Hamid and to tell the Sultan what the American people thought of his behavior. This solicitude led to an attempt on the part of European powers after World War I to give the United States a League of Nations mandate over Armenia — but that is not a part of the ambassadorial story.

The number of American embassies had grown to eleven by 1920, including Brussels, which was raised in recognition of the heroic stand of King Albert against the armies of the German Kaiser; and Poland, which the American people hoped would live up to its ancient heritage. By 1925, the date of my first vice consular commission, there were six embassies in Europe and six in Latin America, but only one — Tokyo — in the entire Far East. There were nineteen embassies when World War II began, but by mid-century the number had rocketed to fifty-eight. That figure in turn has since been nearly doubled as the bits and pieces of Africa joined the free-dom procession.

The proliferation of embassies during the 1940's was due to our Latin American Good Neighbors, but the architect of ambassadorial inflation was Sumner Welles, with an assist two decades later from a former governor, gone native on Kiliman-jaro. Welles, as deputy to Secretary Cordell Hull, was in charge of relations with Latin America, then as now a source of Po-tomac preoccupation. Then as now, there were complaints from below the Rio Grande, to the effect that whenever a Good Neighbor sought to catch Uncle Sam's eye, *Tío* Sam behaved like the headwaiter in a crowded restaurant, taking orders for steak *châteaubriand,* and *knedlicky,* and *sukiyaki,* and even for Hungarian *goulash,* but never (oh never) for *arroz con pollo.* Secretary Hull dutifully turned up, to be sure, for cere-monial bonfires at the Pan American Union. But let some Good Neighbor diplomat try to deliver a note at the Secretary's hotel: the Carleton doorman would likely as not toss him clear across Sixteenth Street. Or so, at least, went the allegation.

Sumner Welles loved the Good Neighbors. He missed few opportunities to polish their bright and shining egos. Meditat-ing on their self-inflicted martyrdom, Welles hit upon a novel idea, which he proceeded to establish as a proposition and then — unluckily for ambassadors — to sell to President Roose-velt.

Welles' proposition had to do with sovereignty. It was to the effect that since all sovereignty is infinite, all sovereignty is equal. Therefore the sovereignty of, say, Nicaragua is the same as the sovereignty of, say, Great Britain or Soviet Rus-sia. That being the case, the distinction between ministers and ambassadors is illusory, and every sovereign country is enti-tled to have an ambassador. Wherefore, concluded the Under

Secretary, all the Latin American legations in Washington ought of right to be raised to embassies, and all the Latin American ministers promoted to ambassadors. Everything, of course, to be on a reciprocal basis.

It seems doubtful whether President Roosevelt, who knew a power play when he saw one, could have been overwhelmingly impressed by a syllogism so charmingly irrational, but Roosevelt enjoyed tinkering with the machinery of foreign affairs. Back in 1933, he had proclaimed the Good Neighbor Policy, and here was an opportunity to promote further good will, at no greater cost to the American taxpayer than new embassy shields to mount over doorways and new commissions for all the corporals promoted to sergeants.

There were fourteen Latin American legations which thus became embassies in Washington, and fourteen legations of the United States that simultaneously became embassies in the Caribbean and in Central and South America. But that was only the beginning. The happy Good Neighbors promptly went Sumner Welles one better by exchanging ambassadors with one another, as well as with the United States. By the time Quito and Asunción and Ciudad Trujillo and Tegucigalpa finished exchanging *Embajadores* with Montevideo and La Paz and San José and Caracas, there were not twenty-eight new ambassadors in the hemisphere, but over one hundred and fifty.

Furthermore, the countries of Europe, which were occupied with World War II at the time of Welles' ambush, suddenly found their own diplomatic representatives — Spanish and Italian and British ministers in South America — outranked not only by their American colleagues, which perhaps could have been endured, but by the Bolivian and Guatemalan ambassadors as well.

The curses of the Europeans echoed from the Andes to the Apennines; their Foreign Offices were beseeched to come to the rescue. The inevitable outcome, once Welles' galloping diplomatic inflation set in, was for the countries of Europe to raise *their* legations to embassies, to buy new shields for their residences and chanceries, and to issue new commissions to yet another pride of ambassadorial lions, who were by now becoming almost as numerous in Latin America as guanacos in Tierra del Fuego.

No sooner had the dust settled on these portentous doings than a further inflationary step was taken, again with the encouragement of the United States. The Pan American Union by unanimous vote became in 1947 the Organization of American States, and the twenty-one members solemnly invited themselves to appoint ambassadors accredited to that institution. Most of them did so, giving the countries concerned not one but two ambassadors apiece in the District of Columbia. The State Department, which had been accused of blindness with respect to Latin America, wound up seeing double.

I was one of the early beneficiaries of the corporal-to-sergeant gambit, my first post as chief of mission being ambassador to the Dominican Republic. After eighteen years on the rungs of the bureaucratic ladder I was eager to enjoy my first taste of ambassadorial grandeur.

I called to say goodbye to Dean Acheson, that fountain of memorable phrases, who as Assistant Secretary of State was outranked at the time by Under Secretary Welles.

"All set to take off for Santo Domingo?" inquired Dean Acheson genially. "And how do you like being one of Sumner's Shambassadors?"

Another development undermining the authority of professional diplomats was likewise promoted by the Roosevelt administration, almost as soon as it came into office. That was to superimpose on the regularly accredited envoys a plague of "Special Representatives with the Personal Rank of Ambassador." They were mostly amateurs in diplomacy, who oftentimes reached foreign capitals with no advance notice to the resident ambassador, no written instructions or terms of refer-

295

ence, and little or no experience in dealing with foreign officials.

The practice of appointing special agents goes back to the dawn of the Republic with Benjamin Franklin aforesaid, but no one made such lavish use of it as the thirty-first President of the United States. Whereas when the Continental Congress was appointing its Commissioners, the rebellious colonies had no diplomatic service and had to devise one, President Roosevelt in 1933 inherited one of the best diplomatic services in the world, already commissioned and serving in every country with which the United States had relations. Under FDR, the Foreign Service took a beating.

Roosevelt's talent for turbulent administration was rarely more abundantly demonstrated than in country after country visited by his Special Representatives, including his so-called Coordinator of Inter American Affairs who was turned loose on the Good Neighbors. The majority of these latter-day circumnavigating Magellans produced either bewilderment or havoc abroad, and not infrequently both. And almost all of them reduced the authority, and hence the efficacy, of the resident representative, by raising doubts about the confidence he enjoyed or the influence he wielded with the government in Washington.

China was a case in point. In China, in 1943, the relations among the American ambassador, the commanding general, and Chiang Kai Shek had become so strained that obviously some remedy had to be applied. But instead of disciplining the American disputants, or deciding between them, Roosevelt summoned the flamboyant Pat Hurley and despatched him to Chungking as his personal representative. Hurley made some recommendations, and the next thing he knew, Roosevelt had appointed him ambassador to China. When I reached Chungking shortly thereafter to be Hurley's Deputy, he told me that any time the President of the United States wanted the job of ambassador to China thrown back in his lap, all he had to do was send out one — just one — Special Representative to start breathing down his neck or looking over his shoulder.

"No Washington kibitzer," declared Pat, "is going to undercut me as ambassador to China."

Not all diplomats, with lifetime careers at stake, are in a position to make stick their opposition to a crackpot Washington proposal, especially if it emanates from the White House. They can protest, and they often do, but they can seldom veto. The Constitution gives the President authority for the conduct of foreign affairs, and so in effect he can send abroad anyone he wishes. But whereas accredited representatives have to be confirmed by the Senate — which always scrutinizes, often comments, and occasionally combs out an undesirable — no limitation affects the short-order enthusiast despatched abroad by the President "with personal rank of ambassador." For him, the sky, or as often the boulevard or the boudoir, is the limit. And the one who is left to do the tidying up is the resident — the regularly accredited but often *dis*credited — ambassador.

Of all the special envoys encountered in nearly four decades of Foreign Service, I can think of only two who accomplished anything that could not have been done as efficiently or economically by the regular ambassador; and those two were able to succeed because they collaborated with the chancery and followed professional advice in their dealings with the host government.

One remedy would be to require the State Department to issue suitable instructions which, by subordinating the special agent to the regular ambassador and requiring the former to report through the established channel of the chancery, would minimize the mischief-making potential of the visitor.

But the best solution would be to stop appointing special ambassadors, except perhaps for such strictly ceremonial occasions as state weddings, state funerals, inaugurations, and coronations.

297

Another matter affecting the authority of the resident ambassador which has come about since the tremendous expansion of State Department personnel in Washington is the propensity of certain middle-grade bureaucrats — Assistant Secretaries of State and their Deputies, for example — to rush abroad on the slightest pretext and there to Get-In-on-the-Ambassador's-Act. Occasionally something useful comes of the visit, which can be educational for a newly-appointed Potomac Traveler. But often he wants to be a personage in his own right; he wants to meet the chief of state, and then the Prime Minister, and then the Foreign Minister and the Minister of Finance, and before he knows it his initiative has got the better of his judgment, so that on the departure of the Foggy Bottom commuter the ambassador is faced with an extensive repair job, plus a series of unnecessary headaches.

It would be more practical to summon the ambassador back to Washington twice a year for consultation, and for the State Department to send abroad instead of Assistant Secretaries, what are called Country Desk Officers, who seldom nourish delusions of grandeur, do not expect to be received by the Queen, and, as competent professionals, are as uneager to rock the ambassador's boat as he is.

Secretarial diplomacy and summitry are germane to the present thesis only in so far as their operations influence the usefulness of the accredited ambassador.

Little conspicuous success, and less permanent value, seems to have attended American adventures in summitry. And there have been humiliating failures. A President should never go abroad to negotiate — as Wilson did at Versailles in 1919. Presidential presence abroad to ratify an agreement already achieved by negotiators on the ministerial-ambassadorial level could conceivably be useful, in order to emphasize to the world the importance or solemnity of an undertaking. But international agreements commensurate with Presidential attendance outside the country are few and far between.

298

Conclaves of Presidents, like the uproarious clambake sponsored by Eisenhower in Panama in 1956, are the sorts of gatherings that no Chief Executive in his right mind ought ever to consider attending.

Secretarial diplomacy can unquestionably be effective, and the presence of the Secretary of State can enhance the authority of the accredited ambassador. But even conceding that the airplane is here to stay, many believe that the Secretary of State ought to remain home and tend the store a good deal more than he has in the past dozen years.

There remains to consider the stampedes abroad by Vice Presidents, the impact of whose enterprise has to be experienced to be believed: haranguing stevedores on piers, and debating with students on street-corners; press conferences while taking a bath; giving *abrazos* to grandmothers and singing "Happy Birthday to You" in a foreign vegetable market; challenging a Court Chamberlain in uniform and dress sword to a footrace to the international airport . . . For the past quarter century some of our Vice Presidents traveling abroad seem to have had difficulty divesting themselves of the notion that the Paraguayans, or the Koreans, or the Pakistani, are not the same raw material for carefree extrovert demagoguery as the lowest common denominator of bingo-players at home — all this to the consternation of our friends, the delight of our detractors, and the humiliation of our envoys.

Countries with royal families usually do it better. The heir apparent, by the time he is wearing long trousers, is an experienced traveler. When he visits officially, he does so with the dignified formality expected of him and his position by his foreign hosts. His prestige is zealously protected. When the heir apparent wants to relax or make whoopee, to pinch a waitress or embrace a hostess, he sets forth incognito, calling himself Count Danilo, and attracting no more public attention than an Ivy League sophomore prowling the rue Pigalle. Press and television are not encouraged to rally around the incognito heir apparent, and the name of his country is not held up to ridicule.

For the traveling Vice President on the other hand, the slogan seems to be All Publicity Is Good Publicity, while an accompanying advertising man dreams up new angles from the geometry book of Barnum and Bailey, and an ambassador of the United States is tempted to reach for the scissors, so he can open a vein before the official Pegasus bearing his exalted visitor lights down in the embassy paddock.

Not all of this can legitimately be laid at the door of the Department of State, which much of the time since Pearl Harbor has been only theoretically in charge of foreign relations. The State Department is an instrumentality of the Presidency. The specific things that have undermined the effectiveness of our envoys have sometimes been confected in the White House, but more often they have been ratified there — like Sumner Welles' scheme to stoke the self-esteem of the junior Good Neighbors by promoting their ministers. Others have been invented by agencies or officials ambitious to horn into foreign affairs, and then peddled to the White House over a bleated State Department protest.

The President is the one who should reestablish the authority of his envoys by first restoring the primacy of the Department of State in matters affecting foreign relations. A tough and determined Secretary of State, supported by the White House, could work a miracle on behalf of American representation. He could block the indiscriminate sending of special representatives "with personal rank," the principal result of whose visitations has been to make more difficult the functioning of the accredited United States agent. He could discourage Assistant Secretaries from living out of their flight bags, and arrange instead for more frequent trips to Washington by ambassadors.

The Secretary of State might even tackle the problem of the Vice Presidential itch for foreign travel. At the least he could encourage those wayfarers to comprehend that droshki-drivers don't vote in Oklahoma, nor the Guarani Indians in Pennsylvania. Whatever the disesteem in which dignity may be held in some of the wards and hustings of our far-flung Republic, a Secretary of State could explain to a departing traveler that our foreign friends set stock upon occasional restraint, and even upon unspectacular behavior.

While accomplishing the foregoing magic, the Secretary of State would do well to set an example by curbing his own ambition to sleep in five different capitals every week, to the end that the seventh floor of his teeming domain might get to know him better, and the Secretary himself develop familiarity with the operation of his own Department.

All those things would help restore the authority and effectiveness of American representatives abroad, and hence be beneficial to the country. They would be warmly welcomed wherever the mantle of diplomacy falls on competent shoulders. But they would not cure the inflation afflicting ambassadorial coinage. To cure that requires a different approach altogether.

The damage to the ambassadorial title was done when the missions in Tegucigalpa and La Paz were raised from legation to embassy. An opportunity to repair the error was missed a few years ago when the colonial areas of Africa began hatching out as separate independent countries. Had the American government then elected to establish legations in Africa, the ambassadorial population explosion might have been contained. Some scheme might then have been devised to control it in future.

It is now too late. In Africa evangelism had been substituted for diplomacy: nothing sufficed except to organize embassies in Mogadiscio and Ouagadougou and Usumbura, each with an ambassador sweating attendance. Only thus, it was possibly reasoned, could the United States prove to the Paramount Chiefs of the Grand Bassa and Pickanniny Cess that each chief

301

is as worthy in the eyes of the American people as the Chancellor of Germany or the Prime Minister of Great Britain.

To complete the picture, embassies were likewise established in Nicosia, Reykjavik and Phnom Penh — well out of reach of the patrons of emancipation.

Since it might now be awkward to demote nine-tenths of the ambassadors back again to minister, the happiest solution would be to establish a new grade of representative to accommodate the responsible American officials in the capitals of the countries that are genuinely important to the United Sates: London, Paris, Ottawa, Moscow, Rio de Janeiro, Tokyo, Bonn . . . a handful more would complete the list.

It should not be necessary to convoke a second Congress of Vienna in order to agree upon an acceptable title for this new and superior representative. To separate present ambassadors into first, second, and third class would obviously be undemocratic, and perhaps invidious as well. But the title Envoy could be used, or Agent; or, if more syllables were deemed more impressive, Plenipotentiary, or Emissary.

"Emissary of the United States of America" would make, after all, a handsome title. "The Honorable the Emissary of the United States of America" would look fine on a franked envelope, and even better on an engraved invitation.

And all the existing ambassadors, all one hundred and eleven of them, plus the sportsmen assigned to shoot clay pigeons in international forums, could go on being ambassadors and collecting their respective salutes — in Cotonou, in Conakry, in Kuala Lampur, and UNESCO — and in all those places where the pavement ends, but where it really does not make a great deal of difference to the United States whether the pavement ends against a palm tree, or against the foot of a glacier.

A penetrating look at the position of the American ambassador has been recently taken by the Jackson subcommittee of the committee on government operations of the United States Senate, mentioned in Chapter One. As this book goes to press, their completed report, "The American Ambassador," has just been released. This sixteen-page study should be read by everyone interested in public affairs. During nearly two years of nonpartisan investigation, this small and efficient committee took testimony from the Secretary of State and his ranking assistants, and from ten American ambassadors, with service all the way from Rio de Janeiro to Moscow, and from Vienna to the Congo.

Distilling from hundreds of pages of testimony the essence of the ambassadorial problem, the committee concludes that if American Chiefs of Mission are to survive the ministrations of the backseat drivers, they must have authority commensurate with the responsibilities they are expected to discharge. The solution is as simple as that, but it will not be achieved unless the President himself is prepared to take action.

The modern ambassador is expected to perform his functions "with less independence and less policy authority than ambassadors once exercised, and with far more people underfoot . . . and he is expected to serve as leader and coordinator of his 'country team,' while lacking power or even much influence over the budgets, the personnel systems, the reporting requirements, and the operating policies of many of the field staffs theoretically subordinate to him."

This goes to the heart of the problem. Although Presidents Eisenhower and Kennedy both sought to fortify the ambassador by declaring his preeminence over all the other official Americans in a given country, their orders did little to make the authority of the ambassador effective. Innumerable Washington agencies are still permitted to dispute with the State Department the right of the latter to have the final word on the conduct of foreign affairs, and the representatives abroad of those agencies, while subordinate to the ambassador in matters of protocol and on ceremonial occasions, still have wide latitude in their activities and operations.

The ambassadorial authority should extend to funds and personnel, including the budgets of other agencies and the assignment of the key officials from those agencies who are to serve in the ambassador's establishment.

No ambassador in his right mind would seek, for example, to control the *mechanics* of the C.I.A. activities in his country. The ambassador should, however, be fully aware of the *objectives* of those operations, and apprised of the value of the assets it is proposed to risk to attain them. And if the hazard seems in the ambassador's judgment to outweigh the possible gain, he should be in a position to veto the operation. Otherwise the executive-coordinating role of the ambassador is meaningless, and he may soon find himself sitting on a bomb, with both the fuse and the detonator in the hands of another American official or agency.

Again, the ambassador should have the authority not only to remove individual members of his mission whose performance he considers ineffective, but he should possess in addition the far more important power to trim excess field staffs, and to abolish or consolidate overlapping jobs, including those abundant slots in the machinery of administration. As the committee sagaciously observes, "understaffing can be the best staffing; if officers have more to do than they can possibly do, they are more likely to do what is important."

Some impressive *don'ts* are listed. The committee would place a long-overdue curb on special Washington emissaries zooming hither and thither, hectoring an ambassador at his post and trying to paddle his canoe for him. Those visitors often succeed only in rocking the boat, or in punching a hole in the bottom. Such commuter trips "are now clearly overdone, and a serious consequence is to erode the prestige of an ambassador in the eyes of the local government."

Instead, the committee recommends that ambassadors

304

should return to Washington more frequently — two or three times a year at least — in order to reimmerse themselves in the stream of policy-making, and to make sure that each embassy abroad is in step with the procession at home.

A "clamp-down on the open mouth policy" is likewise advocated, so that it is the ambassador accredited by the President who is spokesman for the American government in a given country "and not a troupe of visiting firemen." Once the firemen have departed, the committee notes, the ambassador may face the "unnecessary and difficult job" of tidying up and putting together the pieces scattered about by his heedless and too articulate visitors.

The ambassador also needs more effective support in the Department of State — what the committee calls "a strong rear echelon at headquarters" — so that when an important issue is raised by an envoy, fast action can be taken in Washington, and a suitable reply cabled back to the ambassador before the matter has died on the bureaucratic vine, or withered on the desiccated stalk of a missed opportunity.

The committee suggests this could be accomplished by increasing the stature of the Country Desk Officer, thus providing each ambassador with a more stalwart working counterpart in the Department of State. Maybe so, but to expand the existing departmental rabbit warren to accommodate one hundred additional souped-up bunnies, each serving as the opposite number of an ambassador abroad, and each lustily thumping the Foggy Bottom terrain, might contribute still further to the personnel "layering" that Secretary Rusk cited in his testimony, without significantly improving an ambassador's liaison with Washington.

It would be simpler to strengthen the five geographic bureaus of the Department of State in which the Country Desk Officers operate, and to raise the rank of the five Assistant Secretaries of State who head those bureaus, so that the officials who are responsible for the substantive aspects of foreign operations can clearly outvote the other areas of the State Department, where much of the bureaucratic delay now occurs.

Finally, national policy begins at home, and no ambassador can be effective if he is kept guessing about the intentions and objectives of the government he serves. Here the difficulty is identified as the "frequent failure of Washington to provide a timely, coherent, approved policy line, and to give the reasoning behind its action — or inaction."

A scarcity of documents is not involved. On the contrary, the archives are bursting with comprehensive planning papers "in which all contingencies are itemized (except the one circumstances will produce) and all possible sources of action are delineated (except the one that will actually follow)." Noting moreover the "dreamlike logic" of the planner's world, the committee concludes that the conduct of foreign affairs will continue to be mainly a matter of "detecting changes promptly and devising action quickly," for which no plan, paper, or professor is a substitute for the strategic and tactical sense of the experienced diplomatist. Therefore, suggests the committee, the ambassador and his staff should make important contributions to policy planning. If they fail, or if they "offer few insights and poor advice, the cure is not to disregard them but to move them — or remove them."

None would subscribe more heartily to that formula than the hard-pressed ambassadors who are the subjects of this senatorial study, which says more in sixteen pages than do most volumes on diplomatic affairs in acres of tedious exposition. The pamphlet is a tribute to the nine participating senators, to the competence of their professional staff, and to the validity of non-partisanship in foreign relations.

The adoption of the committee's recommendations would not only strengthen the ambassadorial hand, it would vastly facilitate the transaction of our government's overseas business.

Otherwise, when a better madhouse is built, the American ambassador is likely to be the first to seek asylum in it.